The Post-Truth Media's Survival Sutra: A Footsoldier's Version

The Post-Truth Media's Survival Sutra: A Footsoldier's Version

P. Raman

AAKAR

The Post-Truth Media's Survival Sutra: A Footsoldier's Version
P. Raman

First Published 2018

ISBN 978-93-5002-557-4

Published by
AAKAR BOOKS
28 E Pocket IV, Mayur Vihar Phase I
Delhi 110 091 India
aakarbooks@gmail.com

Laser Typeset at
Arpit Printographers, Delhi

Printed at
Sapra Brothers, Noida

Free India's bitter battles for content control. Can the market itself
tweak marketization of news? How our print media successfully
defied the digital demon. Who killed the grand old Super Editor?

Contents

Foreword by Sanjaya Baru 9

1. A Footsoldier's Version 13
2. Reporters' Travails 16
3. The Early Pioneers 31
4. Celeb to Owner's Fixer 41
5. The Survival Sutra 63
6. The Snake Was A Rope 89
7. The Rebellious 60s 99
8. Under the Hot Metal 112
9. At Menon's Weekly 125
10. Cut-'n'-paste Magazines 133
11. Fall of Media Charmers 140
12. The Crusader Journos 148
13. Pretenders on the Prowl 163
14. Pariahs and Press Dharma 174
15. A Muffled Watchdog 182
16. Why is it Dysfunctional? 193

Glossary 201

Index 203

Foreword

Mr. Raman, and that is how every young reporter would deferentially refer to him, was no faceless footsoldier. He was a war hero on the battlefield of political journalism in New Delhi. It is a different matter that he, along with some of his contemporaries and comrades, chose not to aspire for the rank of a brigadier or a general. Early in his professional life as a political reporter he chose not to seek a managerial role in the media and remained a lifelong reporter. But, boy, what a reporter!

It was a mere happenstance that Mr. Raman's request for a foreword to this book arrived in my email inbox just as I was finishing my book on "1991" and the role of Prime Minister Narasimha Rao. Mr. Raman was very much on my mind as I wrote that book. To refresh my memory of 1991 I spent the hot summer afternoons of 2016 in the cool environs of the Sapru House Library at the Indian Council of World Affairs in New Delhi. I went on a nostalgic trip back to my early days in journalism reading the hard copies of *The Economic Times* of that year. Ever so often I found myself engrossed in a news report or column penned by Mr. Raman. He had his ear to the ground. He knew what was happening. That was the kind of political reporting a businessman's newspaper needed.

No one is more interested in authentic political reporting than a businessman. Living in Mumbai or Kolkata or Chennai even the best networked business leader is a keen reader of authentic political reporting from the corridors of power in Lutyens' Delhi. They do not want to read partisan stuff. They want real news. Mr. Raman offered that fare. That explained why a pro-market and pro-business financial newspaper would hire an avowed left-winger like Mr. Raman. He had his politics, he had his views. But he never allowed them to interfere with his reporting.

One of the casualties of the insidious trend towards non-serious reporting, and the evolution of news media into infotainment business has been that good political reporting is all but dead. The deadly combination of partisan and non-serious political reporting has meant that few political journalists are able to focus on real change in the ground. There can be no other explanation as to why so many in the New Delhi media did not expect Mr. Narendra Modi to sweep the polls in May 2014. Most political pundits in the Delhi media had lost touch with the ground reality.

In these essays that are part memoir and part reflection on contemporary India, Mr. Raman offers an authentic account of the evolution of journalism, especially political journalism, in a rapidly changing India. He bemoans, like many, the growing role of money power and the craze for the high life and social visibility of many editors and media personalities.

Mr. Raman also offers a fascinating account of how journalism has changed as a profession from the days he had to wire telegrams from remote villages while covering the election campaign of even someone as important as Indira Gandhi to the present when mobile telephony has wiped out the distance gap in live reporting. Today news comes to us on our mobile phones from the remotest parts of the country. Barely three decades ago political reporters like Mr. Raman had to not only find their way to some distant village but also befriend the local telegraph operator to ensure that he worked late enough into the evening that Mr. Raman could wire his report for next day's newspaper.

It is in telling these tales that *A Footsoldier's Version* presents an authentic account of the tremendous change in the media and in society at large within our lifetime. India is an ancient civilization in the midst of the most dramatic social and economic change. Every family across the country offers a case study of this phenomenal transformation. It the capturing and reporting of this change that makes journalism such an exciting profession. Certainly, many evils have crept into the profession as they have into others. Yet, if a reporter has her eyes and ears open and is alive to the reality around her and has the capacity to write about it, almost every journalist can become a chronicler of change.

Mr. Raman is a chronicler of change par excellence. His journalism always rings true and tells it as it is. He may fell slightly let down by what he sees around him today but his account of the journalism of his times should inspire every young reporter even today. What I recall most about Mr. Raman was the fact that he never insisted that his news report should be displayed prominently. The battle for space is an everyday phenomenon in every news room. The more aggressive journalists manage to secure more space, in print, and more time, on television. Which is one reason why good news reports often get buried. Mr. Raman never pushed his case in news meetings. He would write his reports and hand them over to the news editor, leaving it to the judgment of the news editor as to where the report would appear. As a result some of his very good news reports often got buried in the inside pages. His grace lay in the fact that he never once complained about it.

I am delighted that Mr. Raman has penned these memoirs. I am honoured that he has asked me to write this Foreword. I hope every young news reporter reads this book to get a feel of how the real heroes of their profession soldiered on, holding the flag of professionalism high above their shoulders.

Sanjaya Baru

Former editor of the *Financial Express* and *Business Standard* and media advisor to Prime Minister Manmohan Singh

1

A Footsoldier's Version

It was some time in 1986. Four of us—C.K. Arora of UNI, Upendra Vajpayee of *The Hindustan Times,* Balraj Mehta of *The Economic & Political Weekly* and me—took a conscientious decision: never to aspire for any executive position in the profession beyond the level of bureau chief. We used to meet at PIB press launch and share the frequent media gossip. Stories of government and corporate pressures on the newspapers, rise and fall of editors, their humiliation at the hands of the owners and the unprofessional work they were told to do. There were disgraceful tales of who got high postings and on whose prop; who were hankering for being nominated as MPs and press advisors and envoys even if to minor countries. All this enslaves you, binds you to one power centre or other; erodes your integrity and sense of fairness; you get identified with power centres and become part of palace cabal.

The moment you fall for the lure of an executive editor or resident editor, the person ceases to be a creative journalist. The very nature of the person's duties and function undergoes change. He or she becomes more of an editorial manager and fixer. The person gets bogged down in staff postings, leave sanctions, recruitment and endless reportings to the bosses and the company executives. They instantly lose the excitement of meeting people, digging out hard stories and intepreting them to the readers. All this was in our minds when we took the crucial decision to keep off managerial journalism. Some of us too had such offers. But we all chose to remain humble footsoldiers of the profession.

We had still more valid reasons for this career option. Our kind of people could do better as a purely creative—or rather destructive at times—journalists. As middle-rung scribes, one need not strike compromises or seek favours like promotions and higher positions. We could also keep off the office intrigues and indulging in the art of pleasing the bosses—the secret of the quick climbers' career success. And finally, no one had ever asked us to push the company's papers with the ministers or secretaries.

Reporting was a mission and interpreting events a passion. The small man in the middle rung has many advantages. We were too close to the editors but less prone to invisible dictats from the corporate office. We were so close to the politicians and bureaucracy, too familiar with their whims and fancies. But we conscientiously kept ourselves too far. We were witness to many ugly intrigues, deception and subversion in the corridors of power. All this enabled the footsoldiers to observe things from close quarters without getting entangled in the murky deal makings.

At a personal level, this writer has taken meticulous care to shun official patronage and inducements. It was imperative for a journalist who ventures into the world of adversarial reporting to follow certain minimum ethics. Those who criticize others should also conduct themselves. If you fancy being included in the foreign or domestic tours of a prime minister or ministers, a bureaucrat or politician, you stand to lose that humble honour. There were more such self-imposed fads like keeping off government-appointed panels, even the innocuous ones like press gallery and PIB accreditation committees. But there were some exceptions. The first was the conducted press tours in groups to specific events and PSU projects. These were formal invitations in groups. The Press Council nomination was done by journalist bodies, not government. Then there was a third: sharing hospitality along with other journos at the jamborees of BJP and Congress.

Here is a pertinent question. Should a political reporter stop having contact with crucial government wings in the name of avoiding professional pressures and lures? No. A reporter must keep all ususal liaison aggressively. There is no contradiction here. In this regard, former *Anand Bazar Patrika* editor Avik Sarkar's words are worth quoting: "Hunky dory, yes. Mata Hari, no." Sarkar's comment came the day we had launched *Business Standard* from Delhi. He had said so in an answer to our queries.

Gone are the days when the government used to make

deliberate leaks to a trusted reporter. Now there are many channels for this. So there is no professional justification for being an embedded loyalist reporter. Second, experience has it that critical stories always emanated from the disgruntled elements—like an aggrieved person or interest groups or rival business entities—within an organization. You only have to tap it with care and caution. This enables people like us to be more forthright without feeling the burden of guilt. The ensuing 15 chapters form a free and fair account of what a footsoldier had seen, heard and felt. It relies on the reporter's daily notings and observations made in my spiral books meant for my weekly column *Realpolitik*.

2

Reporters' Travails

"Mahanaadu... Kangress mahanaadu..." (session, Congress session) "the *tongawalas* (horse carriage) were at their shouting best. They had taken over the entire narrow road to the railway station. And one of them took us to the venue of the Congress session. All along the way there were anxious crowds, most of them in dhotis and lungis. They came on their own—not ferried by trucks—to have a look at the big mela. It was the historic Avadi session of the Indian National Congress in 1955.

A Seva Dal volunteer took the newsmen to a counter a few metres away from the decorated main gate. The man at the desk examined the editor's handwritten letter, made some markings and handed a press badge and some background papers and folders. Another volunteer led the newsmen inside the 'nagar'.

Behind and either side of the main pandal were rows of thatched sheds of different sizes. Narrow *galis* divided them. They all had doors made of plam leaves. A little away, clouds of smoke arose above the rows of sheds and clanking of utensils. That was the kitchen complex that served food to the Congress delegates and invitees. Adjoining the kitchen was a couple of dining halls—all thatched with palm leaves and bambo frames. Plastic was unknown and there was not a shred of it anywhere around.

"This is the Press room," the volunteers told the newsmen. It was nothing but half a dozen telephones kept on a raw wooden desk and a dozen chairs around it. In one corner were two mud *kujas* and a few tin mugs. Near the 'Press room' were more thatched sheds.

"This is your bed," the volunteers pointed to the plain bamboo coats arranged in two rows. "Keep this with you for personal use."

Beside the coats were kept an iron bucket, a tin mug, a *kuja* and a glass tumbler. There were five coats in the shed. Three were occupied by journalists of Telugu dailies. Tea, coffee and food were available at the common dining halls. All this were the common facilities for the delegates and newsmen. That was the kind of Press facilities for the journalists at the famous Avadi session.

This was how the reporter of *Navajeevan* wrote after the session. *Navajeevan* was a Malayalam daily from Thrissur edited by renowned literary critic Prof. Joseph Mundasseri who was also Kerala's first education minister. The paper had 8,000 circulation. A few of us students were working as trainee sub-editors at the daily after college hours. We the green horns were listening to the senior's accounts of his experiences at Avadi with rapt attention. He talked about how Jawaharlal Nehru, U.N. Debhar, Jagjivan Ram and other senior leaders mingled with the delegates and newsmen at the dining hall. He spoke highly of the press facilities and camp life at the Avadi session 'nagar'.

No one had any complaint about sleeping on creaking bamboo coats without a quilt. Most delegates had brought along bed rolls, blankets and their own *kujas*. That is what they did at all Congress sessions. PTI, the only wire agency on which the regional dailies relied for news, had a few reporters. May be the special representatives of the big English dailies also lived in the sheds. No reporter complained about living under the thatched halls. They bathed under the makeshift water taps behind thatched palm leaf hedges. They shared snacks and food with the khadi-clad delegates.

For most reporters, there was limited scope for reporting. The copy had to be short. True, the telephone department officials at the 'Press room' were very cordial. In any case, reporters of the regional language dailies were not familiar with typing out telegrams in abbreviated words in English. Most had confined their reporting to covering the speeches of their local leaders. They sent reports by post which, incidentally, reached their offices the next day.

The press room in those early days did not even have typewriters. They kept carbon papers, lead pencils and writing papers. The latter was the kind of government stationery with twin diagonal lines across. This was to prevent misuse of paper for personal purposes. There were also pins, writing ink in huge bottles with 'fillers' and a jar of resin gum which emitted a thick stink all around. Ink bottle because ball point pens were yet to arrive. You have to fill your fountain pens with ink. After all, what else did a reporter in those days need? And there was the 'blotting paper' kept along with 'steel pens'. A steel pen is a pencil-sized wooden stick to which a writing nib is attached. After writing a sentence, you might wish to press the copy with the blotting paper to absorb the excess ink.

A couple of postal staff sat at the entrance of the press room with the ubiquitous red post drop box. They accepted written reports from the newsmen, put them in GOI's brown covers which the messengers rushed to the rail postal van for quick delivery. Trains with nomenclature ending 'mail' (like Howrah Mail) had moving mail vans attached to them. The postal staff sat in the moving train, sorted out the mail bags and dropped them at the railway stations. That was the system. This enabled quick collection and delivery. The postal vans in mail trains continued till the turn of the past century.

For reporters, the fastest way to send stories to their newspapers was by land line telephone. But it was so cumbersome, an almost impossible task. You first write down the report and read it out to a sub-editor on the other end. For this you had to book a 'trunk' call with the man at the telephone exchange. STD (self-dialing) from Madras to Delhi was introduced by around 1963. 'Express trunk' had a higher priority and was faster. The operator at the telephone exchange gave you a token number. It took anywhere between ten minutes to hours depending on the route, to get the contact with the desired number. The operators had to put through several telephone 'calls' en route. Disruptions on the route were common because in many places there were no underground cables. The problem was once you booked the trunk, you had to keep waiting. Once you got through, you had to quickly dictate the text to the sub-editor who had to take it down. Often disturbances made it impossible to make out anything. And after every three minutes, you had to ask for an extension. Some newspaper offices had introduced innovations like tape recorders to make the news transfer faster. They then played back the recorders to transcribe the text.

That, again, was not so smooth. Recorders in the early days were rather clumsy with two huge spools. Cassette discs made their appearance decades later. In those days, many cash-starved newspapers could not even spend money on dispatching reporters to cover such events. They all depended on PTI which produced full text of the resolutions at the session with embargo. They sent extensive summaries of speeches and sidelights. PTI also had a cheaper service customized for small and medium dailies.

Things were certainly more smooth by the time the Congress session took place at Bhubaneshwar in 1964. The STD facility was spreading to more centres with less voice disruptions. Better cable networks and the 'Cross-Bar' French technology had made land-based telephone communication a bit more hassle-free. Telegraph facilities had penetrated deep into smaller towns and large villages. Teleprinter machines were fast replacing the Morse code system in bigger telegraph offices. Separation of posts and telegraph had led to better concentration on tele-communication. For active newsmen, the system of press telegrams was a real relief. The rates for the press telegrams were less and the respective newspaper offices issued press authority cards to reporters. Under this system, reporters did not have to pay cash at the counter. It was done by the newspaper offices as part of an accounting arrangement.

About three decades later the press room at the Calcutta session of the AICC in 1984 certainly had a better look. Incidentally, that was Indira Gandhi's last AICC session. There were rows of STD phones, all functioning. And it was free. Some friends did misuse the facility to make free calls to family and friends. Tele lines were specially kept streamlined for the event as the telephone minister himself was an AICC office-bearer. There were experienced teleprinter operators to 'through' the line. PR officials were frequently asking newsmen whether they faced any difficulty. Another advantage was that all major newspaper organizations, including *The Indian Express* which this writer represented, had their own offices in Calcutta with regular direct teleprinter lines.

However, the status, demands and expectations of the media crowds had also soared. If their 'fathers' at the Avadi session had comfortably slept on the bare bamboo coats, bathed under the open makeshift taps and ate the camp food, many among the new generation journalists at Calcutta were fighting in public for free five star accommodation. Initially, the reception committee had put most of us in small-time guest houses on Chowringhee Street.

We were given the room numbers at Delhi and taken to the rooms promptly. But few were satisfied with narrow rooms. Some of them mobbed Priyaranjan Dasmunshi when he came to see the arrangements. They charged him with 'discrimination' and practising 'casteism' by accommodating big names in five star hotels. Soon most newsmen had moved over to better hotels. And a few news cameramen and I were left at dingy guest houses. This writer did not change the accommodation for operational reasons. The place was within walking distance of the session venue and *Indian Express* office and hence free from Calcutta's traffic hassles.

The differences were not confined to facilities. Rajiv Gandhi's Congress session in Bombay in 1985 was really a grand show for the media persons. It was there that Rajiv had made his famous appeal to get the organization rid of 'power brokers.' The size of the press corps attending the Bombay jamboree had swollen by leaps and bounds. More media organizations had sent their own reporters. Regional dailies were present in strength chasing local issues. It was really the heyday for the presenters who along with their friends and fiancés had managed to occupy the best suites in the Taj. Many of those moving with press cards (Delhi) were totally unknown to us who had been covering the AICC from the Jantar Mantar days, i.e. before the Congress split in 1989. Among them were known dancers and self-styled artistes and writers. Press cards were liberally issued from the AICC office quota to friends and favourites of the leaders. There were also rumours of extending free air tickets to the favourites.

The change was more visible at the vast media centre set up at the venue. 'Press rooms' of Avadi had become 'Media Centre'. Avadi's mud cups and plantain leaves for snacks had given way to branded cold drinks and coffee stands. Sand floors under the thatch were no match for the cool, carpeted floors with stylish sofas. The whole place had a modernist look—reflecting the young Congress set's lavish style. The 'Doon pals' or 'computer boys'— Arun Nehru, Arun Singh, Suman Dubey and Mani Shankar Aiyar— had introduced several novel facilities for the media. Computers and fax machines were displayed at the venue but few had the skills to operate them. Moreover the other end at our offices did not have the infrastructure to receive them. Even the two agencies continued to use their 'Hindustan' teleprinters with an array of reporters and sub-editors at one side of the air conditiond Media Centre.

For media, the Bombay Congress session also marked two novel trends. The surge of women correspondents was so conspicuous. This even for the more conservative regional dailies. Until the 70s, women journalists were mainly sub-editors or doing such soft beats as art, theatre or fashion events. Some did book reviews and covered seminars. Conservative editors had denied them such tough and hard beats like crime and politics. The attitudinal change was a gradual process. The resistance was more from the old generation middle-level functionaries like news editors. However, once the gates were thrown open, all apprehensions evaporated. Some women crime reporters had a better record in covering the anti-Sikh riots of 1984 and such events. By the mid-80s, large numbers of women had begun doing political parties and Parliament. At one time it seemed there was higher representation for women among the outstation correspondents than men. This trend was widely reflected at the Bombay Congress event.

The other trend Bombay had signalled related to the power of the regional press. One could observe this qualitative change in the very media mix. With rising literacy and post-emergency political awakening, Indian language dailies had emerged powerful in both circulation and with regard to public opinion-making. So far, election ticket seekers and position grabbers in the party had relied too much on the the Capital's English dailies for grabbing the Delhi bosses' attention. For them, time was coming to improve their image back in their respective states. Such support from the regional media alone could get sufficient cooperation from the local party leaders. Moreover, reports in regional dailies also began influencing the Delhi durbar's attitude.

The best manifestation of this revolution was the emergence by the mid-80s of a new crop of Hindi journalists, smart and skilful, as political writers and special correspondents. They were the products of political upheavals like Jayaprakash Narayan's 'permanent revolution' movement and anti-emergency struggles. The JP movement had led to the closure of educational institutions for months—as much as about a year in Bihar. From them emerged an activist generation, fairly well read and with a sharp political antena.

Jansatta, the Hindi daily of the Express group was a pioneer both in terms of technology, layout and writing style. Its illustrious editor Prabhash Joshi had picked the JNU types and posted them at crucial places. Their Left grounding provided them with analytical ability and a different world view. Then there were the Hindutva stream. After the emergency, Samachar Bharti news agency with an abundance of RSS-oriented recruits, were also visible on the scene. After Bharti's final collapse, many of them had joined the regional and mainstream media. Then there was a third strain in Hindi journalism—moulded by *Dinman,* the Hindi journal of *The Times of India* stable. Its celebrated editor Raghuvir Sahay, a reputed Hindi poet in the Lohyaist mould, was a role model for his generation of aspiring writers in the Hindi world. He inspired thousands of youth writers. His was a highly modernist generation. Raghuvir Sahai had to resign and *Dinman*—the popular weekly shut subsequently—for still unknown reasons. But *Dinman* had by the time rendered a new dynamism to Hindi journalism. Rajendra Mathur, who died as editor of *Navbharat Times,* was the one who had contributed immensely to giving Hindi journalism a modernist perspective and look.

Before the Gen X's arrival which coincided with the *Jansatta-Dinman* phenomenon, Hindi dailies were a dull imitation of their English sister dailies. Owners had mostly picked known Hindi writers and litterateurs as editors. Though well versed in their domain, many of those selected by the English chains for their Hindi dailies lacked the world view of a versatile editor or the necessary journalistic skill. Things were better in Hindi dailies under regional media houses. In the Delhi press corps, the earlier crop of Hindi special correspondents looked rather dull and lazy. They were mostly of a Sanskritized Hindi background. They wrote reports in that style. *Janasatta* editor Prabhash Joshi often lamented that generation's 'lazy' life and the writing style. Their special correspondents attended for all formal briefings and media events but hardly did any value addition to the agency version. Rajendra Mathur had once called them 'Sanskrit Masters'.

The post-80 generation changed all that. As a result, Hindi dailies began giving story-breakers, something unthinkable in yesteryears. Many young Hindi journalists from Allahabad and JNU became visible in external affairs and economic/finance briefing. With deep domain knowledge, they often excelled the 'angreziwallas'. It is another matter that many of their stories were dumped down by their hyper cautious editors. I remember once a *Hindustan* (*Hindustan Times* group) correspondent narrated his frustration over rejection of such a story-breaker by his office. It was at the central hall of Parliament. *The Statesman*'s D.P. Kumar and I got the details from the reporter and confirmed with the source. Our stories had appeared on page one—mine as second lead in *The Indian Express* and his as bottom anchor. The irony did not end there. The next day, his bureau chief asked him to follow-up our stories. This post-80 makeover had often forced the 'angrezi' media scribes to look for Hindi dailies for follow-up. English journalists, even some star-studded ones, had begun tying up with what they had earlier dismissed as 'Hindiwallas' for the regular information tap.

For non-Hindi regional dailies, it was a mixed bag. Representatives of Bengali dailies like *Anand Bazar Patrika* and the defunct *Amrit Bazar Patrika* were traditionally active in the Delhi press corps. And so were some Marathi dailies. This may be due to the impact of the formidable English dailies in their home states. But then what about Tamil? Despite the predominance of *The Hindu*, Tamil language dailies did not believe in deputing active correspondents in the capital. At least that was the position until recently. That apart, the regional dailies, by and large, thought of having a presence in Delhi only by the early 1960s. The Indian and Eastern Newspapers Society (IENS), had offered rooms for all major newspaper establishments at what is now INS building on the Old Mill Road (now Rafi Marg). This motivated them to have a presence in Dehli. Initially, the regional newspapers had posted a manager to look after their interests in Delhi. Their work included pursuing import permits for machinery, newsprint quota and central government advertisements. They kept in touch with the headquarters back at home and facilitated visits of management officials and editors/owners to Dehli. They also began occasionally acting as journalists.

Representatives of many regional dailies had told this writer how hard they had to lobby for a posting in Delhi. The mindset in the states in those early days was that they need not waste resources on Delhi. Some early arrivals in IENS offices had to do part-time liaison work for business establishments to supplement their income. In any case, their eight-pagers (or ten-pagers) had limited space or interest in hard politics of the capital. However, the regional reporters got help from the MPs and union ministers friendly to the respective media house. They promoted the reporters, who in turn, tried to give them a good projection. So much so, many early correspondents from the regional dailies stayed with their patron MPs and ministers in government flats. They specially covered the speeches of union ministers from their respective states and stories with a state angle. The reporters also had to keep in touch with the visiting chief ministers and state officials for special stories. The more industrious ones sent periodic Delhi letters to their dailies. By the mid-70s, almost all newspapers with an office in the INS building had their own correspondents in Dehli. Some had made arrangements for part-timers and some retired PIB officials. Yet most confined their work to scanning the morning dailes and rewrite stories relevant to the state. All Gjuarati dailies had a front page column variously called 'Dilli ni Vat' or 'Dilli Durbar'. These were supposed to be a personalized narration of interesting happenings in Delhi designed to the taste of the Gujarati readers. Part-time correspondents normally picked stories from the English dailies and put them in the personalized style. I have seen some of them simply marking a few items in the *Evening News* and asking the teleprinter operator to creed it. Someone in Ahmedabad made it in Gujarati.

'Local angle' has always been the lifeline for the regional correspondents in Delhi. If an Andhra man is among a hundred victims of a train accident, the Telugu dailies are sure to highlight the kinsman's background. For the lazy ones, 'local angle' comes in handy to compensate for their professional laxity. We had many juicy stories on this theme. A reporter of a Maharashtra daily was fast asleep even hours after Sanjay Gandhi died in a morning air crash. Finally his editor in Bombay had to wake him up. Not to be left behind, the correspondent came out with a 'local angle' story on the tragedy: Sanjay was wearing 'Kolhapuri chappals'. His daily had an edition from Kolhapur in Maharashtra. This may purely be a joke. But 'local angle' had often gone to such ridiculous extremes. *Mumbai Samachar*, one of the oldest surviving regional language dailies, had the distinction of refusing to have its own correspondents in Dehli. As late as 1990, its owner had told this writer that his daily was well off without a reporter in the capital.

This was at a time when competitive coverage of state politics and local interest stories had reached a feverish peak. A tip on a leadership change in states or airdashing of a PCC chief or chief minister to Delhi was enough for the state reporters to rush to their respective Bhavans and Houses. They mobbed the general secretaries in charge of the state for clues. A cut in Plan allocation or approval for a project in the state were considered big exclusives. Apparently, in the face of competitive coverage by the provincial media giants, the respective editors back home pestered their Delhi reporters for exclusive details. All this gave Delhi representatives of a regional daily a special status. This is born out by the fact that bureau chiefs of nearly a dozen regional dailies were called back to take charge as editors or executive editors. Examples: *Mathrubhumi, Anand Bazar Patrika, Bartaman, Janmabhumi* group, *Andhra Prabha, The Hindu, Deccan Herald.* The Bombay Congress session had signalled the emphatic arrival of an energetic set of Hindi and other regional representatives. The 'angrezi' crowd was clearly losing their predominant position.

By the time the Thirupati session of the Congress under P.V. Narasimha Rao as president came up, things were much smoother for journalists. The new media centre was a testimony to the impressive strides in communication technology. There were better typewriters and plenty of them. Telegram counters had very few takers. Instead, fax had emerged as a far easier tool to rush stories. You only had to type out or write down on plain sheets—in any language. These reached the newspaper offices instantly. And it cost just Rs. 30 a page. The only problem perhaps was at times some lines went blank. But you could ask them to repeat. We in *The Economic Times* had then made it a point to send two copies of the same report at a time. We could thus avoid the bother of checking with Delhi office for confirmation. The Thirupathi media centre also heralded the arrival of computers and e-mail as new modes to rush stories. Bombay had a couple of them as exhibits. But no one could use them. At Thirupathi computers were online and some reporters with functioning computer systems at their offices had used it. But only very few. For, in most offices the e-mail service was still at an experimental stage.

The era of telegrams as the quickest mode of communication had lasted far too long. Even the metro-based biggies had relied on telegrams for over half a century. In its early phase, things were never smooth for the field reporters or those at the news desk. The latter had to decode the text and do drastic editing. In the news room, sub-editors were the first to sense, rather smell, the arrival of the much-detested press telegrams. They appeared in clumsy packets from the telegraph office, bringing with them the odour of resin gum, often still wet. At the telegraph office, the press telegrams emerged from the primitive teleprinters. They came out in the form of narrow strips, line by line. The peons would then cut the strips and paste each line on official foolscap letterheads. Lack of space between the pasted lines made it impossible to make corrections. Often the ink from the pen would not stick on the gum-coated paper.

Abbreviations for common English words were another problem. It was standardized and a list of the code and words was pasted at the news desk for ready reference. For instance, when they wrote 'the man ex-Bombay', the sub-editor had to give the elaborated version: 'the man coming from Bombay'. But some smart reporters invented their own abbreviations. It became a bigger nightmare when handwritten copies (instead of typed) came from the telegraph office. Untrained mofussil stringers with their awful English made the decoding more hazardous. Sub-editors had to often consult colleagues to find out what exactly the reporter meant. The position improved when the telegraph department agreed to lay direct lines to the newspaper offices. Since then the telegrams began appearing on regular teleprinter rolls.

However, longish reports and newsletters continued to come by mail. Some reporters from smaller state dailies continued to send their newsletters to their editors even till the 90s. They found it easier to send them by post. Urgent exclusives alone were sent by telegram. Correspondents and stringers were given envelopes printed with their newspaper's address and labelled 'Book-Post'/ 'Urgent'/'Press Matter'. Postmen always treated 'press matter' with urgency. Despite this, some big newspaper chains had stuck to the practice of dispatching their edit page articles to far away resident editors by own 'container' service years after they had set up their own teleprinter network. The Delhi editorial headquarters simply scheduled the edit pieces for each day and sent the intimation on TP to the resident editors. Editorials were, however, sent on TP. Despatching by mail was considered more reliable even as late as the 1970s. 'Container service'—a cylindrical aluminium box—was found necessary to send and receive items like 'press matter', advertisements and blocks. Cylindrical because the cargo often included full-page flongs to be cast and added to the day's paper. Incidentally, the term 'news despatch' had its origin in this pre-telegram practice of sending stories by post. Many such revolutionary technologies of yore now remain fossilized in newspaper titles: *The Mail, Telegraph, Interfax* and possibly *Post* as in *Washington Post.*

Field Reporting from distant places was a wild goose chase for the reporter, especially from areas without a telephone link or telegraph office. We still shudder to think of those frustrating days. The present generation with text messages and OB van facilities will sympathize with their 'grandfathers' for their professional travails. We would start on our reporting expedition armed with a Press Telegram Authority Card, the PIB card and plenty of cash. Remember, it was much before the ATM era. Even banking had not spread to interiors. If you were a smart reporter, the first task after reaching the venue was to spot the telegraph office and alert the department's local teleprinter (TP) operators about a longish story.

The problem was the TP operators were not used to handling long stories. They only did brief messages: "Father died stop start immediately stop." The sight of a reporter at the telegraph office meant longer copy and tiring work. So the TP operators would look for ways to evade us. Line trouble, machine snag and power cut are the usual excuses. I too had learnt to counter such pretexts with my own counter defence. First is to gift a new ballpoint pen (precious in those days) to the operators and the boss. Second is to assure them that I would myself 'punch' copy on the TP machine.

"Take care of this, please," I tell them. "This is a baby typewriter. After the function I'll rush back here to punch the copy. Also keep ready some tea and snacks—for all of us."

Baby typewriter was our own version of the present-day laptop. We had first to type out the story, divide it in 20-word sections so that the account clerks could easily fix the tariff before handing it to the staff. For language journalists, there were more problems. They had to write in Roman letters. Punching itself was a latter day innovation. The TP operators punched the text on an electric typewriter and out would come a narrow paper tape with innumerable pin holes in them. These holes were the codes for the letters and words. The punched tape was fed to the teleprinter which instantly transmitted the data in alphabets to the destination. Once the work was over, I would thank and pay the tea stall owner's bill. Once a young TP operator grabbed my bag and came up to the taxi. He sounded me for an operator's job at our office.

Till the mid-90s, election coverage in daily newspapers was fairly exhaustive. Opinion polls were yet to begin. Field reports by journalists should indicate the voters' preferences. Even the headlines would give you an idea about the stirrings on the ground. Editors wanted more realistic assessment even if we had to spend more time in a region. Sample the headlines: 'No cakewalk for Devi Lal,' 'Congress on sure wicket', 'Close tie at Indore'. Evasive reports like "women outnumber men" or "huge turnout likely" were despised. Undoubtedly, predictions were easier in those days. Political divide was more definable and less complex. Parameters were narrow, and if one was shrewd enough to read between the lines, it was far easier to sum up things after meeting half dozen politicians of different hues and local elders. Moreover, we still had old politicians—mostly of Congress—in Hindi states who could give you a tehsil-wise voting pattern. The old guard began losing track after new undefinable forces emerged on the scene to make things more complex.

It was on the eve of my departure for the election tour of eastern UP. V.P. Singh had emerged as a big challenge to the Congress. I got a call from an old friend in the INS building. He suggested I file my private assessment of the electoral situation in UP to him after my return. He then introduced me to a friend who offered Rs. 5,000 for the story. It was relatively a sizeable amount in those days. I was surprised.

"Don't do it," Janardan Thakur warned me. "This may be for IB or a foreign agency. They have done so with others. People like us should not do it." I was told some small time scribes in those days were giving poll-eve assessments for a price—some even faking their travel.

While on election tour, you are totally cut off from the office and home. Press telegrams were a sure-shot. They promptly reached the office and the newspaper carried it the next day under bylines. But it was a one-way traffic. We could send messages all right. But there was no way to get responses from the office. This is because we were constantly moving from place to place without a telephone or telegraph address. Back home, our families learnt about our movements from the datelines of the stories carried by the daily.

Those were the times when you had to use your wits to surmount the news transmission hurdles. Often we had to resort to not so ethical means to rush the stories to our newspaper offices. To beat the midnight deadline, filing pre-written stories was a standard practice for some of us. For this you should have direct contact with the office. Any failure to stop a misfired story would have disastrous consequences. My experience in Baroda was of a different kind. Indira Gandhi was out of power after the post-Emergency Janata sweep. Everyone had written her off as a spent force. I was among the reporters when she began her campaign trail in Gujarat. Valsad, then Bulsar, was her launch pad. At the circuit house in Baroda were Congress leader Raof Valiullah and Indira Gandhi's security man Dutta. The latter showed me a copy of the synopsis of her address at the late evening's Baroda rally. Dutta was DSP security when Indira Gandhi was prime minister. After she lost power, Dutta resigned his government job and worked for her as a private person. I had a quick glance at the paper and decided to take a big risk. I rushed to the telegraph office, befriended the TP man, punched a report and kept it with him. I was right.

That evening, Indira Gandhi, seeing a massive crowd, was at her aggressive best. She alleged that the charges being levelled against her by the ruling Janata Party leaders were so absured. "They say I have even stolen eggs and chicken", she thundered. Her fiery speech proved to be a game changer in politics as the Gujarat offensive gave her the confidence of a fight-back. The rally ended at around 10 pm. I positioned myself at the end of the maidan on the way to the telegraph office—not at the press enclosure. This was to save time wading through the crowds into the street after the end of the rally. Ensuring she had stuck to the synopsis, I rushed to the Telegraph office, produced the card got a receipt and released the pre-punched tape. Next morning, only *Patriot* had carried the landmark speech with full thrust. None of the local dailies had it.

Even the daily chores of a reporter at the capital were arduous. For routine stories you had to rush back to the office, sit at a heavy typewriter and type out the reports in tricplicate. Any major mid-course correction or addition meant you had to retype the whole sheet. The first copy went to the local news desk and the second one to the TP room to be creeded to other editions. Unlike today, you could not make a few clicks and send the stories on the mobile.

Late night stories were more frustrating, especially for those who were passionately committed to the profession. The best way to transmit a midnight story to the office was by telephone. For this you should have access to a landline phone. Then you need the prompt backup of a sub-editor back in office. Most occasions they avoid such requests due to the fear of error. Even if we managed to dictate to the desk, they could not send it to outstation editions.

Once at 10 pm we got a tip that Vasantdada Patil was summoned to Delhi by the Congress high command to ask him to take over as Maharashtra chief minister. His PA Ojha confirmed his airdash to Delhi but could not shed more light on the move. This writer rushed to Patil's bungalow at Willingdon Crescent and waited for his arrival and got the confirmation. But one had to carefully word the story so that you would not be wide off the mark even if it misfired. The best course was to alert the chief sub-editor and Bombay office about the story-breaker. The quickly typed page one lead was carried by Delhi and Bombay editions of *The Indian Express*. But other editions missed this exclusive. Had this happened two decades later, one could have thumped at the mobile sitting in Patil's visitors' room and sent it with more details. And all editions might have carried it.

3

The Early Pioneers

Newspapers in India had two distinct origins. English dailies set up by the British owners and those initiated by enlightened Indian citizens. The former had arrived in India almost as part of the colonial steel frame. Though privately owned, they had the empire's solid support—both financial and functional. The British rulers had always provided special treatment to their editors. The newspapers in British colonies followed the same style and production technology of the dailies back home. They had even transplanted the similar sounding titles and logos and layout scheme. Editors from the home country came to take charge of production. Each of the main colonial administrative provinces in India had its supporting British-owned English dailies: *Civil & Military Gazette* (Lahore), *The Times of India* (Bombay), *The Statesman* (Calcutta), *Pioneer* (Lucknow) and *The Mail* (Madras).

The indigenous newspapers, however, had a different origin and a rich tradition of their own. There were over a hundred such periodicals, all small and tiny—a few of them dailies—at a given time during the last century of the colonial rule. Most were in regional languages and were launched by enthusiastic academics, intellectuals or freedom fighters. Business gain was never the motive. They mobilized some funds and became its editors. But most of these idealist pioneers could not sustain their publications for long periods.

Struggle against the colonial rule was the major motivation for most Indian newspapers of the early era. Every province and princely state had such publications. They together had a tremendous impact on the country's national movement. One could ignore them if going by their poor circulation, low level of technology and quality of the content. Some of them were too small to be counted—a thousand or so copies print order. It is doubtful whether any of these had a circulation in five digits in the pre-1940 period. Yet their cumulative impact—the message they spread and inspiration they provided—on the polity, especially the nationalistic sections, was much larger than the circulation.

I remember in 1960 Baba Sohan Singh Josh saying that some of the Urdu and Gurmukhi journals were being printed in crown 1/8 size on locally fabricated treddle machines—page by page. Printing ink was often made with charcoal and turpentine oil. That was the kind of technology most of them had. The bigger ones launched by veteran personalities may have had a regular printing press. Yet the editorial content of such protest journals was less than mediocre. Most had too much sloganeering and were reproductions of old articles or speeches by favourite leaders. They often wrote their own poems and articles. Theirs was more self-expression of intense emotions. But for them, the very running of such periodicals, their production and distribution—often in secret —themselves was part of a great struggle.

Printing, stitching and taking the copies to like-minded comrades at distant places was itself a nationalist campaign. Some were handwritten 'magazines' and those printed on crude litho 'stones' by hand—like the old compositors taking proof sheets for correction. It was common for the most fervent ones to simply copy by hand an entire article or poem from a borrowed journal. A few had more resources. Take the case of *Ghadar*, Lala Hardayal's journal published from the US. It had editons in Hindi, Urdu, Punjabi and Marathi, and was quite popular among sections of people here and abroad. Its copies were smuggled into India in concealed cloth cargo. A move to smuggle a printing press to India had failed at the last minute.

Payam-e-Azadi, in Hindi and Urdu started in 1857, was a fiercely revolutionary kind. The colonial rulers confiscated the periodical when it made a public appeal to the people to fight against the British. *Samachar Sudhavarshan*, first Hindi daily, and later in Urdu and Persian, were prosecuted under sedition rules for carrying Bahadur Shah Zafar's *firman* during the 1857 rebellion. Sedition was frequently used against such publications in English as well as regional languages. Most of such early era journals had a relatively short life. Many shut down within a year, others dragged on for some time before finally winding up.

Simultaneously, there emerged a neutral sort of journals that were inspired by causes other than nationalism. These had scrupulously avoided criticism of the Raj. Take the case of *Kavi Vachan Sudha* started in 1868. It had even published a poem eulogizing the visiting Prince of Wales. Some others had also welcomed the visiting emperor. However, in the case of *Kavi Vachan Sudha*, it was found that each line of its poem on the prince had also conveyed a highly negative meaning. This had annoyed the colonial rulers who promptly discontinued funding to *Kavi Vachan Sudha* and all such Indian-owned magazines. It took years for them to restore the old cosy relationship with the Raj and the financial benefits it had entailed.

In this category were more serious nationalistic publications sponsored by the eminent personalities of the day. Ganesh Shankar Vidyarthi launched *Pratap* from Kanpur. Swami Shraddhanand started *Tej* and *Vir Arjun*. *Kesari* in Marathi was launched by Bal Gangadhar Tilak in 1881. It was Govind Ranade who started *Gyan Prakash* and *Indu Prakash*. *Hindi Patriot* was launched by revolutionary playwright Girish Chandra Ghosh. Later Ishwar Chandra Vidyasagar re-launched it with more features. A contemporary of *Hindi Patriot* was *Indian Mirror*. The 19th century saw the birth of *Amrita Bazar Patrika* from Jessore. It was later shifted to Calcutta. Lala Lajpat Rai initiated publication of *The Punjabi, Bande Mataram* and *People* from Lahore. Subhas Chandra Bose and C.R. Das (1906) had journals like *Forward* and *Advance*. *Vandemataram* was established by Bipin Chandra Pal. Sardar Dyal Singh Majithia had brought out *The Tribune* (1881). Bipin Chandra Pal had also edited *The Tribune*. A.G. Horniman made *Bombay Chronicle* a powerful daily. Sachidananda Sinha's *Searchlight* in Patna had Murlimanohar Sinha as editor. *The Hindustan Times*, launched by nationalists in 1924 had a rich tradition of intellectual editors such as Madan Mohan Malviya, K.M. Panikkar and Devdas Gandhi.

What about the more established *desi* newspapers with better resources and wider reach? Did they play second fiddle to the Raj for their survival? Barring rare exceptions, most sponsors and editors of those successful dailies too had lent support to nationalistic activities. *The Hindu* was originally launched by five public spirited lawyers of Madras. When they handed the journal over to Kasturi the only condition was that it should continue to enhance nationalistic aspirations.

The Bombay Congress session in 1885 that had marked the launch of the Indian National Congress, had a galaxy of eminent editors in the front row. Its first four resolutions were proposed by senior journalists of the day. Noted journalist Dadabhai Naoroji was among the sponsors. The very first resolution was introduced by editor of *The Hindu* G. Subrahmanya Aiyar. At least ten Congress presidents, including Feroz Mehta, Malviya who had launched *Bombay Chronicle*, C.R. Das, Gokhale, Dadabhai Naoroji and Lajpat Rai, were editors or launchers of newspapers. Some others had combined editorship with political activism. This rich tradition continued till the commercialization of news began getting better of it after the liberalization.

However, the pre-independence periodicals had a very high attrition rate. Most of them lacked sound financial back-up. Many had to wind up soon after the exit of its celebrity founders. Yet a few nationalist Engish dailies and language newspapers did manage to survive and establish dominant positions in their regions. Like *The Hindu, The Tribune, The Hindustan Times, Tej, Vir Arjun* and *Kesari*. Some surviving journals were launched just a few years before independence. Yet they could establish themselves against all odds. Conversely, British-owned papers that had changed hands after independence, had a still higher attrition rate. The Bennet, Coleman and Co under domestic ownership has been able to make it to the very top. But all the others languished or closed down. *The Statesman's* British editor Evan Charlton continued till 1966. Yet that daily as well as *Pioneer* are not in the pink of health. *The Mail* (Madras) had an early demise.

It is often asked how a few Indian-owned media houses managed to sustain themselves while hundreds of others had a short life. Then there is the other riddle: how the Indian-owned media houses without a sound capital base were able to compete with the British-owned dailies? The main reason was that at some stage along the way the control of such newspapers had passed on into the hands of a family or families. This naturally vested the owner with increased commercial interests. This does not necessarily mean that the family took it as purely a profitable business. In most cases, the owners tried to combine social and nationalistic obligations with minimum commercial responsibility. For the family, ownership of a newspaper gave a high status in society. Such owners in the course of time invested more resources in the business and began developing them into a financially sound proposition. The need to induct more capital compelled many family-owned newspaper houses to borrow money from businessmen and industries. Many of them were made minority stakeholders. The Second Press Commission provides details of the financial stake the industrial and trade firms had in *desi* newspapers—big ones as well as regional. This factor too had injected more financial discipline and more clout for the stakeholders.

It is interesting to note that by the 1930s and 40s of the last century major Indian-owned English dailies and language dailies adopted the same production technology, modern layout, editing practices and news network as that of the British-owned ones. Incidentally, this period was also marked by the emergence of many new English dailies—like *The Indian Express, Deccan Chronicle* and *Deccan Herald*—each with the best available production technology. They were able to compete with the established dailies, both Indian and British. For instance, *The Hindustan Times* introduced linotype setting soon after *The Statesman* did. Similarly all major dailies had rotary printing almost the same time. However, smaller language dailies, not the giants among them, were slightly behind in technology. Many of the small and medium dailies apart from the trash or scurrilous kind—continued to print on roller press till recently. This was due to the lack of enough print order. The point is that the success of the later era Indian newspapers depended on their ability to compete with others.

In this game they were not behind the British-owned dailies. Some Indian-owned newspapers had even managed to get similar advertisements in their dailies. The *desis* too had got the prestigious advertisements of the day: like 'Westend Wrist Watch Rs. 3, nine jewels; Wall Clock Rs. 2; Hurricane Lamp Made in Germany 8 annas. All these with blocks depicting the product. Another advertisement carried by both Indian and foreign-owned English dailies was: 'Print your own letters and address at home.' It contained rubber types (fonts) of alphabets and numerals, a board to fix them and an inkpad. Altogether it cost 'Rs. 3 and four annas, postage extra.'

Simultaneously, Indian-owned newspapers had also to learn to live with the prevailing political and administrative system of the Raj. They had to metamorphose themselves into serious newspapers from their position as anti-colonial campaigners. Hence they followed the rules of the game. The coverage of news and presentation had to be as per the contemporary social mores. In those early days, crime stories were to be played down. News pages were full of politics. Speeches by leaders, academics and holy men were regularly covered and played up. Accusations and scandals were often ignored unless they became part of the official record. Reports and photographs had to conform to the highly conservative social convention and mores. In fact, much of the contemporary media *dharma* went well with the Raj's Victorian tradition as well as the conservative Indian mindset. Hence they all had appropriately projected government decisions and policies. This was seen as 'responsible' journalism and earned them high respectability. Most *desis* did so even while upholding the nationalist sentiments.

For instance, they reserved their right to take a discreetly critical view of the colonial rules in their editorials. A careful look at the different kinds of treatment of landmark developments by the two sides—British-owned and Indian—of the spectrum proves this point. Take the case of the Congress Working Committee's (CWC) crucial declaration that its aim was 'full independence'. Nationalist dailies like *The Hindu* and *The Hindustan Times* did not conceal their glee and welcomed the declaration with gusto. *The Times of India* carried the story on page one. But its correspondent after a few paragraphs found fault with the CWC decision and doubted whether Indians really had the ability to do so. Another notable point is that all *desi* dailies were not uniformally nationalistic. Some of those in the princely states were more loyal to their maharajas than the Congress. Some had even mildly ridiculed the politicians' claims to rule the country. Only the maharajas or foreigners could do so. Such *desi* media houses were also soft on the Raj.

There is need to mention the exemplary role played by a Calcutta journal. Little known to the 21st century generation, Ramananda Chatterjee's *The Modern Review* in English and *Prabasi* in Bengali were intellectual institutions by themselves. Chatterjee was an ardent nationalist and liberal. His journals functioned as a platform for intellectual debates on widely varied subjects during the first four decades of the 20th century. Its contributors included Rabindranath Tagore, Jawaharlal Nehru, Mahatma Gandhi, C.F. Andrews, Lala Lajpat Rai, Subhas Chandra Bose, Premchand, Sister Nivedita and Jadunath Sarkar. The journal, however, had to be shut after its visionary editor's death.

Looking back, life moved at a snail's pace. Places were so distant. Information travelled by word of mouth—or dak. It took about a week, if at all, for the report of a devastating earthquake in Assam to reach a hinterland village. That was how things worked up to the 1950s or even into the 60s. Telegrams were an emergency service limited to cities and bigger towns. Postmen on bicycles had to take text to far away villages.

Apart from the telegrams, the post and trains were the fastest mode of communication. Even All India Radio, still in its nascent years, had to rely on telegrams to rush news. AIR was certainly faster but even most tehsil towns lacked radio receivers. It worked like this: first a spot report must reach a news agency through telegrams. The agency then released it to the subscriber newspaper which carried the information to the readers in remote tehsils and villages. The process took about three days. In 1948, Mahatma Gandhi's assassination reached this writer's village in Kerala through a radio broadcast in Malayalam—five hours after the incident. The village had one radio set which the householder's wife could not operate. The news arrived through a bus passenger.

In the early years, more than half a daily's circulation was dispatched to the subscribers through the post. Similarly, almost all news despatches came by post. The post was the lifeline for newspapers. Therefore, newspapers had their own numbered 'post boxes' kept in the local post office. When dak arrived, all items addressed to the newspaper were put in that box. Newspaper offices frequently sent messengers to collect dak items from their post box. If we still find 'P.B. No xx' in postal addresses, it is a hangover of that system. And so is the term 'dak' edition. Printing of the 'dak' edition was timed to suit postal timings. The remaining copies were delivered in cities or towns and their perepheries. As the number of outstation subscribers increased and transport facilities improved, the proportion of postal copies came down.

Newspaper agents began direct delivery only when the number of direct subscribers reached a viable level. Part-time booksellers in small towns were the first to act as newspaper agents. Newspaper offices dispatched small bundles to them by train and the first morning bus. The bookseller picked up the bundles and distributed them to the few nearby subscribers. In most cases, the buyer got them only by the evening. As for neighbouring villages, a cobbler or shop assistant brought it when they returned home after work. Yet for the village subscriber, what they read in those dak editions was fresh news. They hastily tore off the wrapper and scanned the headlines which were anyway written three-four days earlier.

Yet there was great curiosity. While one member began glancing at page one, others grabbed the loose sheets and started reading them. It was a normal practice and no one found separating newspaper pages strange. There were other kinds of reading habits. At wayside tea stalls, literate persons read out the dailies for others' benefit. It was a common sight in workplaces like bidi workshops and street corners. At such community readings, every news item evoked loud comments. "Who is this Gandhi? Who is Nehru? Only the British can rule the country. Or our maharaja." Such were the common comments by the loyal conservatives. Nationalist sections would ignore such puerile noises. The politicially conscious readers —or listeners—in those days used to cut out the badly block-printed photos of national heroes and pasted them on the walls. Those were the only photos of the heroes available to them.

There was no dearth of people who had a pathological hatred for newspapers. "Do you think all that they write is true?" the cynics would ask.

"It's always half truth and half lies," was another comment.

"Don't spoil your children's minds. They have already poisoned our youth with all sorts of funny ideas."

"First it was *kaappi* (coffee). Then the bloody soap came. Now they are wasting money on newspapers. They rob your cash and spoil the youth's mind..." says an old Tamil folk song. Coffee, soap and newspapers began getting popular almost simultaneously. And they could be bought only by hard cash, not barter. Those were the days when monetization was in its infancy. Daily wages were in foodgrains and barter trade was still prevalent.

There were also people who took to newspapers as a fashion, a show of modernity and exclusivity. Some newspaper readers thought foreign reports and stories about national leaders were more stylish. They flaunted their knowledge about what others were not so familiar with. For them, local stories were low grade. There were many such tales about semi-literate pretenders of different denominations. One was about a primary school dropout. He would always carry a newspaper claiming to be its local reporter. People began calling him 'sampadak sahib'. There was this retired teacher who walked miles daily to the railway station to fetch his favourite daily.

At railway platforms one could find small bundles of the previous day's daily newspapers waiting for delivery. Time and dates were not a concern for the readers in those days of slow life. Post-dating of the dak editions was an accepted trick resorted to by the editors to fool the distant readers. The newspapers simply added the next day's dateline. At the newspaper where I had worked, when datelines were advanced, all 'todays' were made 'yesterday'. There was an oft-quoted joke about a dull sub-editor. He mechanically applied the rule even in the case of sentences like 'Dr. Radhakrishnan said India (today) *yesterday* was at cross-roads...'

Sometimes some smart hawkers grabbed the post-dated dak editions meant for outstation centres and called out at busy bus stops: "Tomorrow's paper today..." Many passersby fell for his unique sales pitch.

Despite the jarring noises by the ignorant conservatives, newspapers were slowly gaining in popularity in the 1940s and

50s. Many began reading English dailies for general knowledge tests and proficiency in language. During student days, we had a story about an English daily addict.

"Can you find one mistake in *The Hindu* editorals?" It was a retired headmaster sitting at a Tamil Iyers' gramam at Palakkad. "Show me one mistake, and I'll gift my Blackbird pen to you." It may or many not be a true story. But it illustrates the kind of people who had canvassed for the English dailies. *The Hindu,* Blackbird pen and Westend wrist watch were status symbols in most part of the south.

"Maiyya mujhko paisa de de, me jaakar akhbar padhoonga. Nahi Chatni..." (Mother, give me money. I'll buy a newspaper and read it..." This was a poem in an old Hindi textbook. It is a testimony to the academics' open encouragement to the students to make newspaper reading a habit.

As the dailies gained in circulation, the newspaper agents began getting a celebrity status in small towns and villages—like the manager of the good old touring cinema. The manager was seen an a miracle man close to the film stars. Likewise, in many towns and tehsils, the newspaper agent was a sort of celebrity. In the early years, he doubled as agent and reporter. This gave them more clout. Often newspaper agents were invited to preside over or distribute presents at the primary school anniversaries.

The story of the mid-20th century newspaper will not be complete without mentioning the product's end use. Old newspapers had a virtual monopoly in packing and wrapping things. Every Ramayana and Mahabharata book had newspaper wrappings. The cheapest and most widely used wrapping material for the grocer was old newspaper. In villages there were only a couple of newspaper buyers. The grocer used to send a boy to fetch the old papers. Remember, it was decades before the polythene had replaced paper as the shopper's wrappers.

4

Celeb to Owner's Fixer

The much celebrated Editor of Indian journalism is dead. Long live the Editor. No more can one find the old kind of towering editors who had enjoyed an independent stature and whose name sold in the newspaper market. Today's printline says it all: 'Editor responsible for selection of news under the PRB Act.' That is the role assigned to todays' editor. Then there are editors for the opinion page, news desk, news network management and a host of other functions—all on behalf of the owner editors or CEOs.

There are media houses where the designations and work of even the senior-most working editors are assigned through frequent office orders by the management executives. The Second Press Commission says the editor is the 'ear and eye' of a newspaper. And now? In many media houses the ones assigned as managing editor or executive editor are only part of a large establishment presided over by a new generation owner. The editor can provide inputs but must carry out propositions coming from various arms of the new smart management team. Otherwise he or she ceases to be the editor. In effect, today's editior is more of a facilitator or enforcer of the ideas dictated by the expert advisers and consumer surveys. In family-owned papers, one of its members is your boss and in the corporate kind of organizations the CEO. That is the difference.

The post-liberalization media—call it New Media—has its own rules of the game and language. News is 'content', copy is 'file', (Delhi) edition is 'market' and circulation is 'sales' and a newspaper is a (consumer) product. The change is so stunning for those of us who grew up in the profession from the 1960s. Those good old days we were fed with a whole range of narratives like 'social responsibility' and 'public accountability' of the media, editorial independence and non-interference by the owners. A colleague once said how M.J. Akbar had thrown out an entire 'intrusive' advertisement while supervising page making at *The Telegraph*. Will he dare to do so now? During the first Iraq war, TOI had rejected a half-page advertisement sponsored by some activists on the ground that it was against a friendly country. But editor Dilip Padgaonkar overruled the objections after making some minor changes. Can a Padgaonkar do it now in TOI?

Make no mistake, capitalist values have triumphed over the old world ethics and lofty concepts. The New Media has rewritten the whole narrative that had dominated the debate during the past half century. True, there are a few dailies that are still resisting the unbridled push by the biggies. But how long can they remain as an island? The demise of the celebrity editor was not an isolated development. It was accompanied by the collapse of a whole lot of journalistic ideas and institutions nurtured by the old world idealists. It is a sad experience for those of us who had lived through both worlds.

"He is so busy," I have heard Sheshan Iyer telling a veteran edit page writer. "Even the (board) chairman has to make an appointment with the editor."

May be the editor's PA said this in a lighter vein. But it amply illustrated the high status of the editor. He was called to inaugurate academic seminars and deliver keynote addresses at universities. I have seen visisting foreign academics frantically seeking meetings with those editors.

In the early years, the very existence of a newspaper rested on the stature of its editor. It became a practice for the owners to scout for men of high reputation as their editor. *The Hindustan Times* had specially brought such stalwarts as Madan Mohan Malviya, K.M. Panikkar and Devdas Gandhi to head its team. Later years, it had even drafted Khushwant Singh. It was more for their name and stature than their efficacy as the head of a daily newspaper. Yet the relationship between the government, owners and editors was rather uneasy. It was marked by frequent tussles for the bigger say. Later years, we also stood mute witness to the gradual decline of the institution of editor. Whenever the equations of the owners with the ruling establishment and their lobby power rise, the position of the editor they appointed weakened. It was as simple as that.

Every new editor, as they arrived, came with big ideas. They wanted to leave their imprint everywhere. They would try for a new layout and masthead. Here lay the first test. If the owners endorsed the rejig, it signaled their readiness to give the new incumbent a long rope. Kedarnath Pandita was the copy editor of *The Indian Express'* edit page for decades. He had defined chairman R.N. Goenka's rapport with his new editor in three words: 'informal, normal and formal.' At the start, the incumbent was allowed to do everything informally. He could ask the general manager for the moon. The editor's word was order. Soon informality gave way to adherence to normal procedures and rules. That was the 'normal' stage. In the event of disillusionment with the editor or a clash with him, it was time to be 'formal', i.e. plain coolness to the person. That was the signal that the person's service was no more needed and he could pack up. We have all seen the process working at many big media houses. Some editors exited after a golden handshake, others under humiliation and each one unsung.

Those were the days when editors were hired and fired by the media barons. Often it was purely for the purpose of meeting different contingencies. When Times House hired H.K. Dua as editor, it had surprised the media watchers. After Dilip Padgaonkar's exit, TOI had not hired any chief editors for years. Then why was this sudden move? Dua was Prime Minister Atal Behari Vajpayee's media adviser. His high level links could have been useful to settle Bennet, Coleman & Company's financial entanglements like the FERA cases against its chairman Ashok Jain. Apparently, Dua's failure to do so led to his subsequent ouster. Later, the Press Council had taken up the case.

When Rajiv Gandhi became Prime Minister, Ramnath Goenka wanted to patch up with the young scion in whom he had found new hopes. That was the time when he had said: "Now I can die peacefully as a satisfied person." The result was the appointment of Suman Dubey, who was earlier derisively described by us at the *Express* as 'Doon Pal', as editor. The other purpose may be to settle the media house's pending problems (officially about 60 cases) with the government. But the honeymoon did not last long. Dubey could not survive the Bofors Tsunami which had altered the entire political power balance in the country.

Making inroads into the Nehru family was not new to Goenka. Quarter of a century before this, Feroze Gandhi, Rajiv's father, was drafted to a high position in *The Indian Express*. Feroze was not very keen on the job. It was known in those days that Gandhi's salary from the *Express* was being delivered at his residence. Was it intended as currying favour with the then prime minister whose son-in-law Gandhi was? Or was it to cock a snook at the family? There were different interpretations about the real motive of the *Express* boss, especially in view of the rumours about Feroze Gandhi's prevailing equation with the Nehru family.

S. Mulgaonkar was the editor of *The Indian Express* when the Emergency was declared. There were doubts about Mulgaonkar's anti-Emergency credentials. To neutralize it, Ramnath Goenka brought in V.K. Narasimhan as editor. Stories about Narasimhan's subtle but sufficiently effective protestations against the Emergency were legion. One day, at the peak of the Emergency, the *Express* had carried a unique editorial. The whole of it was made up of intelligent quotes from poet Rabindranath Tagore without any comments. But it had sent a sharp message. The censor was angry but could not do anything due to its very subtlety.

Despite such sterling service, Narasimhan was summarily removed days after the defeat of Indira Gandhi in the elections. The *Express* owner did not show the minimum courtesy of informing his editor about slaughter. That day a shocked Narasimhan found his counterpart S. Mulgaonkar again sitting in his chair. He came to know about the change in the printline only when someone had brought it to his notice. Apparently, Narasimhan's utility as editor of *The Indian Express* had ended after the exit of the Emergency regime.

Why was Mulgaonkar brought back? Again, to serve the claimed purpose of 'restoring' the *Express'* credibility with the readers. Such was the kind of owner-editor tension in the decades after 1960. The story did not end here. After some time, Goenka had a change of heart for reasons best known to him.

"Bring him back," one day Goenka asked Kuldip Nayar. "I think he is the best man yet. We can put him in *The Financial Express.*"

Kuldip Nayar was then with the *Express.* The new move had surprised him because Narasimhan was known as a stubborn stickler to ethics. Nayar tried to reason with Goenka. But he was firm. The whole episode was narrated to us by Kuldip Nayar during an evening chit-chat after a media seminar at Nainital. Among those who listened to Nayar recount the story were Upendra Vajpayee, H.K. Dua, Devdutt and John Dayal.

When Nayar reached Narasimhan's residence at Srinivaspuri in Delhi, he was sitting on a mat watching Doordarshan in his humble drawing room. He welcomed Nayar but went on watching Doordarshan. Nayar finally put across the new proposition to him. He suggested that at least he should accept the editorship of *The Financial Express*. Narasimhan, according to Nayar, did not utter a word. He only waved his hand in disapproval. But Narasimhan had poured out to an *Express* chief sub-editor who had met him weeks before Nayar's mission.

"When we (editors) are thrown out, not even a proof reader gathers courage to meet us," he was so overwhelmed to see his old chief-sub.

Perhaps with the help of Kuldip Nayar, Narasimhan was drafted to *Deccan Herald* as editor-in-chief. Years later, he went to Puttaparthi and worked as its media coordinator.

S. Nihal Singh had initiated several improvements in *The Statesman*. Once the pride of Bengal, it was a time when the daily was languishing due to technlogical and editorial inadequacies. However, C.R. Irani's meddling in editorial matters had caused immense heartburn. Soft spoken Nihal Singh was so dignified a person he quietly bowed out without making any fuss. This was in sharp contrast to what B.G. Verghese had done at *The Hindustan Times.* Its owners hired him both for his editorial acumen and his rapport with the Indira Gandhi establishment. Later Verghese was humiliated and shunted out because he declined to undertake certain unprofessional work for the owners. And one day the editor-in-chief was prevented from entering his cabin. A gentleman to the core, Verghese took the issue to the Press Council which had in its exhaustive verdict elaborated the owners' misdemeanours by naming the Birlas.

After his exit from *The Statesman*, Nihal Singh was brought to head *The Indian Express.* He has vividly narrated the kind of friction he had with Arun Shourie who most of the time enjoyed Goenka's patronage. But affable and highly professional, Nihal Singh continued till the end of his contract. Goenka then hired B.G. Verghese who was asked to restore the credibility of the *Express* which was damaged by the pamphleteering kind of articles by Arun Shourie. We in the *Express* held a party for both the gentlemen editors—outgoing Nihal Singh and incoming Verghese. Normally, ousted editors left unsung. At the *Express*, Verghese later said at the regular bureau meeting that while trying to restore the daily's credibility, we should continue with the investigative stories.

Kuldip Nayar in his memoirs has recounted why *The Statesman* owner C.R. Irani had turned against him. For the owners, every editor had a utility. Once the purpose was served, the person becomes dispensable. So much so Nayar's powers as resident editor were reduced and lowered to the status of a consultant. Soon his office phone and peon were withdrawn. And finally Nayar was evicted from his cabin at *The Statesmen.*

At one time, Arun Shourie was a big crusader against corruption and misdeeds. Sections of opposition counted on him as a great hero. At the peak of his glory this courageous man of ethics was also forced to eat humble pie. One of his longish pieces exposing a leading Congress figure was edited and made ready. But in the nick of time, an order came from Goenka at the *Express* guest house to hold it back. Apparently, the article had some link with a business friend of Goenka. Shourie was furious when he found the article did not appear in the next day's paper but was wise enough to reconcile to the reality on the ground.

This writer has first hand information about the insult suffered by another great editor. After Chandra Shekhar became Prime Minister, Dilip Padgoankar, editor of *The Times of India*, was offered a special interview. He was so elated that he informed his owner about the call from the PM. Hours later, the young owner of the media house personally handed him a file that was to be pushed while meeting the new head of government. With his high stature among politicians, it was too much for him to do such things. To resolve the moral dilemma, Padgoankar decided to cancel the interview. But the PM's aides later asked this writer why the editor had backed out. Those days, this episode was very much in the media grapevine and some gossip columns had carried it.

The Times of India had the distinction of being the first British-owned daily to fire its Indian editor. Frank Moraes was the first Indian editor of the TOI after it came under its desi owners. Before this, Moraes had also worked in a Goenka daily. He started well at TOI but suddenly one day he was forced to put in his papers. Later at a Delhi Press Club function, Frank Moraes revealed the reason for his exit from TOI. The Dalmias (it was before BCCL was gifted to Ramakrishna Dalmia's daughter and her husband Shanti Prasad Jain) had tried to use him for business lobbying with the government which he had refused. Unlike today, the Dalmias and Jains were counted as two big business houses with many factories and mills under them. However, soon after Moraes' exist, Goenka hired him for *The Indian Express*, his second stinct with the group.

Those were the decades that were marked by repeated musical chairs of editors in half a dozen newspaper chains. No purpose will be served by narrating who was where and why it was so. But the incessant hire and fire denoted one crucial fact: the media owner's dependence on an eminent personality as chief editor to enhance their newspaper's reputation. Goenka, as quoted by Nihal Singh, had said he wanted Frank Moraes as 'my race horse'. He had dismissed Arun Shourie as a 'two-legged horse'. That was the kind of purposes they served.

Even the long-served TOI editor Shyam Lal had an occasional brush with its owners. In those days there was no dearth of such stories in the capital's grapevine. However, his high reputation (famously, 'Shyam Lal is a Jat among the journalists and a journalist among the jats') and the kind of friends he had in government, saved the situation. Girilal Jain, that veteran of the Times House, had his own share of humiliations. He had a fairly good equation with Ashok Jain before his unexplained exit as chairman of BCCL. This long relationship made him emotionally side with the newspaper owners when they were under attack from entities like the Press Commission and other advocates of editorial independence. His pro-owner editorial on the Second Press Commission's recommendations had surprised even his close friends.

Yet during his sunset years at Times House, he had frequent runs in with the NewGen owners. Unlike in the past, Girilal Jain's ideas were summarily spurned. One day, Girilal with due respect presented to Samir Jain a set of carefully drafted proposals for improvements in the daily. The latter had a quick glance at it and without a word threw it on the editor's table—right in the presence of some junior staff members. This was a big humiliation to the veteran editor and he gave a piece of his mind about it to his friends. Appointments were made to the editorial and reporting sections without Girilal Jain's knowledge. Editor or chief editor is supposed to be the 'ears and eyes' of a newspaper and he was the authority to make appointments and posting of staff. But the young owners began producing separate pullouts and released them as part of the daily without the chief editor's knowledge. Once Girilal had given an interview to a periodical revealing that his paper would soon have as many an average 36 plus pages on all weekdays. It was normal for yesteryear's towering editors to make such claims. But the GenX owners of TOI were harsh to him on this score, and he got a public snub.

Kuldip Nayar in his memoirs narrates how a thoroughly frustrated Girilal Jain sought his help. One day he rang Nayar suggesting he should persuade Ashok Jain "to get Samir Jain, his son, off his back." The anecdotal reference was to the *Vikram and Vetaal* tales where the devil menancingly clings to the back of Vikramaditya insisting on correct replies from the hapless king. And pouring out his woes, Girilal told Nayar that Samir's behaviour was increasingly 'humiliating'. When Kuldip Nayar later met Ashok Jain at Bombay to put across the suggestion, the latter was passionately adamant. Samir, who was by then the vice-chairman, raised BCCL's revenue base by as many as eight times. "With such abundant funds we could hire any number of editors," Kuldip Nayar recorded Ashok Jain as saying.

Finally, Girilal Jain retired as a sad man. He was dubbed a misfit. He had often poured himself out to his old colleagues. There were reports that Samir and Girial did not even greet each other when they happened to be together at a function a few months after the latter's retirement.

There was another episode in TOI credited to the veteran editor Inder Malhotra who was its resident editor. One day, to his surprise, Malhotra had found several senior TOI journalists, including the resident editor, sitting on the floor at vice-chairman Samir Jain's office. They were writing out names of invitees on cards being sent out by Jain. This was a widely known gossip in those days. But its first person confirmation by a credible person like Inder Malhotra was really shocking even to Samir's acolytes. I remember once Dinanath Mishra, a former BJP MP and former bureau chief of *Navbharat Times* narrating another story. While sitting in editor Rajendra Mathur's cabin, he had found Samir dashing in with TOI's then resident editor Ajay Kumar. Mathur, a highly reputed editor, did not stand up to show respect. Most others were doing so in those days. After a brief talk, Mishra says, Samir directed the resident editor to go and fetch his brief case from his cabin on the fourth floor. And Ajay Kumar did it obediently.

Then there was this story about an obituary that had appeared in TOI. Samir was so furious when he was told that it was approved by his resident editor whose tenure was proved rather short. The vice-chairman's argument was that by carrying the obituary, BCCL lost that much paid advertisement on page six. He directed that thereafter no free obituary—unless, of course, of big celebrities—should be carried free by TOI. The hapless RE was told to give a public apology in the daily for the purported sin. And he did so.

The Economic Times editor T.N. Ninan was credited with the re-launching of the daily in its present form and giving it the unique 'pink edge'. But the truth was that it was Samir Jain who had introduced pink when Ninan was on holiday. He came to know about the change when a friend congratulated him for the '*Financial Times*-like look' of ET. Ninan, known for his dignified behaviour, did not make it an issue. Incidentally, neither Samir nor Ninan could take the pink edge credit. For, old timers will tell you *Anand Bazar Patrika* had pink even before the two were born.

Decades before this, there was another interesting case though somewhat different from the present context. Reputed economist Sanchin Chaudhury was the founder editor of the *The Economic*

Weekly published from Bombay. It was owned by Sekhsarias, a group of cotton merchants. The owners had differences with editor Chaudhury and they decided to shut it down in retaliation. However, about 200 intellectuals and thinkers of the day met and decided to run the weekly under the management of a trust to which academics contributed Rs. 500 each. Thus emerged the Samiksha Trust that relaunched the journal as *Economic & Political Weekly (EPW)* under the same editor. In *EPW*'s case, the owners, who were more in the role of a kind of venture capitalists, did not even think it possible to change the editor. For, the weekly owed its existence in Chaudhury's name. In any case the cotton merchants of the early 60s thought it was not an attractive business proposition.

The latest in the pantheon of martyr editors has been Krishna Prasad, editor-in-chief of *Outlook*. The weekly, known for its bold exposition of fresh ideas, often unpalatable to the powers that be, came out with story-breakers which others had avoided—week after week. That was *Outlook*'s forte. Its readers, week after week, waited for the journal to see the 'other' views. Its founder editor Vinod Mehta had in his memoirs narrated how the owners (Rahejas) had come under threat of raids when the weekly carried the Radia tape story. However, Narendra Modi is not as tolerant as Atal Bihari Vajpayee. And one day in August 2016, Krishna Prasad was told to pack up—as unceremoniously as his predecessor editors like Mankekar, Frank Moraes, V.K. Narasimhan, B.G. Verghese, Mulgaonkar, S. Nihal Singh and Kuldip Nayar.

The big media houses' attitude towards their Hindi publications was not different. There were many stories about the *Hindustan* (HT's Hindi daily) and their other publications from Bihar. *Dinman* was once Times group's most significant Hindi journal. Its editor Raghuvir Sahay was a poet and a cult figure for the aspirational youth of the Hindi hinterland. The journal had given exposure to hundreds of young Hindi writers and journalists. Many active journalists and literary figures had their first lessons in *Dinman*. Then at the peak of its glory, Raghuvir Sahai was removed and ordered to take up a humiliating function at the *Times* stable. No one knew why the owners decided to punish him and eventually shut *Dinman*.

At *The Hindustan Times*, it was Shyam Manohar Joshi's turn. Joshi was looking after *Saptahik Hindustan*, the group's highly popular weekly, as well as its morning English tabloid. However, one fine morning Joshi found someone else sitting on his chair. Then he was told to sit at home where his salary was sent. What was this talented editor's fault? Government pressure? Owner's or their friends' whimsical displeasure? He was never told the reason.

At Times House, one day the *Navbharat Times* journalists found a management executive sitting in the associate editor's cabin. His job was to superwise the editorial function over and above the normal hierarchy. Since Punit Jain was the CEO's man, no one, even the editor, could question his dicta.

"Why didn't you carry the photograph along with the story?" he asked the chief sub-editor. The executive was referring to a court report in the daily.

"Sir, sir..." the chief sub was grappling with words. At Times House, men from the fourth floor have an overawing presence. "Sir, they don't allow photographers in courts."

"But the hearing was held in camera," the executive insisted.

Even if it was just a joke, it amply illustrated the kind of direct editorial meddling by the new owners had tried to impose and the management executives' unfamiliarity with journalism.

D.R. Mankekar in his *No My Son, Never*, so vividly narrates the idealist editors' struggles for existence. The newsprint merchant to whom the editor-owner (not owner-editor) owned huge sums of money became the owner. Later the ownership passed on to the stevedore at the port. None of these 'venture capitalists' had much interest in journalism or newspaper business as it was not seen as a profitable busness in those days. Lobby power was non-existent. This has been the genesis of the existence of a dominant editor and subordinate—so to say—owners in Indian print media. Thus owner-editor arrangement continued to prevail until the emergence of the post liberalization new media.

In the 1960s, we the sub-editors had seen the owners dashing in to the editor's cabin for meetings. In those early days, eminent editors had the upper hand. A major change was that the business houses had by then recognized the lobbying power of the media.

This development was coincided by sharp divisions in Indian polity over the Nehruvian economic and foreign policies. On one side, Rajaji was furiously opposing the public sector and campaigning for freedom of free enterprise.

Throughout the 60s, the Swatantra Party was seen as a growing force and main opponent to the Congress. Its leaders had generic links with the business houses. The Swatantra Party's lavish finances were attributed to the business support. In this sharp political divide, it seemed the big media owners were siding with the Swatantra Party albeit discreetly. On the other, editors, by and large, were with Nehruvian persuasions. Business-owned dailies were carrying articles critical of the government's economic policies by the known writers of the economic right. Thus the owners began pressurizing their editors to provide more space for the economic right. But the editors with the backing of the powerful Congress establishment resisted the pressures, again, discreetly. This had ensured the continued domination of the editors as against the owners.

By the second half of the 60s, there broke another testing time for the Press. The bitter war for domination between Indira Gandhi and the powerful syndicate bosses had caused the first vertical split in the ruling party. This had its echo on the business-owned newspapers as well. The owners were clearly with the rather business-friendly Syndicate that had established control over all major pradesh Congress committees. Pro-syndicate articles were thrust upon the editors by the owners of *The Hindustant Times* and *The Times of India*, to name a few. The Syndicate also had the backing of some dominant regional dailies. *The Statesman* and *The Indian Express* did not have that probem as their editors and owners had more or less similar ideas. Nationalization of banks and abolition of Privy Purses by the Indira government had heightened this confrontation. It for once, appeared that a business-friendly establishment under the Syndicate was finally emerging in India as an alternative to the Nehruvian model. This had led to a fresh bout of editor-owner tension. There was a lot of coffee house gossip about how the editors rebuffed the owners. One was about Birla's PA personally handing an edit piece to his editor who held it over as the language was 'awful'. According to another story, Ashok

Jain handed an article critical of the abolition of Privy Purses to an assistant editor. That too did not see the light of day.

Looking back, traces of schism between the owners and editors could be found even during the last years of the 1950s. The First Press Commission is replete with such references. It expressed concern over the 'concentration of monopoly' in newspaper ownership and called for 'a sense of responsibility and public service among those engaged in the profession of journalism'. It called for building 'a code for highest professional standards'. Such suggestions had later developed into a bitter campaign to end the 'monopoly control' of media. Nehruvian socialists, the Left, liberals and academics of the era had found it necessary to strengthen the institution of independent editor to frustrate the owners' hegemony. The main thrust was that a few monopoly owners of the newspapers should not be allowed to dicate national agenda.

The harshest move against the big business press came when the latter was seen by Indira Gandhi as lining up against her opponents. Her information minister Nandini Satpati had drafted a press bill to discipline the monopoly media. It had proposed dispersal of press ownership and shares to others. This was to break the hold on media by a few big business houses. With the big biz at the helm, media's 'social responsibility' was in danger. Under the Satpati bill, trustees were to be appointed to replace the monopoly control of the media. Instead of media owners appointing editors, elections were to be held for the posts of 'independent' editors. In an angry editorial, *The Times of India* had dubbed it as a move for 'state control' of the media through the backdoor.

Soon came another fiat to end the monopoly domination of media. This was to introduce 'price-page' restrictions. As per this provision, the price of a daily newspaper should be proportionate to the number of pages it has. It meant every newspaper would be forced to choose between more and more news and advertisements. It would hurt dailies with huge advertisement revenue. A more blunt verson of this was to impose a uniform 60:40 ratio for news and advertisements. However, such sweeping proposals had to be dropped when some of Indira Gandhi's advisers doubted the constitutional validity of such provisions. Moreover, it was pointed out that the opposition parties could also use some of these provisions to wrest control of the press.

I remember *The Times of India* in a 1978 editorial lamenting why even the 'liberals' like the then Prime Minister Morarji Desai and Information Minister L.K. Advani were harping on the 'editorial freedom' as different from that of the owners. The Janata government came to power in 1977. But the tenor of the media discourse had not changed. For, even the Advani-appointed Second Press Commission had echoed a similar kind of discourse: editorial independence, media's social responsibility and public accountability, pattern of ownership and financial structure of the media, interference of the owners in editorial matters and editorial integrity. *Times* editor Girilal Jain was infuriated even at the commission's terms of reference. He had shouted at Janata Party leader Chandra Shekhar when he met him: "Is the editor a *Brahman* (divine essence)? Editor's freedom for what? To defy the owners? Disregard his own senior editorial colleagues?"

However, the discourse had begun changing from the early 1980s. The political divide had become more complex. Proponents of diffusion of media ownership and free editors had got themselves divided. Sections of those argued against monopoly control began viewing Ramnath Goenka more as a fighter against authoritarianism. All media houses were not on the same page. Some were 'good' and some 'bad' depending on their political shade. Thus even the rhetoric on editorial independence had become more confined to the media circles and activists.

We the footsoldiers could discern the process of the devaluation of the editor. Unlike earlier, there was a growing tendency to keep the editors away from functional managerial matters. 'OSD's and general managers—the old era designations—became curt when the editor's PAs contacted them. An editor of *The Hindustan Times* once got such a snub right when he was holding his morning meeting with his senior editorial staff. This was what senior assistant editor C.P. Ramachandran recounted to us soon after the incident.

The other shift relates to the tenure of the editor. Time-bound contracts to hire editors with fixed tasks had become the order of the day. This marked the end of permanent, long duration editors.

The contract editors were so eager to prove their capabilities. They always arrived with a set of fresh ideas to improve the paper. Some of them even wanted to have new mastheads, types and layout. In *The Statesman,* we were told, the owners had intervened at the last minute to restore the old masthead when the new editor changed it. This had happened soon after the dak edition was released.

An independent editor as an institution had exited almost by the end of the 20th century. Then what kind of an arrangement has substituted this system? We are at a stage when three models or their variations are working simultaneously. In India, most major media houses are family owned. Under this model, the second or third generation scions of the old owner-patriarch function as editor. In effect, this forms part of the family's 'partition' arrangement to distribute crucial positions in the company to its members. If one takes charge as director-editor, the other looks after business operations. May be a daughter or daughter-in-law is assigned the charge of the women, children or film publications of the group. *Jagran* had this arrangement long ago. And so *Malayala Manorama* and most other publications. Here it is unconcealed *advaita* (not two) or the theory that the roles of editor and owner are not separable—like the philosophical *atma* and *Brahman.*

As against the owner-editors, we also have editor-owners. The latter had a different origin. They began as professional journalists and launched their own newspaper or became directors of the media company in due course. Some have had a financial stake. Veteran editor Edathatta Narayanan launched his own ventures—the long defucmt *Link* and *Patriot.* His was more of an ideological mission with the backing of influential ruling politicians of the day. Cartoonist Shankar Pillai had set up his iconic *Shankar's Weekly* which was wound up during the Emergency. T.N. Ninan began as a chief editor of *Business Standard* and became its board chairman. All such editor-owners have been journalists in the first place. *The Tribune* of Chandigarh always had an independent editor under a trust. But we are left with very few cases of the trust model. In recent years, M.J. Akbar and Shekhar Gupta were drafted to *India Today* with great expectations. But the arrangement did not click.

The Times of India has always been on a different pedestal. It can certainly take the credit for dumping the institution of celebrated editor. When the BCCL vice-chairman Samir Jain said at a staff meeting that he considered editors as simply 'skilled labour', and he could run newspapers without a chief editor, we had laughed it away. We never believed a big multi-edition daily like TOI could manage without a super boss as chief. But soon Samir proved right. For over two decades, TOI could produce a fairly readable newspaper without a chief editor. What kind of a functioning model has replaced the editor in Times House? Does the fourth floor regularly micromanage the editorial work? These are the questions frequently asked in media circles.

It took over a decade for TOI to evolve its own working model. In the early years, micromanagement by the senior executives from the 'fourth floor' (FF) was very real. When I was in Times House a proposal had come from the above to intrôduce what was then called a 'swap system.' Under this, the senior editors were to be sent to the management floor and work there for some time for 'a feel of it.' Concurrently, management executives were also to be deputed to the editorial to learn how things work there. It was suggested that such exchanges would help familiarizing with problems by both segments of the organization. It would lead to 'harmonious integration'. The Jain brothers had reiterated the efficacy of the 'swap system' in some of their rare interviews to foreign journalists.

We have in those days seen the assistant editors of TOI waiting for the clearance of the editorials from 'FF'. Some edit pieces never came back. For some time, a senior executive who was recruited from a multinational company engaged in consumer goods business, was directing the senior editors. Later some have written about the humiliation they suffered at the hands of the 'FF people'. Former Times staff have many such stories to tell. Some of these may seem exaggerated. Or may be smacking of ill-will. Still many had put it on record.

As against this, the serving staff and TOI's admirers have an altogether different version. "Shobhna Bhartiya (of HT) is a bigger meddler," a journalist holding a senior position in the TOI hierarchy told this writer. The two Jain brothers (Samir and younger brother Vineet), they claim, do not bother about the micromanagement of editorial department. There was hardly any interference with the professional work, even in the event of frequent policy finetuning, some staffers assert. However, the truth may be somewhere between the two contrary claims.

It is necessary to explain two of the widely held misconceptions about BCCL's editorial management model. First, it is wrong to assume that the editorial content or presentation is tightly micromanaged from the FF on a day-to-day basis. There was such a practice earlier. Now no such institutional mechanism exists. Second, it is also incorrect to claim that the professional editors have full authority or control on the entire daily as the way the celeb editors once had.

Dealing with the issue of micromanagement first, certainly there was frequent interefence by the vice chairman and other executives at one time. Now the V-C is more withdrawn and evinces less interest in editoral matters. Basically, the Jain brothers detest power politics which was not their cup of tea. They had always spurned requests from top politicians and foreign dignitaries for meetings. This had happened even in the case of Barak Obama. They also feel uncomfortable in the company of business leaders. Samir Jain was known to be camera-shy. Instead, the two scions of India's largest media empire have been concentrating on the business build-up of BCCL.

If they had brazenly demolished the institution of editors, went ahead with mixing news with business and made the editorial staff subservient to the considerations of commerce, it was all for this single-minded pursuit of raising BCCL's turnover. Acolytes at Times House cannot deny this simple fact. Look at what Vineet Jain had told the *New Yorker* on record. *The Times of India*'s business success, he said, was due to the demolition of the "wall between the news room and sales department." Vineet does not conceal the owners' strong presence in the daily, even in its presentation style and construct of the content. He says: "I am a content architect." It was his idea to have small boxed 'Times' View' editorials and too many bit news on page one. He says he had later extended it to *The Economic Times*. It was he who had directed Arnab Goswami to adopt an 'attacking style' for Times Now channel.

However, the Jain scions have repeatedly asserted that 'agenda setting' or playing gurus to political parties were not part of their busness. They have set the broad policy frame for their what is described 'sklled labour' of the editorial section: Be on the safe side of the reigning establishment and its adjuncts in all matters. Avoid criticism of the regime or negative reports on them as far as possible. Try to dumb down negative stories and criticisms of the establishment or push them into inside pages or as adds-on to some other stories without separate headlines. But when such stories do gain public attention, go along with the tide and begin highlighting them. Under this paradigm, the PM—of any party—and his senior party bosses are holy cows that should always be treated with great respect. Rahul Gandhi was such a holy cow until May 2014. Then the tone changed and stories deriding him were allowed. On economic and foreign policies, the framework follows the general pattern of the mainstream Indian media: pro-Western tilt and going by the corporate line. By that token, secularism is treated as modernist. Editors of the opinion page, editorial and news network can work freely under these broad parameters.

The changing political situation and unexpected twists and turns do create problems. Then scribes are always attuned to sense the moods of the owners and company bosses. But when policy shift becomes necessary, signals come from the FF. And the senior editors readily take the cue. At the initial stages, TOI did not have a designated team leader. The present team leader 'Jojo' is also a director. Thus he functions as editor or considered as one.

In a way the present Times model is largely patterned on India's times-tested family model of newspaper management with minor variations. The incumbent director-editor is a versatile professional. But under the loose system at TOI, too many senior editors with fancy designations seek to directly deal with the owners or their close executives. Rahul Kansal, an executive president and Brand chief, referred to this fact in a published interview to a foreign journal. This explains too many zig-zags in news coverage and presentation. Insiders cite some eager-to-please types at crucial positions in TOI tinkering or dumbing down stories unfavourable to the present government. It becomes an issue when others play up such stories. There have also been cases of in-house criticism of pre-election bias which had put TOI in an embarrassing position, especially on Bihar. Often FF had expressed displeasure at such unnecessary tilts.

Going back to the properterial control of the news pages. TOI's daily pullouts like 'Delhi/Bombay Times', which mostly have as many pages as the main paper, are totally out of reach for the editors. 'Brand managers', 'Medianet'wallas, etc can come down any time with demand for reserved space even in the news pages of the main paper. It may be for Bennet University or advertisement-related stories like awareness campaign on internal pollution, dengue-mosquito menace or any such campaigns. At a highly publicized 'run against pollution' at Delhi's India Gate, participants found smartly-dressed girls and boys from the consumers' companies distributing handbills and ice cream to children. It meant the TOI campaign was so well dove-tailed with commercial interests. This was followed by more and more advertisements in TOI and allied dailies. In some cases it was at regular intervels. We do not know whether it was also part of 'ad-for-equity' scheme.

Professional editors are obliged to welcome such unethical intrusions into news pages, something the liberals and free media enthusiasts in the West consider as sacrosanct. Some time ago innocuous stories appeared in TOI's news pages making the startling revelations that internal pollution (inside home and offices) was even more dangerous than the threat from atmospheric poisoning. The theory was so convincing that families debated whether they should keep the windows open or shut to prevent outside pollution. Then days later, advertisements about the gadgets that could cleanse air within homes and offices appeared. Such commercial-related reports are regular and routine. TOI editors have practically no option but to allow them. I have a friend here who spent a few minutes every day to study the commercial links between news stories and advertisements in TOI pages. He would then scan the ad-for-equity list of BCCL to connect it further. There was a proposal to give the list as annexure to this book but the researcher wished to use it for his own publication.

Then there is a less known fact. It is about the way the crass commercialization of media has created so many new social fads and converted obscure community practices into national festivals. Take the 'Akshaya Tritiya', 'Rakhi' and pre-Diwali Dhan Tera. The former has been neatly linked with the government's gold deposit scheme. The Akshaya Tritiya gold rush has even penetrated into the south where the practice was earlier unknown. All such festivals get wide media publicity weeks before the event with prompt advertisement backup. These are major biz opportunities for manufacturers and e-tail giants. Festivals have been turned into a sales pitch with surprise gifts from a faraway brother or friend. And in the case of BCCL's 'ad-for-equity' firms (details about it in the next chapter), it is a double whammy.

Devaluation of the editor, by no means, was not an isolated trend. Along with it, several other crucial institutions underwent degradation. Special correspondents were once regarded as the ones with a special status in the hierarchy. With their top-level contacts and the editor's trust they enjoyed, their stories were treated with priority. This writer's late night special stories were readily carried by the chief sub without even referring them to the news editor. It was never trampled upon or added to other stories. And now? Special correspondents in most dailies are becoming just input providers. Multiple byline stories alone tell the special's great fall from the high pedestal. We had a long tradition of the special correspondents becoming edit page writers and columnists. Many politicial commentators appearing at panel discussions on TV channels had come up from the ranks of specials. Has this century produced any such analyst? At one time, many editors had come from the bureaus or the ranks of assistant editor. The belief now is that inhouse experts are not worth for edit or oped pages. Such pieces must come from those with a think trank address or foreign universities.

All this is part of the growing mistrust of the established system. In our time, we had post-mortem analysis of the newspaper on a daily basis. Autopsy is now passé. Instead it is full biopsy, i.e. rigid pre-screening before publication. I have seen at 9 pm the deputy news editor at *The Indian Express* reading out stories to Arun Shourie at home for his approval. Now in many media houses, every major story has to be vetted, added or re-written by the trusted copy editors.

It is also incorrect to conclude that the economic reform was the only factor that had hastened the metamorphosis of journalism as a mission into a total business proposition where a newspaper has become a consumer product. The post-1991 *laissez faire* ambience did give it a big push. There can be no dispute on that. But there were also more compelling factors. First is the emergence of a bold new generation of newspaper owners. They are energetic, foreign-educated, active and prepared to take risks. They are determined to take full control of the entire operation of newspaper business, not the management part alone. Unlike their elderly patriarchs, the young owners deride the big editor halo. They have successfully established their own editorial management system with talented journalist staff under them and proved that newspapers could be produced without an iconic editor.

Second, new communication and printing technology acted as a booster dose. The old generation editors' resistance to change had made the new generation owners to force it on the system. I was at Times House when Girilal Jain had famously dismissed Samir Jain as an 'upstart' who was bound to destroy TOI's long-earned lead in the industry. He was critical of the scion putting in so many resources in advertisement and marketing departments. There was unusually massive expansion of the two with huge recruitments. Looking back, it transpires that the TOI became the biggest business proposition due to those initiatives.

The post-Rajiv shift in balance of political power was the other reason for the makeover. The institution of independent editor has always been a tool to bend the media to the establishment's favour. Suddenly, the media houses found the coalitions and shaky governments incapable of hoodwinking them. Thus they felt themselves free to act—even to wrest the direct control of the editorial management.

Then there was that tectonic shift in the establishment's game plan to discipline the erring media—from class action to arm-twisting of the individual media owners. Unlike in the past, the governments have found it easier to ensure media support through subtle threats like an Enforcement Directorate notice and CBI phone call. And who is not a sinner? May be Indira Gandhi was the first to invent this tool. But both the UPA and Modi governments have used it to the best effect. It is always a quiet deal. Look at Arnab Goswami, the roaring lion during the murky days of the Lalit Modi scandal. He had sent his teams to Jaipur and Ajmer to dig out the muck. Such an all-out attack on the ruling party stalwarts was a big puzzle in media circles. How could a media house so keen to be seen on the right side of the ruling establishment allow such adversarial dramatis, and so virulently? Then suddenly the guns went silent. Apparently, the owners under pressure from the establishment asserted, and the lion of Times Now turned out to be a mouse. Some of his staff told this writer how shattered Arnab was when the shut-up order came. He has now confined his moral anger to an odd Bihar MLC or a railway TTR. All his subsequent exposures were on the basis of friendly government leaks, often with CDs. Clearly, Goswami is not a B.G. Verghese, V.K. Narasimhan or Nihal Singh. And you have no Ramnath Goenka around.

5

The Survival Sutra

The dawn of the 21st century found India's print media in the throes of a twin challenge. It has valiantly fought back the first set of onslaught—initially from the 24-hour news channels and then mobile-based social media and online news. The feat also marked a stunning circulation triumph for the print media. Instead of any drop in circulation, Indian media had scored an average annual circulation rise of 4.87 per cent during the past decade. In absolute terms, increase in circulation during the decade was as much as 2.37 crore copies. Even the English newspapers had scored an annual circulation raise of 2.87 per cent. This sharp surge comes against the backdrop of a circulation fall of 12 per cent in the UK, 6 per cent in Australia and 2 per cent in the US. But then there is a caveat—modern technology is infinite and can strike at any time with more devastating fury.

The second challenge is more real and is threatening to shake the very foundation of the contemporary free media. Everyone in the profession knows the space for free media is rapidly shrinking. Growing market monopoly stimulated by crass commercialization of newspapers, partisan bias, covert gags and dumbing down of inconvenient stories—all this together form a fatal mix. This can be as deadlier as the official blue pencil. For all appearances, the print media has a free run: the governments seem sanguine, watchdogs like the Press Council ineffective, self-regulation non-existent, professional bodies and owners' associations like the Editors' Guild and INS virtually moribund and statutory regulators non-applicable to the newspaper industry. Yet those in media are constantly under unseen restraint as to whether to carry this story or wait for the 'clearance' for that one, and how unobtrusively can those be presented in news columns.

The First Press Commission in the mid-50s had warned against big business monopoly in Indian media. Since then the whole discourse for decades has been on difusing the media ownership and strengthening the institution of independent editors to free the media from monopolitistic control. The concern those days was limited to the combined monopoly of all big business houses. What is now happening is the worst kind of media domination. Just one media house—Bennet, Coleman and Company Ltd—now commands more than half of the English language newspaper readers in India. *The Times of India* is the largest circulated daily in the world. BCCL's total daily print order is well over 6 million copies. According to *India Today*'s Magic Eye, BCCL's annual turnover is over Rs. 4,000 crores. The latest figures might be still higher. It also commands half of the English language advertising. TOI has already overwhelmed the Delhi 'market', pushing its formidable rival *The Hindustan Times* to the second position. This was after decades of cut-throat competition accompanied by predatory price cuts and such other unfair trade practices. The media house has since applied the same tricks of the trade to push *Deccan Herald* in Karnataka 'market' to a distant second position. The stranglehold is getting tightened on *The Tribune* in the north-west and some other 'markets' in the south. Significantly, the circulation gap between the biggest and next in most of such besieged markets is already getting rapidly narrowed down.

Spread of monopoly is more intense in the Hindi hinterland with disastrous consequences. Two Hindi giants—*Jagran* and *Dainik Bhaskar*—are invading district after district across Hindi-speaking states. Region-centric Hindi dailies with local flavour and political and cultural diversities are facing decimation under the combined might of money power, predatory price cut and better technology. Some time ago, *Jagran* bought Madhya Pradesh's most significant multi-edition Hindi giant *Nai Dunia*. This has given the former awesome market power in MP and Chhatisgarh. Latest circulation and readership figures show that in Hindi-speaking regions, the gap between the dominant daily and its second or third rivals is rapidly widening—a clear indication of the growing market monopoly of the two Hindi giants.

This trend is a major threat to the concepts of heterogeneity, flow of diverse informtion and political dissent. Media imperialism leads to brute hegemony where a single owner can dictate the social and political agenda with their increasing hold over the respective administrations. There have been cases of the giants playing down or exaggerating incidents at will to suit their political predilictions and business interests. Media portals have in recent years cited many such specific cases of news manipulations by the biggies. Under the sheer might of circulation, alternative ideas and diverse versions get dumbed down. The establishment, at the centre and states, loves monopoly because it provides a one-window service to the administration to armstwist the media and thus doctor public opinion. Media barons, in turn, use the domineering power to bargain for more benefits like cheap land and concessional facilities. We all know how certain media barons had got involved in the notorious coal scam that had enabled them wrest natural resources at cheap rates. They often dabble in politics and seek membership of official panels. Many get legislative council or Rajya Sabha seats. In some cases, such *quid pro quo* has been happening for decades—both under the Congress and BJP. Fortunately, newspapers in other Indian languages have shown better resilience to monopoly invasion with rival media houses in states successfully putting up resistance in business and circulation.

The media monopoly is not confined to numbers alone. It has already begun giving new meanings to the concept of news and its presentation. The Bhagwat Gita dictum that '*Yadyaacharati shreshta tatta devetaro jana*' (people follow what the great men do) or the old 'domino theory' is very much in operation. When TOI had cut the price of the daily to Rs. 1.50 in the Delhi 'market', the rival *Hindustan Times* followed it immediately. The latter had also hurriedly put together its own 'HT City' when TOI began winning over the Bollywood fans with its 'Delhi/Mumbai Times' pullout. 'Medianet' is a Samir Jain venture designed as BCCL's money spinner. As per the latest figures available, it accounts for well over 4 per cent of the company's annual revenue. It is essentially a platform for paid news or what in the US they call 'ad that mimics news'. An internal BCCL note made available to the reporter of the *New Yorker* explains how its Bollywood-style colour pullout carry 'brand building' stories for film and such other celebrities, of course for a price.

These paid 'advertorials' are written by the Times staff, not the sponsors as in other journals, for a huge price. This also involves serious ethical problems and leads to cruel ironies. The practice has now crept into the regular sponsored supplements. Writeups sent by central or state governments for their supplements appear under 'Timesgroup.com' or Times staffers' byline. This provides a false sense authenticity to the stories, of course, again, at a huge price. Logically, the group must own up the claims made by its own staff in such pullouts. In May 2017, a TOI editorial had valiantly disputed the claims made by its own staffers about the actions of the Kerala government which it carried under 'consumer connect initiative'. Recently, there was another paradoxical twist. An article distributed by the Press Information Bureau appeared under the byline of a senior staff.

True, such innovations proved to be a major financial as well as circulation bonanza for BCCL. Like the *'yadyacharati'* syndrome, many others in the profession were also forced to launch their own copycat pullouts. Incidentally, some of the weaker rivals were compelled to produce the pullouts free or without the cash-for-news arrangement. This was purely to meet the reader demand. Such has been the force of the BCCL's innovations. The whole 'Medianet' platform runs against the Press Council's guidelines for tariff fixing and payment for advertisements. Moreover, this predatory platform due to its domineering position makes their rivals commercially non-competitive. And the biggies take advantage of this huge financial cost for strangulating the smaller rivals through price cuts and lavish production techniques. BCCL's latest strategy is to introduce high-cost gloss paper which gives its dailies a better look. This is being experimented in selected 'markets' like Delhi. Like introduction of colour pages last decade, even the financially weak rivals will now be forced to opt for glossy paper.

'Private Treaties' or 'Ad-for-Equity' is another innovation that has rendered rival media houses commercially non-competitive. As per this arrangement, BCCL has treaties with a claimed 350 companies which could insert advertisements in its publications for one-third cash payment of the normal tariff. The rest is converted into BCCL equity in the respective companies. Already, BCCL's stake in those companies ranges from 1 per cent to 20 per cent. This is another what the Press Council calls unethical practice that gives undue financial edge to the media house as compared to those newspapers that stick to old ethics. The ad-for-equity system alone accounts for over 15 per cent of the BCCL's advertisement revenue. This too has a contagious effect on the entire media. Some media houses are already trying to copycat the practice with varying rates of success.

The relatively weaker newspapers are the worst victims of the manipulative monopoly. The biggies are brazenly leveraging their clout as the market leader to force advertisers to deny insertions to rival local newspapers. This is what an unnamed senior BCCL executive told Ken Auletta of the *New Yorker*: "We tell advertisers that if you want to be in *The Times of India* you have to drop our Marathi competitors and take the ads to our Marathi paper...We told advertisers that if you want *The Times of India* in Mumbai, you drop *The Hindustan Times*..." This is a classic case of brute monopoly using its stranglehold to stifle the competitors. Talk to smaller dailies, especially those in the Hindi belt. They will narrate innumerable cases of such predatory tactics resorted to by the invading Hindi giants. Years ago there were complaints that some dominant media houses were armtwisting the agents and hawkers in some 'markets' to prevent them from lifting the newspaper bundles of weaker or new entrants in the region. When 30 years back *The Hindu* launched its edition from Delhi, Kasturi himself went round the major newspaper distribution centres in the morning hours to supervise his marketing team. There were complaints of hawkers refusing to lift *The Hindu* bundles, obviously due to the biggies' armtwisting.

Another BCCL executive had revealed a perfect economic model to deliver TOI virtually free to the subscribers. That is to make the daily's weight as much as the *raddi* price. This is not a laughable matter. For, TOI is progressively adding more pages, advertisements and pullouts. Once this plan is put in place, sheer market forces will make it overwhelm the newspaper market. The way TOI is gaining thickness in Delhi, it may not be an unachievable target. This is going to be a major challenge to its rivals.

All this should sound a grim warning as to how the brute

monopoly could use its commercial might to destroy every instrument of free expression. We have elsewhere dealt with the price wars. Vineet Jain of BCCL has put on record: "If 90 per cent of your revenue comes from advertising, you're in advertising business." The power of advertisement revenue (as against the share from circulation) apparently provides immense holding power to the biggies to resort to price cut as a means to grab circulation from high-priced dailies. Take the case of the Delhi 'market'. Why should one pay Rs. 10 for *The Hindu* with 24 pages and Rs. 5 for *The Indian Express* with 28 pages when TOI gives you a hefty 48 plus page paper at a mere Rs. 4.50? During the festival season and many such occasions, TOI crosses the 100-page mark. For many, it might be as simple as that. In Bangalore, for some time TOI was sold at just Re 1. This is the kind of enduring commercial might the 'Medianet' and 'Ad-for-Equity' have provided to the biggies. How long can this unequal war go on?

The stranglehold of media monopoly has already hindered free flow of information. It invariably puts restraints on the citizen's right to objective news. It works at three levels. First, there are cases where the giants, mainly English and Hindi, tinkering with news unfavourable to their own business interests or their business partners. We have found BCCL alone has 350 business partners. *The Hoot*, a respected media watch website, had long back cited the case of an elevator crash in Bangalore in which two workers had died. TOI covered the news all right but carefully concealing the builder's identity. Clearly, BCCL has an equity stake in the company and was keen on averting any damage to its business reputation. A doctoral study by an investigative journalist of *The Caravan* describes how TOI had treated the industrial strike in the Honda plant in Gurgaon. He cites how its reports remained repeatedly partisan by highlighting the company's concerns while conspicuously ignoring the issues raised by the workers. This, of course, was for obvious reasons. Similar was its treatment of Gurgaon's Maruti strike. When the affected workers won in a court, that fact was dumbed down or ignored altogether but when the appellate court turned down their plea, it was a three-column story. This has another variation. Playing up or provide disproportionate coverage to others ventures of the media house or sister publications. Frequent stories about the 'Bennet University' is a case in point.

The second is the biased coverage and presentation of news by such media houses to suit their perceived reader base. We have already elaborated this aspect elsewhere. The reigning philosophy is: 'publish what sells' or carry what interests the English-reading urban elite. Cherished ideals like objectivity and fair play about which the press commissions and Press Council were so eloquent, are the biggest casualty. For them, the media's role is not 'informing and educating' but 'informing and entertaining'. Pick up stories that have entertainment value or simply make the news entertaining to the readers. You may call it 'formula journalism'. P. Sainath describes how the TOI editors had rejected his pieces on rural distress. "How is this relevant to our readers?" the news managers at helm had asked him. Write about successful business achievers and aspiring middle classes, the TOI editors had advised him. In an interview to a foreign journalist, former *Indian Express* editor Shekhar Gupta made the point so succinctly: "Seeds of the problem lie in the idea that you call focus groups where you figure out what it is they like to read in a newspaper and then tailor the content accordingly." Arun Purie of *India Today* conceded that his organization too have entered into barter deals with companies. "But we don't say we won't write negatively about you," he had said in a recorded interview.

The third is the *'yadyaacharati'* syndrome or domino theory. Arun Purie refers to the advertisers trying to persuade him to adopt certain other practices of the TOI: "If even *The Times of India* does it, why can't you?" He then asserts that he need not do all that those at TOI do. Surely, the domino theory is very much at work. Commercialization of news is spreading fast. On the issue of 'paid news', more newspapers are falling in line with the dominant media houses. This can happen for two reasons: either under market and commercial compulsions or due to sheer pressure of a dominant trend. Under the force multiplier effect, many lesser fry follow the biggies without even deriving any accompanying commercial benefit. We have elsewhere discussed Times House's problems with the Press Council and its subsequent blackout. But then why even others who are not in conflict with the Press Council join the boycott? Why should those newspapers which have no advertisement contracts or such things as ad-for-stake deals, also try to black out the council's verdicts of journalistic ethics?

A crisis of credibility is looming large. The direct properterial control on news and their growing nexus with the media house's business partners have left us in a curious situation. Every bit of news has become suspect. When a BMW crushes a boy and the rider's name not mentioned in the report, it becomes a suspect. Does the daily hiding the name to protect its partner firm? If a report talks of an MP's name in the possible list of ministers, wags speculate about the person's business links with Medianet. Any tax raid, sceptics scrutinize the names as to whether identities were being withheld and why. 'Brosnan ad as per contract: Pan Bahar', was a double-column headline in TOI in October last year. This was on page one. What further surprised the media circles was that the very next day another story on the quality of the products of the same firm appeared under an even a bigger headline. Naturally, this evoked more speculations in blogs and social media about the media house's links with the firm.

Last year another story appeared in its news pages. It was about the harm caused by the use of wrong paints. It was based on a survey which said those living in homes painted with fume-emitting paints were prone to respiratory problems. After some time, an advertisement of a paint free of such harmful chemicals appeared. It may be an accident but it gave enough grit to the critics to allege a neat PR operation using mass media. All this may be on mere suspicion or hearsay. Or at worse, on sheer mistrust spread by rival media groups and former staff. Yet wider sections of enlightened readers fall for scepticism. For some, call them incorrigible cynics, looking for the concealed truths in newspaper reports has become a pastime—like the daily cross-words and Sudoku. Owner's direct news control provides a fertile ground for such endless speculations. Fear of something being held back is so prevalent. And it is so disturbing for the discerning readers.

Media's collaborative acquiescence with the establishment is another topic of speculation. This comes up even during the idle chats at club tables and drawing rooms. A senior opposition leader makes a frontal attack on the PM (whoever it may be). If you get to read a headline and intro highlighting the ruling party's rebuttal and the actual opposition allegations as an add-on down below, it only tends to highten the incredulity. At times, as it happens in news rooms, such treatment of a story may be purely unintentional or accidental. Or it might have been overdone by a senior executive editor to prove his loyalty to the CEOs above. In either case, the end result is unbalanced or distorted presentation. Then there are cases of intentional rewriting of stories to tone down the effect.

"Always keep in mind how do those 'above' respond to the sensitive stories," a professional news coordinator says. "This was the golden advice I got from the executive editor on the very first day." 'Those above' means the brand manager or whatever you call the person. The coordinator could not survive there longer. Another practice is to simply hold back adverse stories and exclusives. A former high ranking investigative journalist at TOI says about 70 per cent of his stories were held back as they were not to the liking of the executive editor and the executives above. He finally left the organization. Then we have this senior desk man who says he had to put in papers due to a news manager's displeasure. All such stories, so frequent in media circles, tend to swell the ranks of cynics.

'False equivalency'—a term coined by *New York Times*' Public Editor (Readers' Editor) Margaret Sullivan—is a device to tone down the impact of critical stories. In the US they cite reports on climate change. Such reports try to equivocate sharply contradictory views because the two lobbies are equally strong. As a result, the actual truth about the man-made destructions get buried deep down. In India 'false equivalency' is applied in cases of political accusations where parity just does not exist. 'Congress, BJP spar over Arunachal': the government had found itself under fire in Parliament following the Supreme Court's indictment on the dismissal of the state government. Resorting to 'equivalency', the report sought to soften the government's embarrassment over the judicial fiat. Another device is filling the report with meaningless clichés like 'targeting PM', 'mounted an attack', 'indulging in slugfest' and attributing too many motivations, too wild and imaginary. In the process, the real points raised by the rival sides in a debate get lost, leaving empty clichés and verbose comments.

It is all the more disturbing when such news presentation becomes selective and as a device to defend the favoured political groups. In the absence of an independent editor, critics naturally put the blame at the door of the newspaper owner and his business compulsions to defend the ruling elite.

The market leaders in print media may dismiss all such misgivings on the part of the conscientious media watchers and readers as the obsessions of a minuscule section still clinging to the outdated ethos. Times, they assert, have changed and the GenX readers hardly bother about the so-called high journalistic values. "We give them a lavish 'Gujarati thali' which has everything for every one... Our growth chart shows the readers are happy with it. If a few great intellectuals wished to order connoisseur items from the menu card, let them," an executive at the BCCL was famously recorded as saying. Their understanding is that when it comes to newspaper sales, a few political activists and a handful of consciencious intellectuals hardly count. Readers seek news that relates to them, that entertains them. How many readers have time to look through all 48 plus pages? This is the gravamen of the new 'formula journalism' which at the moment is on a winning spree.

Elected democracy and Western liberalism were considered essential virtues of the 20th century capitalism. Dictatorship and communist regimes disallowed free speech and put the state-owned media under strict control. This has been the Western liberals' signature tune throughout the last century. Now there is considerable uneasiness in the West at the collapse of this established narrative. This has happened at two levels—the 'Post-Truth' shock and the erosion of public accountability of news. 'Post-Truth' is a recent political phenomenon that has badly shaken the power elite of the West. It is described as an adjective "relating to or denoting circumstances in which objective facts are less influential in shaping public opinion than appeals to emotion or personal belief." The term got currency after the upset outcome of the Brexit referendum and Donald Trump's stunning victory. Both had challenged the established political elite's tight hold over public opinion and the very effectiveness of the traditional media in shaping the voters' mood. Both had taken advantage of the people's post-liberalization disillusionment and misery. Both had also cultivated a nationalistic style with a xenophobic overtone. Hence the adjunct 'national-populist'. The rather noisy social media and Trump's brash campaign style made it difficult for the citizenry to distinguish between truth and fantasy. In such a narrative, facts no longer form the foundation of truth. This is the genesis of the term 'Post-Truth'.

None of this is new to India. There is a difference though. Here we have perfected the art of turning truth into an increasingly dispensable illusion with the aid and active involvement of the sections of mass media. Every Indian political *messiah*—Indira Gandhi, Rajiv Gandhi, V.P. Singh, Atal Bihari Vajpayee and Narendra Modi—had arrived with the same kind of hysterical fantasies that carried the middle class voters. They all had resorted to a massive campaign blitzkrieg that had cloaked the rival's achievements and projected themselves as the *messiah*. However, in the 12th and 16th general elections, many influential media houses allowed themselves to be willing partners in the image building projects of the winning prime ministerial candidates.

We in India are faced with a more worrysome trend. The usual poll-eve doctoring of the information order is now being successfully replicated with stunning effect to sustain the chosen establishment. An elaborate machinery affecting every walk of life has been crafted with a view to evolve truth into an increasingly dispensable illusion. In this game of knowledge war, what really matters is one's ability to make the gullible believe the illusions you spin with the help of an obliging media. None of the demonetization's objectives—detecting fake currency, checking terrorism and drug traffic and unearthing black money—was achieved. Lakhs of people suffered. Yet a decisive number of people endorsed the gambit during the subsequent elections. This is the best case to establish the efficacy of post-truth. This cannot be achieved without the willing involvement of the media. Things like communication skills and charisma could be propped up only by the right projections and tight source control, the latter being equally crucial. During those days, clips of the best poise and impressive oration of the messiah with the right audition were rushed to two dozen TV channels for repeated airing. Owned by loyals, channels still remain the most effective vehicles of the emerging information imperialism. We are in the midst of an interesting experiment in imposing information control without official censorship or state ownership of the media.

Making media behave is just one aspect of the new media management regime. The other is an elaborate system of source control. Flow of adverse information should be plugged at the very source by all means. This makes the task of media control much easier. In April-May 2017, there were stories of large-scale retrenchments by the IT firms. This was more due to introduction of new technologies like cloud computing, artificial intelligence and 'internet of things'rather than the Trump effect. Honchos of all IT majors had formally let out the figures of job loss to reduce the shock effect on their staff. The pro-establishment channels had safely avoided the story. When sections of print media carried the details, hell broke loose. Government spokesmen charged the media with spreading panic; Nascom was forced to deny it forthwith. The minister summoned the honchos of the IT majors for a pep talk. And the guns fell silent. Thus the truth was effectively suppressed without censorship. Unfortunately, media had failed in its responsibility to unearth facts and present them dispassionately after cross checking.

Stone walls are erected at every source. Uncomfortable information is kept as guarded secrets. The source control has all the attributes of a totalitarian state. Take the case of the Zika outbreak in Ahmedabad. For six months from November 2016, the information was concealed from the media when public awareness and community efforts are key to checking its spread. Finally, WHO had to break the state secret in May 2017. A Gujarati daily had it but its owners were pressurized to hold it as it would tarnish the 'national image'. May be the government wanted to avoid the bad omen on the eve of the vibrant Gujarat Summit of foreign investors which the PM was to open. It might also have spoiled the nationwide Swachch Bharat campaign which was then at it peak.

Simultaneously, the practice of selective leaks are being institutionalized. Earlier reporters had to dig out scoops. Now as part of the source control, there are invisible special window services in all major government departments, including CBI and enforcement agencies. They effectively stonewall unwanted information and disperse the leaks to the right channel or daily. Even the army PRs hand clips to the favoured channels as part of the new information order. By mid-2017, for many of them, leaked patriotic stories and exposures of opposition leaders have become established practice. This has made a senior analyst call them 'saffron channels'. Columnist Aakar Patel named it 'channel Jihadi'. Fortunately, rigours of the market pressure were such that even the most dominant media houses have invented a new model to overcome fall in ratings. While maintaining the tabloid-style pro-establishment, agitprop character of the existing channels, new ones are being launched as a newsy, non-partisan and fair alternative. Incidentally, the latter is picking up fast.

But there is one crucial difference. In the West, fantasies overwhelmed truth in spite of the traditional media's stiff resistance. But in India mainstream media itself was part of the project. They colluded with the myth creation and fabrication of false images. The media took it as its duty to create a strong leader capable of running a stable government. In some cases the media's honeymoon was rather brief. Neither the global recognition to 'Post-Truth' nor the word's inclusion in the Oxford English dictionary adds to our concern. It was with us for four decades.

For the Western liberals, direct proprietorial control of the newsroom without an independent editor is as bad as the state control of the media. In this regard, India is often cited as the worst case scenario in the 'free world'. Take, for instance, the Western liberals' cherished goal of public accountability of news. Liberals and advocates of free speech continue to persistently advocate some kind of institutional mechanism to prevent news control by private owners and corporates. They cite the Organization of Newspapers Ombudsmen (ONO), a world body, with 270 Ombudsmen or 'Public Editors' as they call it in the US. The institution still commands immense moral powers and authority.

And out of 270, how many Ombudsmen do we have in India, the home of the world's largest English daily? Just one for the print media. *The Hindu* alone has a 'Readers' Editor' equivalent to Public Editor. No other daily. News portal Thewire.in and Scroll too have readers' editors. Unfortunately print media has been zealously avoiding any such independent scrutiny of free flow of news. In

1989, *The Times of India* had appointed former chief justice P.N. Bhagwati as its Ombudsman. This was under the reign of BCCL's GenX leaders. This had surprised the media observers. But then it transpired that the appointment of the former CJI was purely as a response to TOI's problems with the Press Council. They simply wanted to prove that rather than a light-weight Press Council they had a top jurist at the helm. As expected, the experiment was proved to be short-lived and Justice Bhagwati had to bow out. Clearly, a newspaper which does not even have a regular 'letter to editor' column was not amenable to the dictates of judicial pontifications. For, TOI Ombudsman had actually become an obstacle to BCCL's young owners' new concept of an editorless newspaper, paid sections and 'ad-for-equity schemes and Brand intrusions into the news sections. Paid by the newspaper organization, the readers' editor has an independent role. He or she functions as interface between the readers and the editor. The person's role is to be a referee in settling the complaints from the readers.

Adequate attention has not been paid to another impasse being encountered by the contemporary free media. It is largely a hangover from the past when the media had a cosy *quid pro quo* relationship with the establishment. Under this unwritten code, media extends full cooperation to the government on issues of foreign policy, internal security and emergency situations like war and natural calamities. Constitutional obligations also bind the media to extend all possible cooperation to the administration in the event of a national crisis. Indian media has, by and large, unreservedly stood by the successive governments during the war with the neighbours. The only exception was the 1962 war with China. Rightist forces, including the RSS-controlled Jana Sangh, Swatantra Party and assorted groups of Indian socialists had mounted an attack on Prime Minister Jawaharlal Nehru right in the midst of the war. True, those who had acted against the country's national efforts at defence were doing so at the behest of the Western cold war forces that were bent on using the crisis to pull down the pro-Soviet Nehru regime. In the formidable line-up were several pro-US Congress leaders like Mahavir Tyagi who had assailed their own government even on the floor of Parliament.

Sections of the media had also joined the jarring voices. This may be the first and last case of the media breaking the good old golden code. Since then the mainstream media had maintained the time-honoured relationship during every war and border clashes with Pakistan. Take the case of the Kargil operation. It has been a well coordinated successful effort under the Vajpayee government. The role of the media, including the nascent 24-hour news channels, has been superb in that it was able to inspire the nation against the adversary. In the process, the media also carefully avoided mentioning the lapses and several pitfalls in the government's war efforts. The media's fraility showed up after normalcy was restored. Ideally, that is the right time for introspection and evaluation of the government's actions.

Like unreserved endorsement of the executive's actions during a crisis, it is also incumbent up on the media to conduct a dispassionate post-mortem of the failures and inadequacies. Both are inseparable aspects of the media *dharma*. If the Kargil operation has been a good example of coordinated efforts, it also unfolded the grim truth about the utter intelligence failure on the part of the same administration. It was so shameful that the government's intelligence agencies were unaware of the wanton occupation and massive fortifications of a whole stretch of Indian territory by Pakistani forces. Initially, the official response was to deny the intrusion and dismiss local reports as a false alarm. Why did the media fail to find out where things went wrong and fix the responsibility?

The task of the free media, both during conflicts and under normalcy, is very delicate and sensitive. But it is also fairly well defined. During the period of hostilities and tension media is bound by its own '*Bhishma* vow' even if the confrontation is due to our own rulers' adventurism and follies. Bhishma too was in a similar moral dilemma. But once the hostilities end and the rulers themselves begin indulging in *bonhomie* with the adversaries, we need not bind ourselves by the Bhishma vow. From that point onwards, the media should end its embedded or captive role. Unfortunately, Indian media or a dominant section of it, did not have an exemplary record on this score. I remember M.N. Buch had complained about English dailies that had kept rejecting his pieces on economic reform in the early 90s just because it was also critical of the executive's failings.

In this context, it is necessary to refer to a recent trend. Take the Indian media's coverage of the foreign visits of the dignitaries and multilateral summits. For all practical purposes, these are not different from the kind of coverage in countries where media is under the state control. Traditionally, domestic media does give a national angle to such events. Every country focuses on its leaders' activities at global conclaves and endorsingly present its official views. This is unexceptionable. The problem arises when nationalistic overdrive blinds us to the actual happenings, especially those unpalatable to the establishment. This happens due to the media's zeal to defend their respective government's official position. But when unfavourable tidings at international fora are deliberately dumbed down, it is certainly a dangerous trend.

Media's nationalistic indulgence in the last three years has become too preposterous. Look at the coverage of events like the G-20 Summit in China, ASEAN in Laos, UN General Assembly, BRICS in Goa and BIMSTEC in 2015-16. The real deliberations at the summits and core outcomes were eclipsed by repetitive projections of the official position. Almost like a coordinated campaign. At BRICS, our preoccupation with terrorism made us oblivious to its crucial deliberations on issues like equitable distribution of global resources, BRICS' own rating agency, railway research network, agricultural research and sports council. Did the Indian media bother to go into the merits of such programmes from our own stand point? This was a grave lapse.

Blatant news blackout of adverse events is the worst form of the media patriotism. Such gestures may be justifiable during war or national emergency. But of late the blackout is becoming the norm even under normalcy. One such incident happened in the midst of our diplomatic thrust after the Uri incident to isolate Pakistan. The state department spokesman made a formal announcement in Washington that the US was not in favour of declaring Pakistan a terrorist state. The PTI story was carried by several newspapers in their blogs. But the reasons best known to the editors, even the same newspapers did not carry this significant report. The story may not be music to our ears. But shooting the messenger is not the solution.

Just before this, there was another similar snub from the US.

On September 12, 2016, the state department spokesman John Kirby was asked: "Where does the US stand on Baluchistan? Because Indian Prime Minister has raised the subject." Kirby's reply: "The US government respects the unity and territorial integrity of Pakistan, and we do not support independence for Baluchistan." Why was the Indian media, barring one, blacked out the story? Similarly, the Organization of Islamic Cooperation (OIC) had in a resolution at its foreign ministers' conference at Tashkent upheld what it described the right to self-determination for Kashmiris. It had also condemned the human rights violations in Kashmir. This story was also blacked out by our media. A few days after the OIC resolution, there was a retort to it on October 24 by the South Block spokesman. This we carried. All this had happened in a span of one month. This has been happening frequently. Is Indian public opinion so fragile to melt away by such seemingly adverse reports? Blatant blackout of unfavourable news is a tool specific to dictatorships and closed societies. The best course to deal with adverse stories is to carry them in full and then expose their perfidy and thus prepare the public opinion to face up to the adversities. Moreover, obligation to project the official position is different from blackout of news however embarrassing it might be to us. This goes against the readers' right to know full facts. Balanced presentation of information is an inalienable duty under the media *dharma*. Such misplaced notions only tend to erode our own credibility.

Clearly, this is not the free media *dharma*. There is no conflict of duty between standing by the executive on major foreign policy and strategic initiatives and performing the role of 'informing and educating' the public. Both can be harmoniously combined. It is the duty of the responsible media to respect the reader's right to know. We as media are obliged by our own professional *dharma* to present the 'other' view and thus alert the polity. Any such conspiracy of silence indulged in by large sections of media will prove to be the biggest disservice to the polity, even to the incumbent executive. We all had early signals about the scams taking shape during the Manmohan Singh government's second term as prime minister. But in their eagerness to please the establishment, the mainstream media—unlike the parallel media—

sought to apply the blue pencil. Similarly, the 'good' media had ignored as unprintable the charges against Robert Vadra. It was left to dailies like *The Hindu* and *The Indian Express* to alert the rulers about the rot setting in. Had the biggies also performed their assigned role as an ethical watchdog at the early stages, the UPA government might have got enough time to take correctives and might have been spared much of the election-eve scam taint.

Finally, there is another pertinent question that begs for an answer: Is the executive's right to media cooperation for its foreign and strategic policies and internal security absolute in the normal times? The Bofors scandal had burst the first fad as early as the late 80s. It had established that scrutiny of government's arms deals no more constituted an 'anti-national' act. Nor does it amount to hampering defence efforts. This apart, a grievous distortion in the nature of the media-government relationship had taken place in the past few years. Before this, the interaction between the two entities was marked by mutuality. It was never unilateral. We have elsewhere referred to how even a bureau chief (UNI) like R. Rangarajan was taken into confidence on major strategic initiatives in yesteryears. Even an authoritarian prime minister like Indira Gandhi had recognized the importance of direct media interaction. A day before the strategic Indo-Soviet defence agreement was signed before the Bangladesh operation, the government had taken senior editors like Girilal Jain into confidence about its details. Jain himself had recorded this fact in an edit page article. Editors of *The Statesman, The Indian Express, Patriot* and *The Hindustan Times* were also called for special briefings. This was the kind of tradition we had. Similarly, soon after the first nuclear explosion at Pokhran, she had specially explained to the editors the circumstances under which the government had to take the decision.

Bureau chiefs who were seen as representatives of the editor were religiously kept in the loop during and on the eve of the wars with Pakistan, including the Kargil operation. The whole idea was to seek the media's involvement in all major strategic initiatives. And now? It has totally become a one-way traffic. The present establishment does not believe in genuine interactions with media. The institution of media advisor to the PM, who functioned as the necessary interface with media, has been abolished. The PM's press conferences, a major media thrust where news persons were free to interact with the government's chief executve and had enabled the government to win public space, is a thing of the past. The PM's recent interviews to the embedded scribes from friendly media houses, are never a substitute for fruitful interface with the entire press corps. Worse, the incumbent government seeks to divide us into 'good' media and 'bad' media. Patronage is bestowed on such extremely narrow calculations. This was never so under the previous governments.

What makes it worse for the free media has been the new government's propensity for abrupt policy reversals. In the past three years, foreign policy has undergone tectonic jolts. Vajpayee and Manmohan Singh had zealously guarded India's much cherished strategic autonomy. This had enabled the previous governments to put up a better strategic bargain with the global players. The Modi administraton has suddenly pushed India into the US alliance in the South China Sea region which the predecessors have been scrupulously avoiding all the while. The UPA government had withstood all pressures for dragging India into multi-lateral joint military exercises against China. The former's golden rule was to welcome bilateral joint exercises with all countries. Now suddenly the Modi government has signed the Logistic Support Agreement (LSA) under which India's military bases will be thrown open for use by US forces. All this was done without any meaningful interaction with the media.

No lively democracy with an assertive free media might have allowed such a *volte face* and retrogression without critical scrutiny and appraisal. Then how is it that the mainstream media in India happen to endorse a whole set of fundamental policy reversals and flip-flops sans even a whimper of demur? This is a living testimony to the stunning success of the unique media management system perfected by the Narendra Modi dispensation. The new government has little use for the old style dialogue and interaction with media. Instead, it has devised a complex web of 'good' and 'bad' media. The whole strategy of the present establishment is to cultivate the 'good' media, especially those controlled by the friendly corporates. The latter has a domineering presence in the broadcast media. These are the ones who take an aggressive role in instantly endorsing the government initiatives even in the event of sudden somersaults. They relentlessly work to create a favourable public opinion through motivated leaks, panel discussions and exaggerated 'breaking news'. When a dozen such channels blare tenaciously, it amounts to creating the tone for the national narrative. This is further amplified by the dominant sections of the print media, including some market leaders. In the face of such massive pedagogy, the free sections of the media find themselves voiceless. Thus they have become victims of the brute domino effect or *yadyaacharati* syndrome on which we have already gone into in detail. The establishment is well aware of this inherent debility of the 'bad' media. Hence they need not care for them. Consequently, the official patronage has become the sole preserve of the 'good' media.

Then how can liberalism and free media be safeguarded in the wake of the spreading monopoly stranglehold and its Domino effect on the quality of journalism? Old remedies like diffusion of ownership, separation of editorial and management controls and price-page curbs are passé. There can be resistance to such moves even from within the media. Therefore, the way towards a free information order can only be through the judicious use of the existing market mechanism. For, competition in the news market has been proved to be the most effective deterrent to the information monopoly and content distortions.

The most stunning evidence of the power of a competitive news market has been the compulsive comformity being displayed by the contemporary Indian print media. It, by and large, eludes the customary Left-Right classification. It was not so during the second half of the last century when a sharp division was so discernible. Those days, foreign media used to quote sections of Indian media like *Patriot* and *Blitz* with the adjective 'Left-wing'. Such sections of media had advocated distinctly different economic and foreign policies. They had even used such terms as 'tycoons' to describe corporate houses. Today can you name any mainstream daily (English or regional language) that does not endorse the post-1991 economic reform? Perhaps this is partly due to the ownership pattern of the media houses. But even on communal and communitarian issues, mainstream media avoids partisan positions.

Some media owners do have distinct communitarian affiliations. But they too are forced to fall in line when it comes to divisive issues. Today's enlightened reader detests mass media pushing extreme views (even if he or she personally air utterly irresponsible ideas through the social media). In November last (2016), the Information and Broadcsting Ministry ordered the shutdown of NDTV Hindi and a TV channel in Assam. There were big protests from the journalist fraternity, including the Editors' Guild. But certain market leaders continued to play down the draconian measues for the first few days. But when it developed into a massive issue, the 'good' media too fell in line to defy the government order. Look at the partisan dailies that have fallen by the wayside despite some of them being reasonably newsy and well produced: *Patriot, Motherland* and *Pioneer* (BJP), *National Herald* and allied publications and Reliance's *Business & Political Observer* that had visibly campaigned for the ouster of the V.P. Singh government. The fact was that even the committed votaries of such dailies looked to other newspapers for reader satisfaction. In today's news rooms, the term 'balanced' has become the every day watchword. Every story should undergo this compliance test. Editorial managers frequently ask: are we going too far? Get a piece from someone on the other side to 'balance' it. The consumer may or may not be the king. But for the 21st century mainstream print media the subscriber is the sustainer. In the event of a hard choice between the government fiat and subscriber preference what will an avidly pro-establishment media house do? Not a second's pause, they will stand by the latter. Such is the power of the subscriber market.

We are living with a highly volatile information system. The old kind of news blackout no more works even if the entire print media in a region shuts off an event. Stand-alone online news portals and social media are there to break the blackout. Social media has emerged as the fastest rumour mill. It has a wide reach. Often puns on frequent biased stories in the mainstream media, both TV and print, are making waves through the social media. This can bring a bad name even to those who think they are unassailable. Think of the situation where readers have to turn to the rival dailies or news portals to know the 'other' side of the story. Recently, TV personality Karan Thapar has advised the celebs to check with the print media for 'true fact' before rushing to react to reports appearing on TV and social media. Many people have fallen prey to such irresponsible information on these platforms. Circulation experts feel that there is a trend among readers to return to print media after having switched to mobile-based news and TV channels. This argument is founded on the increase in percentage of circulation rise of the print media. Even if the premise is too premature, it should alarm even the mightiest market leader. This means the conspiracy of silence will not go uncontested. Watch the way even the most trusted brands and oligopolic markets crumble under the weight of new industrial products. In the media world too, no market leader can hereafter run roughshod over with news blackouts. Moreover, news as a saleable product is different from other factory-made items. The latter has well definable features and hence easier to maintain quality. In the business of news, consumers' expectations are not static. So the brand managers have to keep a constant watch on readers' preferences and shifting mood on emerging issues. Take this case: this year, the Congress spokesperson came out with a Rs. 2.5 lakh crore pulse scam involving Jayesh Patel and Adanis. Some biggies did try to dumb it down. Soon, under the pressure of the news market, the dominant 'good' media too had to carry a follow-up of the story without, of course, naming the industrialists.

Such 'fine-tunings', as they call it, has become part and parcel of the dominant media's content management under oligopoly. The market leaders first holding back a critical story and then forced to do a followup the next day, talks volumes of their vulnerability to the competition from the liberal media. Let us not overlook the reality that the free sections of the media still have an imposing presence in all 'markets'—like *The Hindu* in the south, *Telegraph* in the east and north-east, *The Tribune* in the north-west and *The Hindustan Times* (if one includes it in 'bad' category) in Delhi and surrounding regions. *The Indian Express*, 'journalism of courage', may be second or third in most markets. But it has a highly enlightened readership with domineering influence on opinion makers.

There have been long debates among such media houses as to

how to deal with the market invasion. Some like the HT seems to have tamely yielded to the Domino effect. But those in second and third positions are looking at a different strategy. For them, no purpose will be served by following or copycating the market leaders in content management. From the Ramnath Goenka days, *The Indian Express* had realized that it does have an enlightened readership, some with esoteric tastes. Some other regional media houses have gone in for a mix of similar content presentation. This includes large sections who seek political alternatives and uncontrolled news flow. If newspapers with double the per issue price and half the number of pages have been able to put up a valiant resistance against the invading market leaders, it simply proves that there is a large section of informed readership that yearn for free and fair information order. Those who buy a second daily do so only to get the 'other' view, things that the pro-establishment media seek to conceal from the readers. They have a very strong, widely spread presence. Then there are the oppoisiton groups—pro-Congress when the BJP is in power and vice versa—that look for anti-government stories. This is a formidable constituency that sustains the liberal media.

Incidentally, the large sections of media that air voices of dissent have a long tradition of critical journalism. Though less in circulation, they have a strong influence on public opinion. They have always been less vulnerable to the pressures by the parties in power. Therefore, for the liberal forces that cherish free expression, the first survival *mantra* must be to strengthen the existing bulwark of free media. Free and liberal media does not necessarily mean anti-establishment. In its pursuit of news, it may have to unearth murky happenings. Critical scrutiny and investigation in good faith are essential characteristics of free expression. Another function of free media is not to shut off information under pressure or for ulterior motives. There have been occasions when free media may not take a decisive editorial position on an emerging issue. But that need not prevent it from presenting differing perceptions on those issues. This is where the liberal media distinguishes itself from the tightly controlled or those uncritically committed to the establishment. Like reasonably balanced presentation of news without prejudice, liberal media must also present a varied fare of views on their opinion pages. Some newspapers are already making the edit and oped pages a platform for diverse views by the domain experts. Here is where it differs from the controlled media. Look at the market leaders. Their edit page pieces must necessarily conform to the official editorial line. For them, free views are anathema. The tone and tenor of their edit page pieces invariably indicate their subtle policy shifts.

Another *sutra* for the free media is to break the various kinds of blackout by the prominent market leaders. Why should the liberal media join the boycott of the Press Council, a watchdog body set up under an act of Parliament, just because one media house had problems with it? The Press Council, with a balanced representation of the Editors' Guild, INS, working journalists, Sahitya Akademi and Bar Council regularly adjudicates complaints by and against the media and administration. At one time, the print media routinely carried the council's findings. These are of considerable interests to the media. The Second Press Commission had even recommended preparation of a compendium of the council's adjudications as a guide to the media. In case the council gives any far-fetched verdict, it is the duty of the fourth estate to criticize it. Healthy debate, not blackout, is the remedy. Many other sections of the polity are also victims of similar boycotts, all imposed due to the domino effect.

Ombudsman or readers' editor is another institution that enhances the strength and authority of the liberal media. As of now, *The Hindu* alone has a readers' editor who attends to the readers' complaints against the editor. 'Public Editor', the term they use in the US, is an important institution in societies with liberal media. Another instrument crucial to the healthy growth of free speech is 'fact check'. During this year's presidential campaign in US, some newspapers had introduced 'fact check' to separate chaff from wheat when the rival candidates came out with tall claims. In India unverified facts and wild accusations are routinely paraded as truth. Business lobbyists and political leaders are often allowed to go scot-free with half truths. If made an occasional feature, 'fact check' can meet the readers' right to verified facts.

Will the online news portals work as a speed breaker to the monopolistic expansion in print media? Initially people laugh at such suggestions. Every newspaper organization has an online service and some have special websites for features and analysis. Then there are over a dozen independent news and features web sites. This is in addition to the ones specializing in niche areas. Yet so far we do not have any conclusive empirical evidence to determine the percentage of print media readers who have shifted to online news. There are people who talk about the growing absence of newspaper reading habit among the smart phone-bound youth. Is this due to the ready availability of the online news? There is also a related question. What percentage of newspaper buyers look at the morning dailies only to recapitulate or confirm what they already know from the TV and online news and social media?

This latter question is more crucial in our quest for clues about the future online challenge to the print media, especially as a bulwark to information monopoly. Already there are nearly a dozen independent online web sites whose primary strength is their essentially critical approach in a refreshening environ of free expression. Some of them do have a soft story mix but they incessantly come out with adversarial stories, happenings in the murky corridors of power and investigative pieces. Some of them provide an unconventional sort of foreign policy analysis highly critical of the government initiatives—something one could never expect from the more conventional print media. As of now, this genre of online news portals looks more like the rebel journalists of the 1960s which cumulatively had a high penetration in the newspaper market. (see 'The Rebellious 60s'). These parallel media were so popular that they could set the political narrative of the era. The portals also seem to play a similar role. Like the old rebel journals, the news portals too enjoy an advantage. With manageable investment and low running cost, they will be free from the arm-twisting by the government and media owners. Neither are they under the Damocles' sword of the ED notices and CBI raids.

A least observed fact has been that the unattached news portals have of late gained much muscle in the market place of ideas. The stories they carry are of a serious nature. Most of them are well documented and well argued. Led by eminent journalists like Sidharth Varadarajan (The Wire), Sevanti Ninan (The Hoot), Naresh Fernandes (Scroll and Quartz), Raghav Behl (Quint), they are seen as serious ventures. Among them at least two can boast of having readers' editors. Dr. Rammanohar Reddy, former editor of *Economic and Political Weekly* is Scroll's Readers' Editor and Pamela Philipose Public Editor of The Wire. This gives the portals added credibility. Clearly, more people are looking to the portals for the additional intellectual kick. With a pan-India presence, one cannot any more ignore their role as a counter-weight to the monopoly hegemony in print media. India now has only a little over 10 per cent internet penetration. The mobile density is still deplorably low. With prices of smart phones declining, there will be a dramatic rise in the exposure to mobile-based online news. In developed countries, the phenomenon had led to a sharp fall in print media circulation. Even if this does not happen here, a bold and credible online news movement is bound to dent the power of the growing monopoly in print media.

6

The Snake Was A Rope

SARPA-SUTRA Nyaya (snake-rope theory) is an expression invented by Adi Shankara to explain the Real (*Brahman*)-Unreal (universe) relationship. A group of travellers were walking on a moonlit night.

"A snake," the one in the front screamed.

"Thrash it with your stick," shouted someone.

"Please don't. Let's take the other route."

Everyone got panicked but the responses were diverse. Some felt scared, others angy till they all realized it was not a snake but a curled up rope. *Advaitis* use this analogy to illustrate the transient nature of the unreal or universe.

That was the kind of paranoia that had gripped the print media when over two dozen 24-hour TV news channels began blaring non-stop. Editors, owners, and public opinion experts went on analysing the consequences of the impending disaster. Who will read the newspapers when the channels give a minute-by-minute account? By the time the dailies come out in the morning they would be at least six hours behind. What is the point in printing the same news stories which are already known to millions of listeners throughout the country?

Reports from the US, UK and Canada about the sharp fall in their newspaper circulation had further sent shock waves at media houses. This had badly hit the finances of the US dailies. Many smaller ones had shut their shops. Some were merged with others. Some became weeklies, others went online. Some media houses had sought details of how the US media had coped with the challenge. Suggestions were also made to equip the daily newspapers with new features and improved storyline.

Unlike Adi Shankara's travellers, it took a long time for the print media to realize that the TV news channels were, after all, not such a life threatening snake but just a curled up rope. B.G. Verghese was the first to take the cue. It was in the thick of the mad rush that this writer had a chance meeting with him. Verghese, who was the chairman of Prasar Bharati, came as the editor of *The Indian Express* soon after I joined their Delhi bureau. I also had the benefit of his association in the Press Council.

"Now India's print media seems quite safe," he said. "This is not because of the media houses' efforts to counter the challenge. The challengers themselves are making it easy for the daily newspapers."

News channels, he said, were planning to go in for a new kind of format. The initiative had come from Star News. They had assigned the task of revamping their TV news to a journalist of a Bombay glossy. She had specifically sought the opinion of Verghese. They were also examining foreign TV news format so that certain features could be borrowed. Star News has conducted consumer surveys and was seeking suggestions from people in different walks of life.

Basically, the new Star format would do away with the news bulletins kind of broadcast. Bulletin format was essentially an audio/video version of newspapers with lead stories, followed by national, state, foreign, entertainment, business-economy and sports, almost in that order. This was the original DD style. It may be rather longish—30 minutes—but it certainly gave a full picture of the day's happenings to the listeners. On days when newspapers were not available, one could fairly depend on the TV news. It had served as a parallel newspaper of the sort.

His information, Verghese said, was that all other news channels have taken their cue from Star News and were planning to revamp their own format in a big way. The idea was to give overwhelming priority for entertainment events and human interest stories. Even hard news had to be packaged in entertainment mode. The channels will be flooded with films, fashion, food, chat shows and other such soft slots and long clips on cricket and sports. Under this concept minor news stories, reports from states, big and small foreign news items would all get eliminated unless they have entertainment and sensational value. If all this happened, Verghese asserted, the print media need not feel any threat from the channels.

His instant prediction proved highly prophetic. Despite so much noise, Star News had failed to give any new definition to news. But other channels outwitted it and moved faster to churn out entertainment-oriented news format. All of them did away with the concept of comprehensive news approach. To give the listeners a full and complete account of the happenings was considered old fashioned. Listeners are interested in hard news, spot news. Not micro details which they could get from sources like mobiles, social media and word of mouth. Scrolls at the bottom of the screen could well take care of this.

In the early days of the changeover, many news channels tried to find their own niche areas. Some even came up with tantric kind of shows and miracle stories eulogizing god men, paid for or unpaid. Some others preferred exaggerated crime stories. They sent the camera men to the spot, took pictures and interviewed – even on routine crime reports like suicides and murders. For this they developed a niche style of narration with horror sound background. Channels may have their own in-house assessment. But the competition was proved to be for who will grab the bigger chunk of the viewer cake. As a result, the newspaper readers felt they could not depend on the TV news for all that they wanted know even if they surfed two dozen channels in the evening. After all this, the next day the habitual readers found a different picture in their dailies.

Apparently, channel planners themselves were aware of such debilities. To compensate for failue to provide enough news, some of them introduced quick news reading—a '100 news' at a stretch. They read them at such a break-neck speed that you fail to make anything out of it. Another TV media house had launched 'Headlines Today' to provide a more detailed account of a large number of news items continuously. This was a major relief to the news hungry TV buffs. Yet for the reason best known to the channel bosses, that too was wound up.

In the final analysis, what the news channels did was to generate their own viewership without so much as to take away the print media readers. For Indian dailies, two other factors are working in their favour. Our literacy rate is still rising fast. Newspaper circulation, especially those of the Indian language dailies, will continue to go up in proportion to the rise in the literacy rate. The other is the belief that proficiency in English, written as well as spoken, opens up a window of career success in India and abroad. The age-old notion has been that English newspapers could give this much needed edge.

The process of commercialization of news by some big media houses had begun much before the advent of 24-hour-TV channels. The latter had only added further impetus to the process. In the normal course, momentous transformations take place after intense debates and compromises. But the tectonic shifts in Indian media were thrust upon without consent of consensus. Stake holders like the employees, legally constituted media watch dogs and the public at large were casually kept out. In the 1970s and 80s, the media owners had fiercely resisted the government's determined moves to discipline the media. The proposed measures included diffusion of media ownership and an entire new bill (see chapter four) to deny full content control rights to the newspaper owners. Now the post-reform New Media has reversed the entire narrative. Forget the Second Press Commission's lofty ideals which were the benchmark for the pre-90 media. Instead, a section of the media owners have reversed the very concept of media being a mission-cum-business. It was suddently made into a full-fledged industry with unbridled freedom to devise its own rules, ethics and practices. The New Media refuses to accept any kind of regulatory measures except those by the judiciary.

The media industry as a collective entity is so powerful that the successive governments have avoided a brush with them. As per the new strategy, the ruling classes find it more effective to bring round individual media houses through subtle signals like an innocuous CBI notice or a phone call from the Enforcement Directorate. That is much more effective to bring them to their knees. This apart, the governments wisely gave a free hand to the crass commercialization and cannibalistic competition now rampant in the print media. But there was one restraining factor: the market. It has been the consumer—readers—intervention and fait by advertisers that had acted as checks and balances in the two decade-long convulutions in print media.

In the 1960s, eminent journalist D.R. Mankekar in his novel *No My Son, Never* had tellingly narrated the bitter circulation wars by the *Daily Wail* and *Daily Wangle*. What we have witnessed three decades later was a worse kind of undercutting and use of predatory practices by rival media giants on a much wider scale. Take, for instance, the cut-throat price war of the late 80s and 90s. A daily newspaper with 24 plus pages was sold at Rs. 1.50 per copy in the Delhi 'market'. This did not even meet the newsprint cost. We have over a dozen regulators for different kinds of industries and a competition commission. We impose anti-dumping duty to protect industries. Why did no authority ever intervene to checkmate such unethical business practices in print media? Clearly, it was intended to undercut the rivals and demolish the status of *The Hindustan Times* as the largest selling daily in the NCR. Initially the latter tried to put up a stiff face. Finally when it began feeling the pinch, it quietly fell in line. And cut the tafiff to the level of *The Times of India*. With relatively less financial clout, the smaller fries were bigger sufferers.

Here too, the only intervention came from the 'market'. At Rs. 1.50, the hawkers' commission also dwindled and they refused to lift the packets. As a compromise, the hawkers insisted that TOI disburse the original commission to them. Thus for years, 'consumers' (subscribers) of the Delhi 'market' had enjoyed the benefit of the competitive undercutting by the two giants. At Times House, the sense was that its arch rival HT was behind the hawkers' protests. After patching up with the hawkers, TOI managers had resorted to pampering the hawkers. They called local news agents and ground level hawkers in small groups. They were given gifts and offered more if they boosted TOI sales. In those days, subscribers found TOI dropped unsolicited at their door instead of their other favoured dailies. Some did not mind, others objected to such forceful newspaper change. At the peak of the circulation war, both giants in Delhi sent teams of boys and girls for a house-to-house subscription drive. Cut-throat 'intoduction' prices—170 years after launch by the TOI and 80 years after the HT—were offered to the subscribers if they deserted the present 'product' or newspaper. The HT had also introduced an annual coupon system with concessional rates.

TOI had got itself embroiled in two other unsavoury controversies. Both had raised serious questions of journalistic ethics. The first was the infamous 'page 6 people'. The allegation was that the media house charged huge sums of money from the movers and shakers for carrying their photos with celebrities on page 6. Taking money for carrying news or pictures in news columns is a wanton violation of ethics. The other relates to allegations that the group had entered into arrangements with some business firms for converting the advertisement tariff amount into equity in the respective company. No one gives any definite reply whether reports to this effect are true or not. If true, it involves transgression of the Press Council guidelines with regard to publication of advertisements.

The rapid technological upgradation was another tool to financially stifle the weaker adversaries. In Delhi, one of the big two had suddenly introduced colour pages. This was accompanied by a big advertisement campaign: 'the colour edge'. This had forced others to raise finance and arrange for expensive colour printing. They found that was the only way to remain in business. Soon the trend spread to other centres and regional language newspapers. True, the colour has brightened the looks. But it was suddenly imposed as predatory tactics to financially stifle the weaker rivals.

In the early years of the marketization, one day the TOI came out with an impressive ten-page colour pullout in a hitherto unknown format. Full of Bollywood pictures, non-serious events and celebrity gossip, it was a big hit among the film buffs and sections of youth. Neighbours who were subscribing to other newspapers would borrow the pullout to relish juicy gossip and provocative photos in enticing posses. This forced the rival *Hindustant Times* to hurriedly launch its own version of 'Delhi Times'. Most others decided not to follow the race. A few others like *Deccan Chronicle* launched a different version of it in another format.

This phase also was witness to different kinds of competition which cannot be described as exactly unethical. But certainly these were intended to stifle the rivals with the sheer might of resources.

After strenuous preparations, TOI launched a new powerful missile: 'Ascent' was a collection of high-end vacancies of big posts in India and abroad. It came as a separate pullout. It was at a time when multinational companies and domestic firms opening shops in a big way. Information technology and management were emerging as a big career opportunity. 'Ascent' had soon become an indispensable retinue for high-end job aspirants. *The Hindustan Times* had put many resources to create its own Ascent. But failed. At one stage, there were reports that a few Indian language groups and *The Hindu* had explored such a joint move to rival 'Ascent'. Then it launched its own modest version of its 'Ascent'. Soon came another marketing gimmick. 'Pay for one, get two Times.' This was an advertisement campaign to highlight TOI's 'Section 2 edge' fortified by extensive lamp post display boards. The additional section comprised foreign news and 'hold over' national stories. But that too proved to be a failed venture.

Catch them young has been a tested tool in the war for winning hearts. TOI had begun way back in the 1980s delivering free copies of its student edition in public schools. That generation of students has grown up with a deep imprint of TOI and HT brands on their subconscious. Soon *The Hindu* has also begun making inroads into the young mind. In this long tussle for supremacy, *The Hindustan Times* scored over its rival in one initiative: *Brunch*. This Sunday supplement is widely read. TOI had tried to counter it with its own version. But it was nowhere near *Brunch* in which HT's both editor and former editor were contributors.

The marketization of news got legitimized by the reform philosophy. Yet it had a chequered history in its wide sweep. It found its feet after a series of panic responses and haphazard experiments. At the early stage, Times House worked hard to build the brand and advertisement. It had neglected content under the notion that the new generation readers, rather than the high quality of the news, went by the brand, looks and advertisements the daily carried. However, after home surverys it had decided to strengthen content as well.

Next, adding 'colour' to the copy and giving 'interesting' (funny) headlines to the stories became the flavour of the season. Editors repeatedly insisted on inventing 'interesting' intros which most often turned atrocious. Headlines themselves became badly opinionated. That too on bizarre premises. All this was done to attract consumers, i.e. readers. The whole concept of intro of news stories made trivialized. In those days, the harassed readers struggled hard to find out what was actually the news in the story and in which paragraph it was hidden down the line. Look at the TOI pages of those days. You will find artificially flowery language and senseless alliterations to dress up silly stories. While the inhouse subs and editors congratulated each other, large swathes of ordinary readers began dismissing them as childish. There were many critical articles by media commentators describing the new trend as 'magazinization' and 'trivialization'. The belief then was that newspaper readers already had all the news from TV and social media and the dailies had to provide adds-on and fresh masala to make it palatable.

At Times House, managing editor Arindam Sengupta had those days put it in black and white. We were colleagues in the Times group—he a special correspondent of *The Times of India* and I political editor of *The Economic Times* and were old friends. Hence he was rather blunt.

"Consumers are interested in the end product," Arindam said. "Who bothers who was the shift in-charge of a product? They go by the quality. Readers want to know what bills were passed and what was it about, not who opposed or who sought amendments. Only a few oldies like you and me may bother about the nitty-gritty of Parliament proceedings."

He looked emotionally involved in the process of the sweeping shifts that had been taking place in print media's concept of news and its presentation. Every readership survey, he explained, showed hardly five per cent readers were interested in the drab, old-style Parliamentary reporting. Why should we waste a whole page (on Parliament coverage) just for the sake of five per cent? In any case, such special interest groups can easily click into so many web sites to get every detail. Arindam seemed fully sharing the changed media philosophy.

"Media is a corporate business and newspapers a consumer product," he said.

"What about 'news'?"

"I know what you mean. Certainly 'news' is a product. You have to sell 'news' in a highly competitive market. Those who live in the 'spot news' days of the 1960s, will be left behind in this bitter war for domination in the newspaper business. Hereafter no one will buy bland news. Our success will depend on how best we can blend news with entertainment."

Arindam talked eloquently about the fast emerging young generation of readers with new aspirations and an obsessive consumerist indulgence. This new generation has already begun dominating the English media 'market'. This is the section he had earlier described as only interested in the 'end-product'.

A few weeks later, it was the turn of resident editor Arun Roy at *The Hindustan Times.* Roy was my senior colleague at *Business Standard.* A thoroughly professional journalist, Roy had a sharp sense of news and an independent mind. We talked about the prevailing paranoia in print media.

"Media planning," Arun Roy said "has already slipped out of the editors' hands. Everything is decided by public opinion experts and readership surveys. Editors have become implementing agencies. Let's see how things develop. You and I can only sit and lament."

Roy conceded his personal assessment was different from that of HT. He made two points: In Indian conditions TV news and social media would not pose any serious challenge to the dailies in the near future. This was because traditionally Indian educated classes have greater faith in printed words. Second, after the present turmoil, the readers will themselves intervene and find the right track in the business of news. He referred to experiments by some big newspapers to give a new sort of funny headings to stories. This was supposedly to break monotony. But they had to revert back due to adverse reader response as shown by inhouse surveys.

He was right. The trend was once again halted by the market intervention. Media houses themselves had to drop extreme kind of magazinisation, trivialization and opinionated headlines. Complaints from the well-wishers and reader responses had prompted the media owners to inject more reasoning and rationality. Over the years ground realities about readers' tastes began putting a restraint on the media houses. Selection of news, coverage and presentation seems to have finally acquired a fairly reasonable pattern. They have realized the readers' interest in intensive coverage of local news and have begun adding more pages. There is increasing recognition that new generation readers are not that averse to hard statistics. Hence we have a daily dose of interesting socio-economic data with charts and graphics. Some dailies have dedicated research teams. All this marks a positive change and new realization. Had the TV snake been proved to be a mere rope, it was both due to the latter's ability to adjust to the new situations and the increasing trivialization by the TV channels.

7

The Rebellious 60s

The 1960s were heydays of intellectual journalism. For once it seemed as if the periodicals and parallel print media had taken over the whole national discourse. Hence the tumultuous decade witnessed proliferation of well over a dozen journals each with its own characteristics and ideological orientation. Most were weeklies. Their editors did not conceal their political convictions. In fact, boldness was their forte. Many of them were known more for their distinct elucidation style and the milieu they represented.

Even those who had disagreed with their ideological tilt enjoyed their writing style and line of argument. The crusader journals, all of them looking dull and colourless, had sprouted from everywhere—from Bombay to the narrow streets of Calcutta. For the *jholawala* generation in their trade mark pant-*kurta* and *Kolhapuri* chappals, plain printing represented super intellectualism. Otherwise how could a 24-page weekly printed on Nepa newsprint without a cover page sell 7,000 copies? In those days it was a fairly big figure. Published from Calcutta, admirers of *Frontier* waited, week after week, for its editor Samar Sen's main editorials and short commentaries. It was hand-composed and printed on a primitive treadle machine. It fiercely projected the extreme left views. On campuses where Naxalism had inspired large sections, *Frontier* was widely talked about and its contents debated.

When the local police threatened the owners of the printing press, the journal had to look for a modest machine in a small garage. Its paper bundles were blocked a couple of times. However, repressive actions only gave *Frontier* more grit and more admirers for its editor from far and wide. Its critics had alleged that the paper was funded by the Chinese, then a proclaimed enemy country.

They cited the lack of advertisements in *Fronteir*. Then how did they manage to raise so much funds to run it? Didn't the Chinese give arms and military training to the north-eastern rebels? But its avid readers refused to believe such wild allegations. For, most work for the weekly was done by volunteers—from proof-reading and stitching to buying the printing paper.

Now was another periodical that had followed in the footsteps of *Frontier*. It was set up by some of those who were earlier with Samar Sen. They left him for ideological differences. Soon *Now* became as popular as its sister weekly. It had the same size, similar layout and rough look. Where it differed from *Frontier* was that it had many talented outside writers and contributors. This qualitative edge made it more informative and rich in fresh ideas. Leftwing economic analysts Balraj Mehta and Girish Mathur were its anonymous contributors. C.P. Ramachandran, a senior assistant editor at *The Hindustan Times* known for his left leanings, had a regular column in *Now* where he lambasted both sides of the political spectrum—the Congress for its opportunism and the economic right-wing for their pro-US advocacy. Some of its provocative pieces had their reverberations in the mainstream English media which otherwise continued to pretend that the parallel rebel media had little impact on the policy and there was nothing beyond the staple they trot out to the public.

It was precisely this media myth that the crusader journals of the 1960s wanted to challenge. The mainstream media's conservative news presentation and refusal to go beyond the officialese were the main factors that made India's post-world war generation to look for fresh ideas from the outside. This inquisitive youth fresh from the educational institutions were not content with the formal government claims, ministers' homilies and official version on government programmes without scrutiny. This was in contrast to the prevailing editorial philosophy that good and balanced journalism meant plain reporting without explanations and comments. The job of a daily newspaper was informing, and interpretations best left to the readers. Even the editorials were more narrarive in style and invariably mild. The edit page was confined to preferred writers with predictable ideas.

The general readers of the day were not satisfied with this.

They were looking beyond the narrow range of diatribe between the two sides of the same bourgeoisie. The rebellious journals free of proprietorial constraints, just fed on this aspirational section's reading passion and quest for what was happening behind the news.

The parallel journals of the era fall under two categories: Left and Right. On the Left were *Frontier, Now, Mainstream, Blitz, Link, Century, Democratic World, Secular Democracy, Delhi Times* and perhaps *Shankar's Weekly*. Then there was Romesh Thapar's *Seminar* which only had a subtle Left tint. A little recognized fact was that Romesh Thapar's anti-establishment journalism had begun at the dawn of independence. His *Cross-Roads* weekly was banned by the Madras government but the Supreme Court in a landmark verdict (AIR 1950 SC 124) upheld the freedom of expression and invalidated the ban.

On the other side were Rajagopalachari's *Swarajya*, Rajmohan Gandhi's *Himmat*, Piloo Modi's *March of the Nation*, D.F. Karaka's *Current* and the US-sponsored *Quest* and *Thought*. *Mother India* was another journal. The list does not include party mouthpieces like *Organiser, New Age* and *AICC Economic Review*. Then there were others like *Economic & Political Weekly, Eastern Economist, Commerce* and *Capital*. By the 70s, the high-priced glossies arrived: *Debonair, Gentleman, Star & Style* and *Society*. There were also more popular ones like *Illustrated Weekly* and *Dharamyug*.

In this partial list drawn from memory, the crusader journals stand apart as a class. They were unapologetically confrontational. Their polemical presentation of facts earned them admirers. They had made it a point to challenge the conventional political fads perpetuated by the contemporary English dailies and sought to inject fresh air. They were not irresponsible in its true sense. They had argumentative pieces based on authentic statistics and government reports. Such factors endeared them to the discerning readers. True, some of these weeklies were uabashedly partisan. Worse, some became tools of the big power cold war. However, such negative factors made them even more popular. Those yearning for information looked to them for the contrarian versions of the two power blocs.

Nikhil Chakravartty's *Mainstream* belonged to the left

spectrum. But it was better produced than *Frontier* and *Now.* With 32-plus pages in A4 size, it had varying fare. Witten by Chakravartty, its 'scrap book' was a quite popular column. Unlike the rugged look of most other left journals, *Mainstream* had two-colour cover pages on which highlights of the contents were printed in 24 point bold. Every issue had different colour tones, obviously to break the monotony. But PRRM Coffee House intellectuals dubbed *Mainstream's* colour change as a symbol of Chakravartty's shifting political loyalties. This was wholly unfair. For, he had never changed his basic ideological commitment. He may have shifted his personal likings to individuals within the groups.

Originally Nikhil, as he was known in the elite circles, wanted to pattern his dream magazine on the lines of *Masses & Mainstream* of the US Left. Beginning as a hardened communist youth in the mid-1940s, Nikhil was in the thick and thin of the party work at the highest levels from the Bombay 'commune' days. He remained with the CPI but changed his roles. For a brief while he remained CPI's media face outside its structure. His India Press Agency and *Mainstream* brought him in contact with the media circles, higher echelons of the Congress Party and the government. In his best days, he was the most networked Delhi 'insider'. In those years, he was seen more as a liberal Left. *Mainstream*'s pages were rich in such information and anecdotes. His own articles and those by eminent politicians and bureaucrats appeared in *Mainstream* under bylines like 'Insider', 'Chanakya' and 'Shakuni'.

Nikhil was a treasure trove of gossip and rumours in ruling circles and bureaucracy. Some of us had got many story-breakers on the tips provided by him. Nikhil's *Mainstream* joined the anti-Emergency campaign in its second half. Some of the articles it carried were highly critical of the emergency. There were lots of blame shifting within the Congress as to who leaked out such internal information. Years later it was revealed that the byline 'stranger' was that of P.V. Narasimha Rao who later became prime minister.

India Press Agency, a non-wire news agency, also belonged to Nikhil's pro-Soviet stable. He and David Cohen, a Left Jew, set up the outfit with its office at what was then IENS (Indian & Eastern Newspapers Society) building. Initially IPA's subscribers were mainly pro-Left newspapers and diplomatic missions. Later many non-Left journals also began subscribing. In its heydays it had to its credit so many story-breakers, including the Thimmaya episode. Superbly written with an eye on fact, IPA was a training ground for many senior journalists.

Blitz from Bombay was the most prominent protest journal of the Left genre. It was also the first and longest survived serious tabloid in India. Launched way back in the 1940s, *Blitz* heralded a revolution in Indian media in terms of layout, presentation, language and printing technology. It broke many traditions and fads perpetuated by the mainstream English media under their highly conservative editors and owners. Its last page, all colour, had regularly carried a three-coloumn colour picture of models, Indian or foreign. Cultural puritans had looked down on such 'dirty' photographs. But it had a large readership, especially of the young. K.A. Abbas' 'Last Page' column in *Blitz* was highly popular. Ramesh Sanghvi also had a widely read column in its inside pages.

Through its juicy stories, *Blitz* exposed superstition and the religious cheats. It was the first Indian newspaper to introduce adversarial reporting. The stories were backed up by big colour displays, pictures of the involved persons, quotes and 'photostat' (photo copies were unknown in those days) copies of the unearthed documents. It liberally used Public Accounts Committee reports and official leaks to best effect. This sort of media activism itself was a story-breaker for the mid-20th century India's media. Some short-lived local rags might have raked up local scandals. But they were swiftly shut down. *Blitz* with the resources at its command and wider reach among the young generation readers was not a rag to be cornered. Those who wished to know beyond what the established mainstream media dished out, found *Bltiz* as a new source. Its youthful looks, flashy display, liberal use of foreign and Indian slang and blunt style of presentation impressed the English-reading middle class. There was freshness even in language. Unlike in traditional media, words like 'rape' appeared in print—even in 36 point bold.

At its peak of glory, *Blitz* had a claimed circulation of 2.5 lakh. It had even got a place in the printer's vocabulary. Demy ¼ was called 'Blitz size'. "This is not your bloody *Blitz*," news editors of big English dailies would warn younger sub-editors. "we had better leak this to *Blitz*," people used to say when they came across a big local scandal. Such was its impact. It was the first crusader journal to put up noisy fights for noble causes. It fiercely defended the Nehruvian economic programmes, his liberal ideas and non-alignment foreign policy.

In foreign policy, this tabloid repeatedly ridiculed those pleading for a pro-West tilt. It did not conceal where it stood in the cold war politics. It repeatedly used terms like 'right reaction', 'kulaks', 'big biz' and 'Yankees'. During the decisive fight in Bombay South which had evoked US media attention, *Blitz* campaigned for Krishna Menon. Naturally, *Blitz's* brazen style had led to many defamation cases. But when they won a case, it became another big story for it.

Speculations about *Blitz*'s finances were aplenty. Some said smugglers—west cost was once a smugglers' den—financed it. But it had regularly carried stories exposing smuggler syndicates, including Haji Mastan. Its owner-editor R.K. Karanjia's links with the Shah of Iran and the money trial from Tehran were legion. Then there was that cold war ususal suspect: the Soviet Union. But all such allegations people took in their stride. For, there were also so many such scandals against other publications and individuals in those cold war days. Seeking CBI inquiry or filing PIL were not in vogue. People called each other Russian and CIA agents.

By the end of the 1980s, Karanjia launched *Daily Blitz*. But the venture failed to click. And soon after the weekly itself began showing signs of fatigue as was its aging editor. The new owners who bought *Blitz* could not keep up its original sting and style, and eventually it had its silent end. Many others had tried to copycat *Blitz*. But in the absence of aggressiveness, none could survive. Incidentally, its layout and style still live in the form of morningers like *News Today* and Bombay's *Midday*.

While *Blitz* was reining high, there appeared *Link*, another Left-of-Centre weekly with an entirely new format. Unlike the brazen *Blitz*, *Link* had a sober look and balanced presentation style. No aggressive words. Even big exposure stories were presented in narrative style. *Link* drew its dignified style and reader acceptability from US *Time* magazine. Its title page cover with thick red borders and logo on the top, the weekly cover story concept and its fixed columns all resembled the contemporary *Time* format.

However, contents and featuring of columns were truly Indian. It had a one-page editorial, letters to the editor in smaller fonts, a half-page O.V. Vijayan cartoon and a 'corridor talks'. This was followed by the week's cover story. 'Capital' was a critical review of the national scene with interesting anecdotes as seen from the left-of-centre kaleidoscope. 'Politics' and 'economy' were *Link's* strong point. In politics, it went on subtly pushing the cause of the progressive elements within the Congress—advocates of planning, strengthening of public sector and self-reliance. Its narrative ranged from attack on the big business control over the economy and the anti-Indira syndicate elements within the Congress Party. It also persistently tried to isolate those elements within the CPI who later formed the CPI(M) in 1964. It did not conceal its tilt against the West in the prevailing cold war.

In the late 50s when *Link* appeared on the news stand, it was a big novelty. Its 'foreign' look and rich fare of inside information and gossip earned it admirers. Curious young readers lapped it up. *Link* had a talented team of reporters and editors. Contrary to wide belief, *Link* was not a Russian project, at least in its initial years. Its celebrated editor Edathatta Narayanan and Aruna Asaf Ali had strong left leanings. They had also worked with the CPI and had great admiration for the Soviet system. But in the political milieu of the late 50s, the two who had a left socialist background, found themselves more comfortable with the 'progressive' sections of the Congress. The new weekly was to be a link between all sections of the progressive block—from the communists to the Congress men. Jawaharlal Nehru and Krishna Menon had publicly blessed the venture. Moreover, among the early *Link* staff, there was hardly any one who could be counted as hard core communist.

Link House began looking for Soviet help mostly after it launched *Patriot*, *Link*'s sister daily. Then they moved closer to the Soviet lobby. Edathatta could manage *Link* with the resources the Congress progressives could mobilize. The daily newspaper was a much bigger project. Edathatta had often revealed such compulsions to his editorial colleagues. His idea was to gradually reduce the outside financial dependence by turning it into a sound business proporsition. This he could not. Again, it was not the Indian communists or what was then called the S.A. Dange faction of the CPI that had brought Link House closer to the Soviets. Stalwarts in the Nehru camp who had a bigger clout with Moscow had played the role of deal makers. Clearly the latter's voice had more weight with the Soviets than the Dange faction. The *Link-Patriot* phenomenon could not survive the operational strains after Edathatta's death. It had ended much before the collapse of the Soviet Union.

When Link House was reigning high, a nondescript weekly had opened shop a couple of blocks away. The owner-editor of *Democratic World,* T.P. Mathai was in the defence ministry. He quit the job to do something big. His weekly carried stories exposing the murky side of MNC operations in India and assailing US policies. It was more of a Gandhian-Nehruvian mould than hard Left. Working out of the basement of the Taj building, this humble venture had served as the kindergarten for two of the best known English daily editors of the century who had the same Bahadur Shah Zafar Marg as their *karmabhumi* in their best of times. There is nothing much to write about this weekly's content, quality or circulation. But it eminently manifested a phenomenon of the era: sprouting of a large number of tiny protest magazines in English and regional languages. For instance, *Delhi Times* of Nand Kishore Nautiyal survived about two years. Nautiyal had later worked at Blitz. Another Left venture was *Broadway Times* from Madras.

There were three more journals which could be categorized as Left. *Shankar's Weekly*, a cartoon magazine in 'Blitz size', had long innings as India's own *Punch* magazine. Its editor Shankar Pillai was a close friend of Nehru and stood by him in politics. His rapport with the government was such that he had pioneered institutions like the Dolls House and Children's Library in their own building on Bahadur Shah Zafar Marg. *Shankar's Weekly* was shut during the Emergency. *Seminar* launched by Romesh Thapar was unique in its layout, type scheme and content. This monthly was a seminar of ideas in the print form. It picked up the month's most significant event and provided a comprehensive fare of different aspects from different angles. If the topic was drought, it began with a brief comment by the editor followed by an introduction of the subject, views by a couple of experts, interviews of leading agriculture experts, field studies, experience abroad, book reviews and references. It dealt with no other subject in that issue. *Seminar* was a serious journal but with a distinct Left imprint. The other was the short-lived *Spectrum* edited by Girish Mathur, a confirmed Left writer. It carried serious analytical articles and commentaries espousing Left precepts. Rather than the impact of such journals, these signalled the generation's idealism and urge for self-exploration.

On the right of the spectrum, the most serious and perhaps the earliest was Rajaji's *Swarajya*, published from Madras. Initially launched to air Rajaji's critical comments against the policies of the Nehru-dominated Congress, It gradually became the voice of the economic right. It had an array of eminent writers as contributors like Minoo Masani and K. Santhanam. In fact, the launch of *Swarajya* itself was necessitated by the mainstream English dailies' reluctance to provide adequate space to the views of the economic right. Rajaji and others were able to make the weekly a platform for the critics of the Nehruvian economic and foreign policies. *Swarajya* functioned as the epicentre for the Swatantra Party and espoused its policies and philosophy. Its critics and acolytes alike looked to *Swarajya* to understand the economic right's protestations on emerging issues.

Swarajya did not disappoint its 4,000 odd subscribers. It was incisive in its criticism of the government's economic programmes, especially its post-Avadi speed. It lauded the virtues of free enterprise as against the centralized planning and command control economy. It was *Swarajya* that had coined the much used phrase 'control-permit-quota raj'. The state, it kept asserting, had 'no busness to run business' and there should not be any controls over business and industry. It lambasted Indira Gandhi for nationalization of banks and insurance and lampooned the government for withdrawing the privy purse to the former rajas. It asserted that this was a breach of trust, violation of a solemn agreement with the former kings many of whom had lined up with the Swatantra Party. *Swarajya* was shut after the party it had sustained it, suffered total rout. It has recently been revived in a different format.

The period also witnessed the birth of a different kind of publishing outfit to propagate similar contrarian doctrines. Bombay-based 'Forum of Free Enterprise' had concentrated on mailing tiny booklets to VIPs, academics and opinion makers. These were delivered by post and at times with the daily newspapers or other publications. Neatly printed in book size, they contained one article at a time by a free enterprise advocate. These were short, in simple language and easy-to-read style, and sought to demolish the government claims. They presented extensive data, some of them unverifiable. The Forum, as it claimed, had adopted the direct mailing strategy due to the failure of the established dailies to adequately represent their views. It was rather hazardous to give a definite tag to *Himmat*, Rajmohan Gandhi's journal. It was exhaustive, sharp and loud when the Emergency was declared. Launched in 1964, *Himmat* ceased publication in 1981.

Flamboyant Swatantra stalwart Piloo Modi was the proponent of the *March of the Nation*. While *Swarajya* and the Forum were known for their bold but persuasive kind of academic presentation, Piloo's journal was combative and acerbic and engaged in a vituperative campaign against the Congress government and Soviet bloc. Remember, anti-Congressism in those days encompassed the Swatantra, anti-Indira Congress(O) or Syndicate, Jana Sangh and sections of socialists. *March of the Nation* was of 'Blitz size' and followed its tabloid language and style. But it was a rather poor copycat. Apart from pedalling the Swatranta line on controls, planning, taxation, foreign trade and MNCs, Modi's journal had targeted more on fighting Indira Gandhi's authoritarianism. This aspect made it the talk of the town. On foreign policy, *March of the Nation* was unashamedly on the side of the US. It kept exposing the 'Soviet socialism' and the futility of siding with the Russians.

On the right were another set of journals—*Current, Thought* and *Quest*. The Swatantra genre periodicals, by and large, managed with their own funds. They did have a different orientation and ideology. But the others were of the crusader category. They perfectly fit into the definition of foreign-funded cold war warriors. They were a direct counter to the pro-Soviet journals.

The Bombay-based *Current* was launched by D.F. Karaka as a rival to *Blitz*. Both were Parsis and both weeklies were of the same size and followed similar presentation style and layout. At one time, *Current* seemed catching up with its rival in reach. They appeared side by side on the news stands. It seemed like a proxy battle as part of the bigger cold war. As a result, many readers began subscribing to both journals to get a feel of rival versions. Scandals broken by *Blitz* were countered by the rival. They launched a bitter war on each other. However, despite the liberal cold war fund flow, *Current* could not sustain competition. Karaka was finally proved to be no match to the more intellectually resourceful Karanjia.

Quest and *Thought* were more pronouncedly US-backed. Both were different projects to counter the growing communist 'penetration' in India. The Bombay-based *Quest* was the organ of the Moral Rearmament Association (MRA), widely believed as a CIA project. It was part of a global venture and hence *Quest* carried a global kind of cold war stories. *Thought* was very much local and unabashedly projected the US side of the story. Its editor Ram Singh, a small time scribe, did not conceal his contact with the US agencies. He was a regular at the coffee house in Connaught Place, then a popular haunt of the middle class intellectuals, and habitual party gate-crashers. *Thought* had its office in Daryaganj. Printed on low quality newsprint and with an awfully bad layout and editing, its popularity was entirely due to its abrasive style and wild stories it had carried.

There were two kinds of stories in *Thought*—well-written pieces with pictures and badly written local ones. Apparently, the first set came from its fund givers. The second was done at Ram Singh's office. *Thought*'s main function was to counter anti-West stories appearing in pro-Soviet publications like *Blitz, Link* and a host of others. But anyone could plant any story in *Thought*. Ram Singh was so liberal. Once it had carried a sensational story about a junior Russian embassy staff handing Rs. 1 lakh—quite a substantial amount then—to a CPI functionary. It was later found that the functionary mentioned had migrated to Poland years before and had died there in a trekking accident. For the rival Blitz, it became another exposure story.

In this decades-long bitter media war between the two cold war blocks, the Soviet side was the clear winner. The journals propped up by the latter were better managed and had a wider reach. They had talented journalists who were armed with the 60's anti-imperialist fervour. Apart from the Left, the pro-Soviet side had the backing of the ruling party. The whole political and academic ambience was in their favour. The socialist idea was still on the upswing. Unlike today, the public sector was seen as the saviour of the economy and provider of jobs for those coming out of schools and colleagues. Every new PSU or their expansion—like BHEL, BEL, Bhilai steel plant and soon—recruited youths. However, many—or most—rebellious periodicals were shut during the Emergency. Some had tried to revive later but the change of politics had made all the difference. Readers looked for better produced journals like *India Today, Sunday* and *Onlooker* for the extra news. High priced glossies were the other alternative.

Soon it was the activism of the decade 1978-88. It was led by the new generation weeklies and fortnightlies of the glossy genre. Unlike the 60s' protest periodicals, the news magazines were highly resourceful and backed by modern printing and communication technology. Launched in 1975 at the peak of the Emergency, *India Today* had led the transformation. Then arrived *Sunday* from the Anand Bazaar group and those like *The Week, Onlooker* and the short-lived one by *Deccan Herald*. Rather sober in language, they had abrasive headlines and provocative display. They had lots of colour and best printing aided by professional designers, something new for Indian journals. They had a network of correspondents, dynamic circulation and advertisement executives. Though a latecomer, *Outlook* edited by Vinod Mehta was among the best survivors.

But the real strength of the new generation weeklies was their out-of-box cover stories and investigative pieces. It was a time when mainstream dailies were still confining themselves to hard news and thus avoiding exposure stories. Hence those yearning for something extra rushed to the news weeklies that dished out spicy stories. For a while, it appeared they were transforming reading tastes and the meaning of journalism. As their contemporaries in Europe, adversarial writing became a challenge to the establishment.

The new journals also broke another fad: dog could eat dog's meat. These magazines, followed by some mainstream dailies, began carrying inside stories about the happenings in newspaper establishments and advertisement firms. They gave details of hiring and firings by media houses and all sorts of stirrings in their dark corridors. Then for unknown reasons, such stories stopped coming out. Perhaps due to a consensus of sorts among the media houses. At one stage, these GenX periodicals together had a massive share in total circulation and impact on public opinion. A half dozen magazines, big and small, went on breaking scandals of different kinds. This led to three developments. First, the success of their exposure journalism forced the daily newspapers like *The Indian Express* to go in for their own well investigated exposure stories. They had made it a routine menu. As those on Antulay and Bofors, the *Express* began stealing the lustre from the magazines. Investigative or adversarial stories still remain part of most daily newspapers.

The second was the launch of a new genre of Sunday broadsheet magazines like *Sunday Observer* and *Sunday Mail*. They appeared on Sundays along with the morning dailies but had their own story breakers and exclusive columns. Some such Sunday magazines still survive. Third, media houses like TOI, that avoided taking to aggressive investigative reporting, began launching their own separate Sunday magazines in broadsheet. Some had launched morning or evening tabloids. True, this was a media strategy to steal the thunder from this segment of the media.

8

Under the Hot Metal

The era of hot metal typesetting and rotary printing was already ushered in when our generation entered the daily newspaper journalism. Both were technological game changers in their own way. Lino types gave the dailies a neat new look. It had replaced the old system of 20 odd compositers hand-picking each letter type and setting them on the 'stone'. In case the twain with which the lead types were held tight broke, the whole page disintegrated. Such was the high risk under the old system.

Hot metal system changed all that. The lino machine cast matter or copy linewise. You press the keyboard and the commanded letters in brass moulds move over to the 'case'. Soon melted lead flushes into the brass letter mould. Thus one line of freshly cast lead type is ready. A lino operator could produce 3-4 columns length matter in one shift. These are then placed in galleys and their proof printouts taken. The proof narrows then go to the proof readers for corrections. Then corrections had to be carried out in the matter kept in galleys. Headlines had to be cast separately on 'Ludlo' machine. Here the brass types are hand-picked and arranged in a 'case' which is then pushed into the 'face' of an oven with melted lead.

Page making under the lino system was quicker and relatively hassle-free. The 'matter' could be easily lifted and arranged as per the chief sub's layout plan and 'locked'up safe in a steel frame. Then the 'frame' goes to the flong machine which presses the wet flong sheet on the locked frame. Flong is a blue colour soft-cardboard cut into the page size. The whole page is thus embossed on the flong which again goes to the 'plate' making machine. This machine casts a cresent-shaped one-inch thick lead plate. Such plates are fixed on the rotary machine as per the page scheme. Once the stytem is put in place, the rotary machine turns out the whole newspaper printed and counted. Unlike earlier, there was no need for inserting pages and folding the printed paper by hand.

The editorial and proof reading sections normally functioned from the ground or first floor with the press mostly in the basement. Life at the desk was slow and dull. Once you join the news desk as sub-editor, chances are you had to do the same work for years. That was how it worked in those days. You might get a fixed salary raise but do the same work. Chances of migration to other dailies were practically nil. In most cases, sub-editors retire as senior subs without even reaching the position of chief sub. But then that was the norm in every profession, in government and private. No one complained. Only the exceptionally smart could change the newspaper and get better positions elsewhere.

The calibre and quality of the editorial staff in those days was rather mediocre. As compared to the present crop of journalists, recruits in those days were very ordinary. Even if some of them were bright and with initiative, the hierarchical hurdles had acted as speed-breakers. Media's failure to attract the best talents begins right from the recruitment stage. Most of the entrants came through promotions from proof readers. Some journalists were PAs to editors. Good and bright proof readers always had a claim to a news desk job. Many of them were fairly good because they, as proof readers, were familiar with copy editing and style. Direct recruitments took place only when such good hands were not available. The main criterion for direct recruitment was ability to handle English. Journalism courses were rare. Punjab University and later Nagpur had such courses. But editors, at least in the early years, looked down on the journalism graduates. Moreover job seekers in those days were not well aware of the career prospects as journalists. The best among the job seekers went in for services like the IAS and army. Others preferred the safer traditional avocations like government jobs or teaching.

In spite of the hierarchical hurdles, a number of the early journalism pioneers managed to reach high positions in the profession. *The Times of India*'s legendary editors Shyam Lal and Girilal Jain had put on record their humble beginnings. N.R.

Chandran was a teleprinter operator and rose to the position of PTI's general manager. His senior in PTI, P. Unnikrishnan, another general manager, began as Edathatta Narayanan's press clipping boy. Later he was posted to Colombo and as *Patriot*'s special representative in Moscow. We know many other big men who would not like to recall their lowly beginnings.

Unlike today newspapers hierarchy and responsibilities were well defined. And so were the nomenclature of positions. Directly under the editor were assistant editors, news editor and bureau chief, and perhaps the cartoonist. No one had heard of positions like executive editor, managing editor, contributing editor, consulting editor and 'joint', 'associate' or 'senior' editors. The news editor had a large empire under him. The chief reporter looking after the local beat and functioned under the NE. And so the sports editor. The commerce page in those days was not so corporate-centric. Stocks rates, 'city notes' or a brief of the company's annual reports, commodity and bullion prices constitued this page. The NE normally put the most dull sub-editor on this page. The 'commerce' became the business page following the growing corporate might after globalization.

The news editor also looked after the teleprinter and proof reader departments. The new generation journalists might not have even seen the proof-readers. An English daily with 10-12 pages (that was the norm) may have at least four proof readers and that many 'copy holders' in a shift. They sat in a separate room because they were 'lower castes' in the editoral hierarchy. The copy holder was still lower in the rank and held the original edited copy and read it out to his proof reader colleague. They marked the errors in the proof sheet and sent it back for correction. There were internationally standardized signs for proof marking. Advent of computer type setting has eliminated this whole tribe. The burden of reading proof has now fallen on the sub-editor.

This writer recently visited his old alma mater IE. What a change! CS table no. can't make out who sits where. We all had (except subs) bulky tables. When I joined there were only fans. *TOI, HT, Statesman, IE* too had only fans. Cooler were first put in the editor's room. By the mid-70s, coolers appeared. ACs came along with computers for the latter's sake.

The teleprinter department was another institution that has been swept away by the information revolution. During our time, the 'TP room' was the nerve centre of news flow. Teleprinters enabled direct connection with far away centres through specially laid cables. So a Delhi daily should have separate teleprinters with each publication centre and with correspondents in major state capitals. Other departments like advertising, circulation and accounts used the TP to communicate with the clients and other centres. The TP men kept bringing stories coming on teleprinters. Teleprinters of UNI and PTI were serviced by the respective agencies but kept in the TP room. They cut the long printed rolls, often as long as 20 feet, storywise and left them in the chief sub's tray. E-mails and smart phones have turned the TP room into a relic.

The old era news editors—do they still exist anywhere with such an aura?—had enjoyed total functional authority over the news desk which was then the control post of the newspaper production. Every shift had a chief sub who sat at a large table surrounded by half a dozen sub editors. Hence the term 'news desk'. Herein lay another vintage institution. Every news story comes in typed or tele-printed sheets. And one can see news in hard copy. The chief sub had around him over half a dozen clip-fixed trays to keep the incoming stories. He screened the paper piles, threw away unwanted ones into a huge wooden basket and selected only a few usable stories. Sports and commerce stories were dropped in their respective trays. The concerned subs would clear them. All likely page 1 stories were kept in a separate tray. The stories of 'local', 'states', 'national', 'development' and 'foreign' go to their tray. Everything was in the form of hard copy and had to be sorted and arranged by hand and edited with a pen and pinned together.

Slow and cumbersome, the system had two advantages. In case some errors crept into the newspaper, the editor could easily find out at what stage it had crept in. It was a normal practice to recall the previous day's copy from the press to fix whether the reporter, sub editor or proof reader committed the error. Under the PRB Act, a newspaper had to keep the original copy and proof sheets of each edition for six months. Police could seize them in the event of defamation cases. The second was that the new sub editors and learners could re-check their copy after the chief sub revised it. For them, it was a learning experience.

At the news desk, the chief sub picked copies traywise and page by page as per the dummy scheme. If he took up the foreign page first, stories and related pieces had to be physically arranged 'take' by 'take'. By the time the NE might have sent the pagewise dummy for the entire paper. The chief sub had to make the layout himself—those days no one had thought of layout experts and designers—fix the lead, second lead and so on and chose the right pictures. Copies were then handed to the subs for editing and giving headlines—all with pen, not on computer screen. Headlines were written on a separate slip of paper and tagged to the edited copy. This was to enable the foreman hand the 'body' matter to the lino operators and headlines to the Ludlo man. Chief sub glanced at the edited copies, marked it on his dummy and sent it to the foreman. Then he took up another page. When the 'matter' for an entire page was ready, the chief sub or a senior sub went to the 'stone' in the press and supervised the page make-up. The chief sub has to approve each page proof. Imagine, the entire work had to be done physicially. Not by clicks on the screen.

In the hot metal era, graphics and cartographics like photos and pictures were a major probem. Even the large newspaper chains lacked their own facilities for graphics. Then an enterprising 'chart maker' at Delhi's *Indian Express* devised his own system to create charts, tables, maps and graphics. He made graphics on a daily basis on published statistics and began delivering them to major dailies, by hand of course. Look at the newspaper files of late last century. You find 'KBK' graphics all over India. Even in regional language dailies. I have seen 'KBK' moving on a Chetak scooter and personally delivering the graphics to the news editors. Later he put up his studio at his Gulmohar Park residence. Years ago I had attended his last rites. The ease of computer graphics has overtaken this unique institution.

Technological antiquity had its toll on the look and content of the hot metal era dailies. They were dull and of shaded impression. In normal days colour was unthinkable. The press was not equipped for printing multi-colour pictures. Single colour was tried on special supplements by the sponsors. But they were so drab. Looks improved with the introduction of photo setting and photo offset printing. The latter came first. Switch to modern printing has been a painful process. Hundreds of press workers engaged as lino operators, proof readers and page makers lost job at each printing centre. Computer setting and page making were introduced in Indian newspapers in phases. In the first stage, computer operators did regular data entry of the edited copies. After correction, columnwise computer printouts were taken on bromide narrows. Such printouts were then pasted on full-page dummy by 'page-pasters'. The pasted full pages were then converted into plates and printed. Soon the sub-editors began page-making on computers and the data entry workers and page-pasters were thrown out.

A few years back when dailies began coming out with display advertisement as page one, many had found it atrocious. But for us, it was not so shocking. Just before our generation, Indian dailies did have the full page one as classifieds. This was a practice borrowed from the British dailies. *The Hindu* had it. Page one as classifieds was seen as proof of the popularity of the paper and its high status. It was discontinued some time in the 50s. During our early days in English dailies we had strict rules. Page one should be rich in news. Advertisements are allowed in the bottom right corner in 20 cm x 3 col. Half or quarter page advertisements were not allowed on page one. There were also 'ear panels' on page one on both sides of the logo. Nothing more. On this point editors of yore were very strict.

English dailies had a highly conservative and ritualistic ambience around them. When we joined the news desk, we had to follow a strict code in selection of news, editing and display. Big dailies had their own style book which the subs were told to read repeatedly. A slight slip, some arrogant chief subs would throw the style book and copy at you. Use of slang was a total no-no.

"Which fool did it?" one day Edathatta Narayanan then 75-plus, rushed to the news room. "No Anglo-Indian English here. Understand?"

Edathatta was known for his emotional outbursts and a cruelly patronizing approach. Soon after the angry bout, he would pat the guilty person on the back: "Follow King's English, not cow boy slang." Beyond the style book, H.W. Fowler was the final authority. His English usage and other works were kept handy for reference. Huge three-volume English dictionaries fixed with nuts and bolts on a hard board were a familiar sight in news rooms. Often senior editors consulted each other on authentic spellings and approved abbreviations. This writer had a collection of old style books of half a dozen English dailies, including *The Times of India* and *The Statesman*. S. Mulgaonkar was no less stubborn in sticking to the code, both on layout and language. He was the one who had introduced three-column single line headings in *The Indian Express*. The only exceptions were first and second lead and bottom anchor.

Down South, *the Hindu* prided itself as being conservative. It had a compulsive reason. Students of English schools and service job aspirants were repeatedly told by their parents and teachers to read English dailies. In the South, street corner typing institutes routinely asked their students to read *The Hindu* for good English and general knowledge. To carry an English daily was a statement of one's academic calibre. Stenos were given practice dictations from the editorials of *The Hindu*.

Many in those days read dailies for its quality of English rather than news. It was seen as a ticket to the elite club. Incidentally, in those days long winding lines with complex and compound sentences were seen as the proof of the writer's proficiency in language. Some eccentrics even stopped you on the way and asked for a grammatical analysis of the sentence in the good old Wren & Martin style. Therefore the early editors always insisted on the purity of language, style and accuracy of spellings.

Reports and headlines should be straight and simple. The old format of pyramid system of news writing was strictly adhered to. There had to be special permission for any departure. The main point of the story had to appear in the intro. Editors never compromised on the five 'W's (Who, What, When, Where and Why) and 'how'. These had to come in the first two paragraphs of the story. This was to help the reader get a gist of the news at the very first look. Following this must come important details of the story. Then other points were in order of importance. This was called the pyramid structure of news presentation.

Remember, those were the days when AIR was the only source of information. Even radio news was only at certain fixed hours and came in bits and pieces. Therefore, readers looked for all the world's news in a morning daily. In those days newpaper offices put up boards displaying 'spot news'. It was both a special service to the people as well as publicity for the media house. Spot news provided three or four news items in the headlines form. They kept updating the content. Passersby paused and looked at the spot news board as a matter of habit. 'I saw it on the spot news' was heard as confirmation of a death or bridge collapse rumour. People used to go to a newspaper or news agency office to confirm street rumours. Such was the importance of a daily newspaper in the pre-mobile era.

Headlines had to be crisp and convey the main theme. Interpretative headlines were totally banned. Adverbs and adjectives in headlines were seen as taking sides and an affront on the readers' intelligence. Headlines like "In face of protests, PM cancels visit" or "After setback, Rahul ..." were never allowed. So were the tasteless alliterations, double meanings and word play in headlines.

"It's Congress in Gujarat," once the Ahmedabad editon of *The Times of India* put on page one when that party won the assembly polls. Soon arrived Shyam Lal's TP message saying *Times* was not 'a bloody tabloid'. Surely, headlines those days were drab and the same words appeared repeatedly. But the counter argument was that 'label' headlines helped readers to quickly grasp the content. Crime, accidents and suicides were covered but in a few sentences. Stories like "father, son found dead" were confined to three-four short sentences, mostly quoting police. Police releases of daily crimes, including accidents, were reserved for 'City Brief'. It was unusual to chase the story and dig into details or get reactions of the kith and kin. All this was shunned as intrusive and insensitive.

City news was covered fairly well. Items like 'In city today', 'news in brief' and 'weather' were unmissable. No mention of the word 'rape' should appear anywhere in the newspaper. It was considered blasphemy. The substitute term was 'woman criminally assaulted'. The old, conservative editors thought that such words were unfit for a family newspaper. What will parents say when kids ask the meaning of rape? That was the logic.

"No, no. Don't do it," the news editor told the chief sub. "I had marked it for the city page. The editor is quite upset."

The reference was to a page one block of a truck accident with the body of the killed pedestrian lying beside the vehicle. The editor had two objections: 'Lorry' was the approved British word, not US term truck. Second, the conservative editors of yore thought that the sight of such ghastly scenes in an early morning daily marked a bad omen for the readers.

Today's generation may laugh at it. But such ideas had prevailed until the TV and social media burst fads. However, I remember as late as 80s-end, the Australian Press Council had canvassed for a ban on such ghastly scenes. These were 'offensive to human sensibilities.' The APC had made a formal request to the Press Council of India to consider the issue. The PCI, however, after discussions decided that the issue be best left to the discretion of the editors. The post-reform generation will be surprised to know that the English dailies had in those days discouraged using private firms' names in print. Instead we wrote: 'Bombay firm fined.' Often big stories on corporate firms were dumped in the 'commerce' page. However, 'company notes' were regularly carried.

This apart, there were also editors who were bold and daring. This writer had such a pleasant experience while on a brief assignment at the Bombay office of *The Indian Express* some time in 1969.

"Are you from Ahmedabad?" SKM asked. S. Krishnamurthi was an all-in-all sort of a man in the Bombay Express. He was more than an editor and a terror to the journalist staff. We were working at the Ahmedabad office. There was a big conjunctivitis epidemic in Bombay and many subs fell ill. We two subs volunteered to go to Bombay when an SOS arrived from SKM. We were working on the day shift when SKM spotted me. Clearly it was just a random pick. He asked me my name and a few casual queries.

"May be you know some astrology," he said as I settled on the chair.

"No."

"OK. Do you read Peter Vidal?"

"Sometimes, yes."

"Look, the Peter Vidal packet has not come so far. You have to do it this week."

Normally Peter Vidal flongs came in a packet of ten from the Delhi *Express* by the office-to-office container service. That week it had not landed.

I was surprised. I told him I was not that familiar with his weekly predictions. He asked me to go to the library and pick up the last years' *Express* file, make some changes and do one for the week. I did so. And SKM liked it. That was how SKM made me an astrologer only for a week.

Those were the days when official statements, hard politics and *bhashans* dominated news pages. One could find it even on the 'states', 'national' and 'development' pages. Special correspondents collected PIB handouts on the activities of the ministries and ministers'speeches, typed them out as their own stories. Editors insisted that government handouts contained useful information and it was an important function of the media to provide it to the readers. For this reason, details of economic decisions were never missed. Here we had a wide range of areas—reports of evaluation panels, public accounts committees, routine CAG reports. They were carried even if there was no big exposures in them. When agencies sent them we too had to make it under our bylines. That was the logic. Stories on public sector units filled the pages. Their PR set could easily push their positive achievements and targets. There were frequent PSU jaunts and one must file a detailed report. Similarly, all major activities in states had to be covered systematically on regional pages. The simple rationale was that the readers trusted you for all the news, and you should not let them down. How many newspapers now carry details of the budget of a faraway state? Those days if a chief sub missed a state budget, it would certainly find mention in the post-mortem file.

Post-mortem file? It was an essential daily litany for most dailies. The editor or his deputy marked major scores and misses of the day in the final city edition. Editing and headline errors, cases of over and underplaying of stories and general observations were the highlights of post-mortem. The editor even went through an entire report and marked the editing errors. The newspaper was then filed and kept on the table. Everyone had to go through it. It was a public document. This also enabled reporters and desk men to sense the nuances of the editorial policies on issues.

Obsession with *bhashans* was legion. If we at the desk missed one, the news editor would mention it the next morning. Often the big shot's staff would complain to the NE. And some of these were nauseatingly repetitive and in the nature of meaningless sermons. Still the hapless reporter had to search for a reasonable 'lead' so that he or she could make sense of it. I remember a PIB officer, now retired, got a punishment transfer for his failure to get the minister's address at a function abroad published in Delhi dailies. In fact that was the one way the minister could impress the watchful high command about the hard work he was putting in.

Stories in those days had to be straight. The desk would mercilessly delete all unnecessary frills. That was the standing instruction. You had to state what he or she said in plain language without comments, comparisons or camouflage. Look at today's style: "Unhappy with the opposition's obstructionist tactics, the NDA government has..." or 'Hardly six months after the PM had launched his scheme, problems have..." In our time, all such writings were called opinionating or editorializing. It was an affront on the readers' power of judgement and an imposition on them. 'Interpretations and criticism are my job. I'll do it in the editorials,' the editors would remind the reporters repeatedly. That meant a report had to be a report, not an article or analysis. The practice continued to prevail until value addition became the theme song at editorial meetings due to the perceived TV scare. Attributing motives and meaningless adjectives were seen as interpretative reporting.

Stories on page one reflected the same editorial mindset. Of course things like big rail accidents and natural calamities were leads. And so were major cabinet decisions and parliament endorsement of bills. But if you did not have such important news for the day, don't hesitate. A *bhashan* of a big celebrity could fill the slots in those days. Possibility of a cabinet reshuffle or the PM's decision to assign a party job to a colleague were always lean-day leads for the bureau as well as the chief sub. We at the desk would happily lap up such exclusives. Not only that. The next day other dailies would come up with a follow-up. Change of leadership in a state was also an all-weather page one story.

Here is another shock for today's readers. It was the media's obsession with bureaucratic reshuffle at the centre. Any such story was a sure-shot lead for page one. *The Statesman,* then a significant daily, seemed specializing in such story-breakers. 'Singh tipped to be cabinet secretary. Patel's chances for finance bright. PM likely to reward Ramaswami with a UN posting.' Such triple-decked leads were taken as earth-shaking leads and came on Mondays. Sample this: "'In view of Chatterjee's familiarity with heavy industry, he is a good candidate for the post of industries secretary. His present place may be filled by Giriraj who had the petroleum minister's backing…" Credibility-conscious editors of yore did not treat them as 'speculative' even if no such changes really materialized. Mind you, nothing happens if positive 'harmless' story misfires. But even a spelling error in the name of a person in a devastating revelation could invite trouble.

Turning to the edit page, editorials of the pre-1977 days were largely evocative. The editors took care not to rub the establishment on the wrong side. Hence they tried to play it safe. Strong editorials were seen as distasteful and uncivil. That was street-fighters' job, not responsible media's. Even if you have to adversely comment, it should be in long winding sentences. Similarly, edit page articles were intended more to emphasize the daily's respectability and balanced approach. Hence they were largely narrative in style. However, it is necessary to highlight a new factor that had begun exerting pressure on the media houses of the early 60s. Some of the big English dailies had begun yielding some space to the right-wing Swatantra Party. With the backing of the big business houses and the old Maharajas, this party had considerable influence on what was then called 'jute press' (some big newspaper owners were running jute mills. Hence the term 'jute press'). However, the newspaper editors, by and large, were in the Nehruvian mould.

Despite this schism, sections of English dailies had begun highlighting the Swatantra attacks on the government. Then emerged the other jarring voice: criticism of the Congress leadership by the Nehru baiters like Mahavir Tyagi. These had found expression on news and edit pages in the 1960s. Some media houses allowed the trend even after the end of the Emergency. So the edit pages had occasional pieces by the free economy writers of the day. In some dailies, the editor or the bureau chief had their columns where the readers could look for discreet criticism of government policies between the lines. Between the lines because forthright comments were seen as hurting the image as a balanced paper. Kuldip Nayar's weekly column was called 'Between the Lines'. Conscientious readers looked at such edit page columns by the editor or bureau chief to gauge the broad trend. They took clues from the overall tone and tenor of such pieces. This was crucial for inquisitive readers at the time when news pages hardly gave behind-the-scene happenings. Then some inhouse columnist began providing brief chit-chat. Even this concession was a response to the blunt comments by the rebellious journals of the 1960s.

9

At Menon's Weekly

"Yours is an independent work," Kakkar said. "You have to produce this four-page blue sheet. It is a diary of the week's events arranged under different heads. Mishraji is here for two more weeks. He will explain further."

B.M. Kakkar was a senior desk man when *The Tribune* was in Ambala. He was the one who coordinated the production of *The Century* weekly. Trevor Drieberg, the founder editor, was about to pack up. T.J.S. George, who was busy writing V.K. Krishna Menon's biography, was already there to take charge from Drieberg.

George dashes in, takes out his baby Olivette typewriter, taps non-stop. Every hour or so he goes out briefly and restarts his work. He had a regular column in *The Century* under his byline. He would also push in a couple of other pieces.

Krishna Menon, whose name figures nowhere in *The Century*, was its guardian spirit. The weekly's 4,000 odd circulation and its very existence owed to Menon who had by then lost his job as defence minister. He never comes to the office but everyone knows it was his paper. A messenger brings Menon's page 1 edit and half a dozen commentaries that go with it. The weekly does not have a cover page. Hence it begins with the editorials. Often Kakkar himself goes to Menon's Teen Murti residence to fetch the typed copy. Quite often Menon also sent articles by unnamed writers which Kakkar rewrites and types out. Menon's standing instruction about unnamed articles was to take the theme, not the articles as such. Such pieces by unknown writers appeared under the byline 'observer'. Some said the articles came from his political and bureaucratic friends in government. Others sourced them to Soviet sources. Kakkar would often ask us to do the re-writing job.

Menon's articles were sharp and incisive. This was the very USP of the weekly. His main targets were the US and its military allies. After quitting the government, he did not conceal where he stood in the cold war divide which took its worst form in the 1960s. His unsigned pieces were minefields of explosive newsbreakers. Very often these became subjects of adjournment motions and questions in Parliament. There was a sudden surge of circulation of *The Century* by 600 copies—a big figure then—the week his editorial on the secret US move to build a naval base on Diego Garcia. The mainstream dailies had to follow it up. Another bomb shell was Voice of America's move for a foothold in neighbouring Ceylon. In India, such issues were politically explosive in that charged cold war atmosphere. Menon did not spare China for stabbing India in the back. He was equally antagonistic towards both US and China. He frequently warned about a US-China link-up against India and the Soviet Union. All this had strengthened the view that *The Century* was among the journals that had the Russian prop.

In domestic politics *The Century* went along the official Nehru-Congress line. It criticized at the Swatantra Party's economic programmes and assailed the business houses for obstructing the growth of the public sector. He alleged that the big business houses were funding the 'right reaction'—a familiar term in disuse after the liberalization—within the Congress Party. In a sharp editorial, he alleged that big money was being pumped in by the right reaction to capture the Congress leadership. The reference was to the Syndicate leaders' clashes with Indira Gandhi within the Congress. Such stories appearing in *The Century* were picked up by sections of foreign media to highlight the kind of power struggles raging within India's ruling party. However, India's own mainstream media had steered clear of such domestic controversies.

Clearly, Menon was drawing heavily from the input from the exclusive diplomatic releases from the Soviet mission in Delhi and their allies like Cuba and North Vietnam. The Russians and China were wooing both these smaller communist countries. At least five other foreign missions, including the US, UK and China, were delivering similar exclusive cold war materials in sealed packets to selected persons. The recipients included a few top politicians, senior bureaucrats and opinion makers. In those days India did not have any private Think Tanks worth the name. The idea was to influence the Indian policies in favour of the respective military blocks. The packets containing details of the rival cold war camp's strategic preparations, secret weapons and alleged designs against India were repeated in different forms. These were delivered at the doorsteps of a dozen or so addressees by CD cars every evening.

Krishna Menon, according to his stenographer, was a fast reader. Iyer, a retired government clerk, says Menon did not want any one else to open the mission papers. He did it himself. After a quick glance, he dropped them in a wooden tray. He picked up a few of them for further reference. Iyer had instructions to collect the rest and send them to *The Century* office. Kakkar handed them over to Lawrence Braddleman, the weekly's literary critic. Kakkar himself was perhaps not sure whether Menon wanted his editorial colleagues to use these in the weekly. So the papers finally got a resting place on a rickety wooden rack. And one day there was a major panic in the congested *Century* office. Kakkar and assistant editor Anil Saari who was also a literary critic were frantically looking for some papers from the dusty bundles. Obviously Menon wanted them to locate a missing article and send it back to him.

From that day, I got a new assignment. The messenger began dumping the papers on my table. I was to go through them and keep track of the contents. It was really engaging to wade through that murky world of cold war slug fest. Within weeks, one could easily decipher the style, attack targets and the kind of materials these rival missions supply to influence the Indian policy makers. Most of them contained newspaper reports or articles, research papers from what was claimed specialist institutions of the home country and secret documents from those like the Pentagon. The Soviet packet called Daily News carried translations of articles appearing in their specialized publications. The Soviet papers justified their stand of the Sino-Soviet recriminations and frequently set forth details of secret US-China collusion against India. The reports mentioned 'secret' meetings of a US official or so with their counterparts in China as proof of the anti-India collusion.

The US documents frequently referred to the famine conditions and shortages in Russia behind the iron curtain. Another theme was the Chinese build-up against India followed by some US expert's warning that ultimately the two communist giants would collude against the 'free world'. So the only option for India was to join the Western alliances. The UK documents frequently mentioned Chinese conspiracy to wrest a foothold in India's North Eastern states. Some of those articles hinted at the Chinese establishing links with the Indian communist groups, apparently the Naxalite elements who were then yet to form a formal grouping. The UK documents referred to details of Mizos and Nagas sending soldiers to China for training and despatch of Chinese arms to them. Indian mainstream media often took a cue from the UK packets, especially their cold war references to the North Eastern states.

Once I had specially noted a piece in the UK packet mentioning the possibility of the pro-China communists in India and northern separatists together holding a meeting within the Chinese territory. It had only talked of the 'possibilities'. Two days later, *The Statesman* came out with a page 1 story saying that such a meeting did take place. The 'special representative' had attributed it to home ministry sources. I showed the UK piece to T.J.S. George. He just smiled. A few such borrowed cold war stories had appeared in some other English dailies. All of them duly attributing such exclusives to Indian sources. That much for our media's credibility. Then there was a startling revelation about another aspect of this war of flea. Rival sides of the cold war were aware of the contents of the packets delivered by the other side to the Indians. Obviously, someone was promptly passing on the materials to the rivals. It all worked at lightning speed. A provocative piece of information contained in the Soviet packet would get a retort just within a couple of days in the UK or US bunch.

The century had three other unique selling points: its usually rich literary fare and an easily fileable digest of events. Both were entirely new features for the weekly journals of the day. One literary feature alone—'Review of the Reviews'—took four to five pages. It contained critical appraisals of the latest English books released in India and abroad. The reviews were extensive and rather longish with special focus on controversial points. The new books, again, came from Menon's residence. Lawrence Braddleman would also bring piles of new books and begin churning out typed sheets. Anil

Saari and Paul Jacob were the other members of the team. It got responses from university academics and writers far and near. Many of those informed commentaries were carried in the literary column. Book reviews of *The Century* were also unique. Which other Indian weekly had experimented with such a lavish literary fare devoting one-fifths of its pages? And it did have a loyal clientele from among universities and academics. The literary pages of *The Century* also gave a synopsis of the new English books. After years, Braddleman left for Canada where he took up a new assignment.

The four-page separate Century News Digest was meant to be a ready reckoner for students and knowledge workers when there was no internet. Subscribers could take out this separate blue-colour pages and file them chronologically week after week. The digest begins with a couple of lead stories of the week in double columns. This was followed by 'national', 'politics', 'Parliament', 'economy', 'neighbours', 'Americas', 'Europe', 'Africa' and 'Australia' and 'obituary'. *The Century*'s third USP was 'Last Laugh', a highly popular column at the fag end of the weekly. Citing its free reach and lucid style, colleagues credited the column to a seasoned Bombay-based journalist. Others say it was by a senior Congress leader with a flair for writing and who knew too much about the happenings around. Despite my best efforts, I could not trace the source.

In production technology and printing, Menon's paper perfectly represented the 1960s' crusader journals. Patterned on the *New Statesman* of yore, it did not have a cover page. The main editorial piece began just below the logo in colour. Today's WiFi-SMS generation cannot even imagine the limitations and strain under which we had to struggle to meet the deadline. Additions and major alterations meant the compositor had to reset by hand an entire paragraph. To avoid major disruption, we had to add the same number of letters—or 'em'—in the copy in the event of any deletion of words. Otherwise the irritated foreman would start grumbling and put the blame on you for the delay. Mind you, those who fiddled with the carbon-stained lead types for hours were prone to get irrigated. 'Em' is a measurement in the hand-setting system to gauge space in a line. Length of a column is measured in 'em', say 11 'em' wide column.

The whole *Century* establishment was stuffed into a medium size hall where one corner was occupied by a bulky roller printing machine. At the other corner was the compositors, 'joiners' and other press staff with their innumerable ink-stained wooden racks, type 'cases' and high stools. Amidst the newsprint rolls and ink drums sat an accounts clerk and a typist. Between them were a few chairs and tables for the editorial staff. Everyone, including George and Kakkar, sat amidst the crowd. No cabins nor screens. Four ceiling fans went on spinning. Noise of the printing machine and the mixed stench of fresh newsprint and tarpentine-based ink made it a messy place. Yet we in the editorial felt the whole ambience free and fresh. Friendly colleagues were there always to help you.

It was not so with our compositor colleagues who spent long hours fiddling with the carbon-stained lead types. Most were hungry-looking and bespectacled with leaning necks. By nature they were prone to get irritated. Therefore, copy editors and page-makers at the desk must take care to avoid too many corrections in the 'set' (composed) 'matter'. Sitting at a two-'case' board, the compositor had to hand-pick the right lead letter-types from the rectangle cavities. Apart from 26 Roman letters and ten numerals, there are separate cavities for dots, commas and question marks. The lower section cavities of the case are for small letters and upper for capitals. Like the 'shifts' for capitals in modern keyboards. The term lower case ('l.c'.) denoting small letters is a hangover of the two-case boards of the hand compositing era. The compositors hold their 'stick' (a 5"x 4" adjustable tray to arrange the types) and hand-pick the right letter types one by one and arrange them on the 'stick' line by line. After about ten lines, the 'matter' (as it is called) is carefully transferred on to the 'galley' which is a 4"x 20" or so narrow tray. The matter in the 'galley' is always securely tied with a thread. The 'galleys' are usually kept on a stand, one below the other. Taking a proof impression of the 'matter' in the 'galley' is the next step. After correction by the proof readers, the compositor will have to 'carry out' (that is the term) the correction in the 'matter'. A second 'galley' proof is taken and sent to the proof readers for final approval. Now the matter is ready for page making.

It takes at least three hours to make a demi 1/8 page in the hand-setting era, something our modern copy editors can do in half an hour sitting at a desktop in cool comfort. And no staining of the hands and dress. For headlines, the compositors had bigger letter types of up to 72 points. These were kept in different cases. And surprise of it all. Types of above 72 points—called poster types —were made of hard wood. Page making in those days was a joint operation by the chief sub editor and the senior compositor who was also called a 'make-up man'. The chief sub also acted as designer. By the way, page designers arrived in newsrooms hardly two decades ago.

While today's generation can make a few clicks and bring out the desired illustrations, photographs and graphics, think of the old generation's travails. We had to decide page design and size of the pictures at least two hours before making the page. This is because photographs/illustrations cannot be put on the page right away as you do now. First, the lense man had to present the prints of the photographs to the news editor. The latter selected the pictures and sent them for 'block' making. At the sudio, a camera transfers the image of the photo on a sheet of specially treated lead. Then the sheet is subjected to another treatment of a red chemical powder. The sheet with the photo image engraved in the reverse is cut to the size and fixed on a wooden block. Hence the term 'block'. Finally, the matter in galleys with headlines and blocks will have to be placed on the printing 'frame' as per the page size and layout. The make-up man needs constant on-the-spot direction by the chief sub or sub-editor. Then the whole 'frame' is transferred on to the 'stone' which is actually the printing plate.

The printing is done 'forme'-by-'forme'. The second hand roller press at *Century* could print only a four-page 'forme' of A1 size at a time. The make-up man places the 4-page forme on the machine as per the pre-determined page scheme. Once the required number of copies are printed on one side of the sheet, another forme is kept ready for printing on the reverse side. To complete 24 pages, they had to make ready six 'formes' and print as many times. It took about two days to print 4,000 copies of the 24-page weekly in six formes. This means the chief sub had to take extreme care while sending copy for typesetting and planning page numbers.

Little was known about the proprietors and funding sources

of Menon's weekly. Soft-spoken S.K. Anand, a businessman doing trade with the Soviet block countries, was its managing director. He was popular among the friends of the Soviet Union as well as sections of the Congress leaders. He moved in an old Fiat car and lived at a modest hired flat. A middle-aged man often came to the cramped hall to supervise the work. No one knew who he was. *The Century* had a few pages of advertisements, mostly public sectaor units and exim houses. Circulation and distribution was managed by the Central News Agency (CNA), a Connaught Place newspaper distributor. In those days, CNA undertook the distribution in Delhi of most regional dailies and journals, including the large ones like *Anand Bazar Patrika, Mathrubhoomi, Malayala Manorama, Thanthi, Sakal, Loksatta* and *Rajasthan Patrika.* CNA staff came to *Century* on Fridays, packed copies in bundles and took them away in a tonga.

The Century, like a dozen or so other protest journals of the era, had filled an intellectual vaccum at a time when the mainstream dailies avoided plain-speaking. The weekly had its last issue soon after Krishna Menon fell ill before his death.

10

Cut-'n'-paste Magazines

Things were quite different at the fortress-like Delhi Press, publishers of *Caravan* (English), *Sarita* and *Mukta* (both in Hindi and Urdu). A hefty chowkidar sat at the heavy door. Two Gurkhas with their *khukris* stood guard. The threesome smoothly regulated entry and exit of visitors to the building. There was no need for a reception or intercom. A messenger guided you to the right man in the two-storey building. It was about two decades before the registered security agencies and uniformed guards appeared on the scene. Simultaneously, the once ubiquitous Gurkhas had also disappeared. In those days, offices had their own staff chowkidars who got the usual benefits of Class IV employees.

The main business at Delhi Press was printing job works. Its owner Vishwa Nath's elder son looked after this work. Publishing was a passion for Vishawa Nath, a gold medalist chartered accountant. Those who today breast-beat over the rigorous labour laws and ease of doing business should learn from this management genius. Without any formal management training, this guru had developed his own labour control system to reward and punish his staff. He did so without seemingly violating the labour laws. Business innovation was his forte. Half a century back when strikes and picketing were the order of the day, Vishwa Nath could run his business through invisible—undetectable—outsourcing and concealed contract labour. He used these to the best effect.

"I'll give you two days to familiarize yourself with our system," Krishan Kumar said. "This is not like other magazine offices. You can't loiter round the office. You will lose half day's attendance in case you are late by ten minutes. No chit-chatting and gossiping in office."

Tall, well-built and fully bald, Kumar was the editorial coordinator. He and Khare, the managing editor, were the only long-serving persons. They were the ones trusted by Vishwa Nath from among the two dozen editorial staff.

"This is a quaint place," the fellow sub editors revealed during the lunch hour. "Kumar can ask you to get out any time. Don't go by the great 'sub-editor'tag. Your job is only to search for illustrations and paste galley proof on dummy. Nothing more. If he finds you good you will get a quick pay rise. If found best, you can work here 179 days."

"One seventy-nine days?"

"Yes, 179 days. Just to beat the rules. One more day, you will get the 'permanent' tag with PF and gratuity claims. They want to avert it. Exactly at 1 noon, the staff must leave the office and return after lunch time."

Fortuitously, I survived in the Delhi Press for a year and a half with quick pay rises and a chief sub's designation. Kumar acted tough and rough. He never smiled. While speaking he looked behind suspiciously at Vishwa Nath's cabin. He kept a handkerchief and frequently wiped sweat on his bald head.

But this cultivated harsh look began changing after a fortnight. When alone, he would talk politely and patronizingly. At times he appreciated a headline or intro.

One day at the PRRM coffee house Kumar poured himself out. He said he was a trade unionist and lost a good job. He had a large family to look after. He bicycled 10 kms, all the way from Sarojini Nagar to the Jhandelwalan office—in winter or summer. He said he had to be rude to please the owner-editor who occasionally watched his staff through a magic eye hole in the door. Remember, the now ubiquitous CCTV cameras had not yet arrived. Kumar said he too would quit the moment he got a better job. Then he would talk about his childhood in the Pakistan part of Punjab, education in a government school in Delhi and how a tufted Tamil priest had tried to molest him.

Years later, I had a chance meeting with Kumar at the Connaught Place coffee house. I had come from Ahmedabad for a short visit. Kumar looked hale and hearty. He talked loudly and cracked jokes with others in the coffee house crowd. He said he had got a trouble-free job at a publishing house in Daryagunj. A former sub-editor of *Sarita* whom he had sacked, had fixed the job for him.

Caravan and *Sarita* were fortnightlies. *Mukta* was a monthly but both in Hindi and Urdu. At one time *Sarita*, a family magazine, was a household name in Hindi-speaking middle class homes. *Caravan* with 11,000 circulation, sizeable in those days, was seen more with the elderly government staff, retired officials and older segment of English educated middle classes. It was fairly popular in cantonment areas and seen regularly in railway book stalls. These were exactly Vishwa Nath's target group. Edits, editorial comments and lighter kind of stories are all tailored to this section's taste. It invariably avoided hard politics but treated politicians as an exploiting class. It frequently suggested that honest civil servants could be better rulers than politicians but disfavoured military rule. Yes, in those days, military rule was a favourite theme among some cynical sections in India.

In national politics, Vishwa Nath showered scorn on the Nehruvian concept of planning and non-alignment. His leanings were with the Swatantra Party. But he rejected the RSS line of Indian history and followed a rationalist way of looking at history. He hated Brahmanism and carried frequent cartoons depicting tufted, obese panditjis gulping ladoos in the name of god. *Caravan* had also carried well researched pieces like 'names in Mahabharata' where all the major characters were bastards. Long stories appeared to prove Rig Vedic people ate beef.

All Delhi Press publications followed the same style and similar fare for the readers. Each issue carried a couple of poems with illustrations. They also had at least two short stories and a longish novel serialized with illustrations. Then there were self-improvement articles, art and films, jokes and funny quotes. Vishwa Nath himself would collect clippings from foreign magazines on home making, personal health and grooming and handed them to outside writers to turn into short feature stories. His readers lapped up all such fare.

All those columns were regular and had separate box files to store the copy and ready-to-paste prints. There was always a huge stock of stories in all 'boxes'. Unlike today's newsmagazines, these had a rather long shelf life. The chief sub (officially designated as 'in-charge') had only to pick the right pieces for the edition and put them on the right pages. A similar system was followed for other sister publications. This smooth and hassle-free arrangement was part of a unique model of editorial management perfected by Vishwa Nath.

It started with his own system of pre-payment for contributions. The group publications received many poems, stories and write-ups as contributions. These were mostly by old fashioned regional writers. Some were translations. Khare weeded out the unwanted ones. Once accepted by Vishwa Nath, he tick marked the approved ones and wrote the amount of remuneration in pencil. A pencil was used because the author could rub it off in case he chose to reject the offer. The amount was as low as Rs. 20 or Rs. 30, a pittance even in those days. The cheque for the amount would be accompanied by a meticulously drafted acceptance form with several legal conditions.

Then the accepted piece became the group's property. It could be used any time, anywhere and in any form. Any group magazine could carry it. A rather curious pre-condition was that Delhi Press could even change the ownership of the 'product' to any other party, including another journal. However, no contributor has ever objected to such outlandish conditions.

The stories were then edited, typed (most articles in those days came handwritten) and sent for lino type-setting. After the proof correction, the ready-to-use prints of stories went into their respective 'boxes'. Simultaneously, the same piece would undergo a similar process for *Sarita* and *Mukta*. The advantage of the pre-payment system is that you got three pieces at the price of one without any obligation.

Another innovation was creation of an 'illustation bank.' It saved mony and time and enabled the sub-editors to pick and choose ready-made illustrations just by thumping through a stitched bunch. After a few weeks of thumping, one got to know which illustration or photograph suited the story and where one could locate it in the 'illustration bank.' It was even easier than clicking different sites on the web. Its negative side is that it is unethical to re-use or truncate a picture that the reader has seen in an earlier article or short story. There is an amount of dishonesty. But the Delhi Press was doing business, not charity.

It needs an explanation to understand the double advantage of the 'illustration bank. In the normal course, the artist would have to make illustrations for each article for which he had to be paid. Then the illustrations or photographs had to be made into blocks. This also costs money. The 'illustration bank' simply short-cuts all such problems. How does the system work? After printing an issue, the page make-up man picks up the blocks of all the magazines and takes their printouts. These are stitched into a book. That is the illustration bank. Stitched bunches are sent to all the publications for use. Each illustration has a number. If the sub-editor wants a lone bearded man sitting at a river side, he can search and pick the one that suits the scene. All that he had to do was to mark the block number. The make-up man will pick the right block from the racks on which these are kept with corresponding numbers. In other words, this simply meant re-use of the same illustration over and again. Worse, sub-editors are often told to combine different illustrations and create new scenes to suit the new articles. This was a clear case of cannibalism. Or call it self-cannibalism. Some discriminating readers had discovered it and protested but such cries were ignored.

Outsourcing of inhouse work and hiring staff on a fixed contract package are practices associated with globalization and liberalization. But Vishwa Nath had perfected both over three decades before. That too, with much more finesse. Articles, write-ups, poems and stories are passed on to anonymous outside entities for editing. One of the outside copy editors was an assistant editor in *The Statesman*. Another was a senior sub in *The Times of India*. They were all quite competent and did the editing in the *Caravan* style. Often the edited copy had to be retyped. Payment for the outside work was done mostly by cash.

The system worked well because the content in all three magazines was not topical in nature. A few weeks delay would not make them out of date. Outside editors made frequent appearances at Delhi Press to meet Vishwa Nath to take briefs from him. For topical articles, there was a different arrangement. The main editorial was probably written by Vishwa Nath himself. A couple of other editorial pieces and a three-page 'national and states' column arrived a day before the deadline. A former sub-editor of *The Hindustan Times* who was working with an advertisement agency in Connaught Place came in the evenings and edited such topical copies.

The system of anonymous outsourcing was followed even in the case of proof reading. Delhi Press had its staff proof readers. But they mostly looked after the 'matter' for job works. For *Caravan*, they did the first proof reading. Outside proof readers—from the *The Times of India* and *The Statesman*—did the final reading. After this, a retired proof reader from the government press on Minto Road went through the final page proof. Thus almost the entire copy editing and proof reading for the magazine was done by outsiders on cash payment. Inhouse sub-editors only had to oversee the process.

Outsourcing the page making of a magazine? Delhi Press had achieved this feat right under the watchful eyes of trade union activists. It was a secret arrangement with the page makers. They pretended to be working as regular employees and signed the necessary papers. But they were actually given a lumpsum for the work.

Today we make pages on the computer screen. In that hot metal era, pages were planned on the dummy sheets of full page size. At Delhi Press, lead types (fonts) were cast instantly on linotype machine. The page-maker's job was to physically pick the cast body types with headlines, intro and blocks as per the dummy layout and arrange it on the 'stone'. At *Caravan*, eight pages formed a 'forme.' The page-maker had to put all the eight pages as per the page numbers on the 'stone' of the machine for printing. The process is repeated for every other eight pages. In a fortnightly, page-makers have irregular work hours. There may not be any page making in the first few days and they will have to be paid overtime in the final few days. Thus the secret contract work saved money for the company.

Under this unique outsourcing system, the job of the two subs and chief sub was to select the right illustration from the 'bank', and cut glazed paper narrows and paste on the dummy sheets as per the layout. Then they had to give the headlines, intro and captions. Everything else—writing, copy editing, proof reading—was done by the unknown outsiders. Even the sub-editor's cut-and-paste job was well structured and defined. Every article or feature had a fixed slot and should go on a particular page. Stories should end in one or two columns or half page. Every piece should have illustrations and an intro or intros. There is very little scope for innovation and imagination. Deviation from the general layout pattern was a strict no-no.

Even this design construct was a part of the outsourcing system under which everyone—from the contributor to the page maker in the press—had a fixed role. It moved as per a strict layout scheme issue after issue. The chief editor's office essentially functions as a control board or like an aggregator as in Uber and Ola. But Vishwa Nath had an explanation even for this fixed format model. Readers of his journals were conservative in their world view. They were looking for regular fare on fixed pages. Wide variations in layout and content would upset their expectations.

Delhi Press had all infrastructure and resources at its command. It had a modern press with the most modern photo offset machine. *Caravan* had 24 colour pages on glazed paper. But Vishwa Nath's bane was his compulsive weakness as a control freak and his inane mistrust of humans. It was this paranoia that had made him construct the outsourcing system. While Vishwa Nath had caught bogged down in his old restrictive management style, a new generation of readers with new tastes and reading habits was emerging. His old style magazines with predictable fare had encountered threats from both sides—the high priced glossies and new generation news magazines like *India Today* on the one side and the blunt and bold kind of rebel weeklies that appealed to the new genre intellectuals. The new challengers had a liberal approach to their journalist staff. Unlike the caged parrots at Delhi Press, reporters of the new magazines walked free and brought fresh stories. Vishwa Nath failed to see the writing on the wall. And that was the tragedy of all control freaks. It is good that decades later, a new *Caravan* has finally emerged. Carry on, friends.

11

Fall of Media Charmers

Enough attention has not been paid to the media management system perfected by L.K. Advani in the 1980s and first half of the next decade. No other politician in the post-Emergency period had succeeded to build such a vast media base. He cultivated and nurtured support both among the middle rung journalists and their editors and proprietors. He put to best use his rapport with the media owners during his tenure as information minister of the Morarji Desai government.

Two aspects of Advani's experiment call for a closer look. The first is how with all his hardliner image he could influence so many non-convert journalists without the support of the state power and any expert PR build-up. Second, how he lost the initiative so suddenly since the mid-90s. Both were equally baffling for the uninitiated. We had many politicians who were exceptionally media savvy. It was an era when national political parties gave a great deal of freedom to the individual leaders to cultivate people and widen their zone of influence. These were not seen with suspicion. Muffles were not so tight nor their movements curbed – whether above or below 75. The institution of spokespersons with monopoly rights to speak on behalf of a political party was a 21st century creation. It had put the last nail on the freedom of expression within India's political parties. General secretaries and senior leaders spoke on behalf of the parties within reasonable limits. Advani had thus begun his media management even while Atal Bihari Vajpayee was the BJP president.

Over the years, there was no dearth of politicians with pampered journalists under their care. H.N. Bahuguna was among the media-savvy politicians. He had a set of journalists around him.

They were regulars at his Sunheribag residence. Some journos had taken undue advantage of his close rapport with Dhirubhai Ambani. Once S. Dharmarajan of *The Times of India*, who had a clean record as a journalist, was surprised to find Reliance PROs at the London airport to receive him when he had gone there in a press party. Bahuguna's hold on business groups had enabled many ordinary scribes get higher positions in newspapers. Those were the days when the business-politcian-scribe nexus was still at a nascent stage.

AICC treasurer (later Congress president) Sitaram Kesari was frequently sighted at corporate floors of the Times House and HT building. This was happening both before and after Ashok Jain's exit. He too had scribes around him. Some Kesari fans did manage to get positions in the Hindi dailies of the two media houses. Journos also flocked to him for minor favours. Wags had it that the best way to befriend Kesari was to fondle his Pomeranians in his presence. Chandra Shekhar as a 'young turk' began with a youth halo. He fought the Syndicate and revolted against Indira Gandhi. A dozen or so of his journalist *chelas* were always there to aid and advise him. Some enjoyed his hospitality at his Bhondsi resort—or call it *ashram*. They helped him produce and manage his publications and organized his press conferences. Among his constant friends were Vijay Sanghvi, K.P. Srivastava and Dev Dutt—all well read scribes known for their intelligent explanations for every political twist and turn.

Arjun Singh had close friends and bitter foes among the scribes. He trusted and helped those who had found virtues in him. But his problem was that he had formidable foes within his own party and BJP. He was a staunch Nehruvian and never abandoned it even when his party bosses humiliated and forced him out. His BJP adversaries, especially from Madhya Pradesh, had consistently harangued him. Many stories had appeared about his 'marble' palace. His statements were often misquoted and twisted. Later a disgusted Arjun Singh made it a point to place a powerful tape recorder while speaking to journalists. And at the outset he would tell the reporters about its presence to warn against misquoting. However, his fatal mistake was that he wasted his energy in convincing the ordinary reporters rather than winning over the media owners. Within the BJP, Murli Manohar Joshi had cultivated his own journo friends. Even Govindacharya before he fell out with Nagpur had a large crowd of admirers. Then there were the chief ministers and powerful state leaders who had their own friendly scribes. Curiously, even the editors were aware of such a relationship and had assigned the respective beat to them for optimum output.

However, in the fine art of media management, no one could rival L.K. Advani. For him, dealing with the media persons was part of his political routine. He cultivated media on a regular basis. He had an innate knack of dealing with different genres of journalists. I have never seen him overdoing it—like rushing for a handshake or a hug. When a reporter enters his cabin, he may not even look at you. Not even a smile of recognition. But after he finishes with his papers, he is a changed man. His style is to be reasonably cordial. He gives the impresson that he gave you time in spite of his busy schedule. But he would never say so. He calls you by your first name. This gives you an inflated ego. If he does it in front of others you feel even more elated. Often he would comment on your 'good' byline story that had appeared that day. Innocents normally fall for such gestures.

There were a dozen instances where Advani endeared himself to those who otherwise had a fierce anti-Hindutva mindset. Take the case of David Devadas, my colleague in *The Economic Times* and *Business Standard.* To us in office, he described himself as an Advani *bhakt*, of course in a lighter vein. He felt so elated at Advani patting him on his back while moving along the Parliament corridor up to the VIP portico. People around watched Advani talking to David, often stopping to make some points. In those days, many like David would emotionally talk about the integrity and reasonableness of L.K. Advani. Among them were D.P. Kumar of *The Statesman* and Prithvis Chakravarti, once a bureau chief of *The Hindustan Times*. Neither was of Hindutva persuasion but admired Advani.

When you met him alone, he would often offer you tips for stories, especially on what was happening in the Congress Party. Or about the gift packet of mangoes he received from the Pakistan prime minister. For a reporter, a gift to a Hindutva leader from Pakistan is a good exclusive. Looking back, I must confess many of my byline political exclusives and stories about the government had emanated from Advani or his authentic aides like Rajendra Sharma. But there was one caveat: he was extremely miserly when it came to the inside happenings of his own party. If you asked him about the BJP, he would simply smile it away. In 1984-85, I remember (in fact recoded in my daily notings) how he was talking highly of Rajiv Gandhi in private. He had met him at a function and the 'young man' was certainly different from the arrogant Congress crowd, he said, of course off the record. He had great hopes of heralding a new era under what others were dismissing as 'computer boys' and 'Doon pals'. Advani was always a good source for what happened at the indoor discussions like all-party meetings and official panels.

His patronizing style was unique. He used it to the maximum effect. Perhaps his personal aides too had learnt the trick of trade. They would often tell you how Advani lauded your article. And you would invariably be taken in. Once he himself had put this idea in an interview to a society journal. In his student days, Advani had told the reporter, he was influenced by Dale Carnegie's *How to Win Friends and Influence People*. He seemed serious about making use of Carnegie's tips. For instance, quite often he himself sought—or his staff telephoned on his behalf—input from us for his address at the BJP's national council or some academic functions. This made you feel important. It was another matter how much of your input he had actually used.

When he was home minister, an old journalist called me up to say that Advani wanted to have a leisurely chat with us. With me, a retired oldie? It was too naïve to take it seriously. And months after, I saw the HM with his entourage crossing the central hall of Parliament.

"Prabhuji," he called out. Apparently, he had called me a wrong name. "Return it after reading." He handed a book to me and walked away. It was Joseph Stiglitz's *Globalisation and It's Discontents*. After reading, I duly deposited the book with his personal staff. This may be his standard way of treating media persons.

However if you are credulous enough you tend to look at the murky side of this affability and cordiality. I was also a victim of such beguilement. Once *Business Standard* editor T.N. Ninan showed me a complaint given by Advani against my stories in the daily. He had attached clippings of my reports with objectionable portions highlighted by fluorescent pen. The packet was personally handed to Avik Sarkar when he visited Calcutta. Sarkar simply passed it on to Ninan. Both were very professional and did not find anything distasteful in the stories. But what hurt me was that hardly three days after this, the same Advani had, after a briefing, lauded the 'balanced' political coverage in *BS*. But then we the footsoldiers of journalism were used to even worse kind of duplicity and perfidy by the politicians, bureaucrats and business. We have taken all that in our stride all through life. They are cordial to you so long as you write what they want. A little scrutiny, they would complain to the owners. Weeks later, friends at sister daily *Telegraph* revealed that the BJP leader had made similar complaints against some of them as well.

L.K. Advani was the one who also believed that the best way to manage news was through the owners. As early as the mid-80s there were stories about Advani meeting Ramnath Goenka for political favours. He sought more coverage for the BJP in *The Indian Express* when it was just a two-MP party. "We also have to sell the paper," Goenka was quoted as telling Advani. At the *Express* editorial meetings, this quote was frequently mentioned to emphasize the need for maintaining the paper's credibility at all costs.

L.K. Advani's media fans belonged to three categories. At the highest level were the trusted big fish—Swapan Dasgupta, T.V.R. Shenoi, Chandan Mitra, Dinanath Mishra and a few others—whose counsel he constantly valued. They advised him on how to deal with the editors and media barons like Samir Jain and suggested useful inputs for every BJP campaign. Feedback from such hard core was highly appreciated during his stewardship.

Just below in the rank was a junior set comprising the RSS faithfuls and those trusted by the BJP, especially the committed Samachar Bharati remnants. They were all loyal journos but did not enjoy the same status as the biggies. In the third category were the non-committed reporters regularly covering BJP. Advani and his aides took special care to cultivate this section. The second rung loyalists helped his handlers keep a close tab on those journos—how close were they with BJP and their reporting style, shifting loyalties and what they discussed in private. Advani had all this background information when he met such uncommitted journos. That was how he had cultivated the unconverted correspondents with amazing results. Advani had carefully avoided a fourth category of reporters—those incorrigible anti-Hindutva types who occasionally make an appearance at BJP's big press conferences and ask uncomfortable questions.

The story of Prithvis Chakravarti was a classic case. He was not a Hindutva type but an atheist and an old Royist. He was active in anti-Emergeny activities. After 1978 he had nowhere to go. Advani spotted him and made a quasi-convert.

"I don't agree with their Muslim hatred," Prithvis would say. "But there are many reasonable people like Advani in the BJP. Unlike those arrogant Congress fellows, he has an open mind. He listens to you. I am sure he will be able to rein in the fringe elements within the BJP." He had said so in the presence of journalist activist Vikram Rao.

"Moonshine," Rao had retorted. This was while we were discussing the Press Council matters. Vikram proved right. That was when the BJP office handed a free air ticket to Prithvis to cover the party's national council meeting at Bombay. A person of high principles, he charged the BJP leaders with 'corrupting' journalists.

Compare Advani's highly sophisticated party and media management with the rigid style introduced by the Narendra Modi-Amit Shah dispensation. Advani, Murli Manohar Joshi and their generation of leaders detested running the party from isolated castles. They mixed with the journalists as freely as they did with politicians of different hues. They did not need to fix secret money deals with deserters from other parties and local vote bank holders to expand the party base as Amit Shah now does. Instead, Advani had worked for a wider appeal outside the converted. Thus his kind of the glasnost had enabled the BJP to rope in an array of liberals like Madhya Pradesh's Arif Beg, K.S. Hegde, General Jacob, Yashwant Sinha and Sushma Swaraj. The Advani line in those days was that the BJP needed a liberal face if it had to expand its electoral base. His media outreach was part of this hard political design.

The Advani phenomenon in BJP has left three unresolved riddles. First, was Advani really keen to rush for a rath yatra in September, 1990, and thus break the V.P. Singh government? Or did he act under pressure from the RSS diehard and his party colleagues? Off-record remarks by Advani and his close aides like Rajendra Sharma point to a different proposition. Notings in my report pad clearly showed that even three days before the announcement of the rath yatra decision, Advani had strong reservations on its timing. He wanted to wait for more tremors within the PM's party. My notings record K.R. Malkani as making this point to us off-the-record. More than this, Advani might have calculated that an immediate rath yatra and sudden showdown might have knocked down his own painstakingly cultivated gentleman image. Jai Dubashi (who became the BJP general secretary later) had compared this to Advani's 'Arjun-like dilemma'. I was with J.P. Mathur and Sunder Singh Bhandari, who were earlier sharing Advani's cautious approach, when they were watching a tempo yatra of the pro-mandir sadhus at Connaught's Place's Shankar Market. "Now you can't stop it", I heard Bhandari saying.

At informal briefings, Advani was eloquent on how the V.P. Singh was trying to take him and Left leader Somnath Chatterjee into confidence on government decisions. At Thursday's dinner meetings, the two opposition supporters had often suggested changes in proposed legislations. My *Realpolitik* column in *The Economic Times* had mentioned such details. Was Advani patently dishonest in saying so at the press briefings and then pushing the government to a corner soon after? We need a deeper investigation to find the truth.

The second is: was Advani really a 'loh purush' or RSS hardliner as has been depicted by the media? The image continued until his rupture with Sarsangh Chalak Mohan Bhagwat on the issue of Jinnah's remarks after the BJP lost power in 2004. Advani did seek better coordination with the RSS. But was the hardline image the result of his juxtapostioning with Atal Behari Vajpayee who was seen as a liberal face of the BJP? This subject is beyond the purview of this media analysis.

Third, how did Advani lose all his cultivated ability for skilful media and political management by the mid-90s? His alleged involvement in the Jain hawala scandal was the first jolt. During the Vajpayee rule, he was discouraged to have his full say in party affairs. Advani did try to put his own nominees as BJP party president. But a few years later something unusual happened. Vajpayee had insisted that he should be consulted even on routine organizational matters at 11 Ashoka Road and nothing should be done without his knowledge. The media had largely ignored the imposition of such a Congress-style PMO control on the party organization. This invariably poured cold water on Advani's initiatives. Then there was a more important factor. Even before moving to the North Block, Advani had bagun losing most of his highly talented aides and think tank. Later, Nagpur's heavy hand on Advani on the Jinnah remarks completed his isolation. Subsequently, small-time apparatchik and family members began getting the better of him.

12

The Crusader Journos

Daily newspapers in India have a tradition of maintaining a symbiotic relationship with the establishment. British-owned newspapers spoke the language of the crown. Most of them behaved as if they were another arm of the empire. One only has to look at the old copies of *The Statesman*, *Pioneer*, *The Times of India* and *The Mail*. This was quite understandable. For, colonial officers had constantly interacted with the media bosses and extended financial support and special privileges.

Indigenous dailies as they began establishing themselves, also learnt to stay on the safe side of the Raj or rajas. The only exceptions were those journals of highly nationalistic orientation. Questioning the establishment was not the media's job. Inform and educate does not mean agitation and revolt. That was the *dharma* followed by the contemporary mainstream media. It may not be the fear of the state as such but mostly a force of habit conditioned by the colonial patronage system. In the early stages, Delhi's accredited press core had an established tradition of identifying themselves with the government. But then how did things take a sharp turn after the Emergency? By the time Indira Gandhi romped back to power in 1980, a big chunk of the Capital's press corps had become partisan crusaders. Clearly, this shift from loyal clients to crusaders had its seeds in the political turmoil in the preceding three decades.

Looking back, the government ifself was smaller in area, size and sheer numbers. The capital elite's southern border was South-end Road. Old Congress leaders and senior bureaucracy cheerfully mingled with the capital's elite special correspondents. The latter were very few in numbers. May be some 15-20. A half dozen from PTI and AIR and two or three from *The Statesman*, *Hindustan Times*,

Times of India and *The Indian Express*. A couple of regional groups also thought it necessary to post a man and office in Delhi. Such correspondents were always more confortable with ministers and bureaucrats from their home states.

You can't even imagine the kind of authority enjoyed by those few PIB card holders. Ministers and senior bureaucrats called them by first name. They were ambassadors of their big editors. The media owners used them for more import licences and newsprint allocations. They freely entered the cabins of ministers and senior secretaries. True, they addressed the ministers and leaders as 'sir'. But this did not denote an inferior status. That was a way of addressing. Whether it is Kaul or Krishnamurthi, the aides at big bhavans greeted the journalists with great respect. This writer before he joined newspapers had the benefit of accompanying PTI's N. Rajamani.

"Come on," he said patting my back when I hesitated to enter the North Block door. He took me through the side gate reserved for the VIPs. The chowkidar stood up and greeted him. No need to show the pass. The journos were so few and everyone knew them by face. Staff chowkidars were found capable of securing the bhavans and blocks. Slightly away, two policemen were sitting on a bench along with their bicycles and bamboo sticks. That was the kind of security in those days. There were no CRPF or industrial security force.

A few feet away, a peon with piles of files greeted the journo.

"It'll be done," the scribe told him with all self-assurance. "I have given him the papers. He had promised me to process them."

The peon bowed in gratitude. In his 40s, the man wanted his relative, a boy from the UP hills, given a 'water boy's job. Those days there were no desert coolers or AC. Every year by February you could see temporary workers making *khas-khas* curtains all along the central secretariat complex. The *khas-khas* curtains are fixed at windows, *verandas* and *balconies*. They remained there until October end. Hundreds of temporary 'boys' were employed to spray water with mugs on the curtains, not water pipes.

Rajamani walked past many doors on both sides. A peon at the minister's cabin opened the door for us—with a polite smile. Ramsubhag Singh (if my fading memory does not betray me) was talking to two men. The minister and the scribe just smiled at each other. Without a word the latter went to the sofa settee and began thumping through at the *Illustrated Weekly*. After some time, the minister arrived and settled on the other settee. The hosts always had their own seat with a white Turkish towel spread on the back. That was where the telephone extensions were kept.

"Hey, a new nice phone," Rajamani exclaimed.

"Yes, they have put it here," Ramsubhag Singh said. "It's called RAX."

"RAX? What's that?" Rajamani wanted to examine it.

"It's a new phone network confined to senior ministers and officers and some VIPs," said Singh. "Outsiders are not allowed to use it. It's for better security."

"We are not outsiders," the scribe reminded the minister. How meaningful and assertive a claim!

"True, we are all part of the system," the minister agreed. "But in any case, RAX phones hardly work."

By the time the secretary came in with a file.

"How is it?" the minister asked while going through the papers.

"Sir, can I refer it to the FM?" the secretary asked. The minister nodded in agreement and the secretary left.

"It was something about the allocation for a mill," the minister revealed.

How informal and casually cordial! That was the kind of relationship Delhi's press corps had some half century back. They behaved as if they were part of the government. Nothing critical appears in the daily newspapers. In case an unpalatable story makes a rare appearance, lest assure that it is a plant by a more senior, influential person against a rival. Never on the initiative of a journo. Even that will be shrouded in politely vague language.

Rajamani dropped me in front of the AIR building on Parliament Street. He came in the minister's car. The AIR buiding was the home of PIB offices before Shastri Bhavan was built. Opposite on the other side of the road was a bungalow where PTI had its office. The present PTI building had come up on that plot.

Ruling politicians had always considered Delhi's elite press corps as their own. K.C. Pant used to quote his father Pandit G.B. Pant having described the government's relationship with media as *advaita* (not two different entities). Both entities are one, not separable. Otherwise how could the government allot the joint secretary-level houses to the scribes in Lutyens' Delhi at nominal rates? For this purpoe, a separate 'Press pool' was created. And this was when the goernment's own officers had to seek private accommodation.

This may be an extreme case of a patron-client deal that had for long compromised the real function of the media. There were two explanations for this. First, the government wanted a dozen or so scribes covering its activities to stay at arms length. Those days in Delhi, many lived in Karol Bagh or beyond Civil Lines. No one had their own conveyance. Government vehicles were sent to fetch the reporters when there were official briefings after 8 pm. How long had this continued we do not know. The second was more specious. The reporters did the government's work and so the latter should reciprocate when their wages were rather low. Such right-based claims for government favours were the cornerstone of the prevailing 'yes-minister' culture. It cut at the very roots of the modern concept of an independent media.

By the 80s, this arrangement became a major scam in the press corps. Some honourable editors got involved. Those PIB card holders and editors occupying the government flats refused to vacate even after retirement. They simply took another accreditation on behalf of some obscure journal. As a result, younger PIB card holders were denied flats from the Press pool. This at a time when the number of accredited correspondents were rising by leaps and bounds. The occupiers of the 'pool' flats included those who shifted residence to other states. There were cases of senior journos subletting their government flats to others in part or full. The Editor of a Bengali daily living in Calcutta had converted his 'pool' flat into a guest house of his media house. Such were the kind of wanton misuse. Some younger journalists had taken the issue to court. A whole list of such gentlemen journalists overstaying in the government flats was made public. Later the PIB had drawn up a seniority list for allocations as and when available. Despite this, a few had managed to wrest out of turn allocations by unethical means.

Another cosy arrangement was the rail travel concession for

accredited journalists in all classes. For this, special coupons of different denominations were printed and distributed. Once there was a move to provide similar concessions on air travel. This was fiercely resisted by the private airlines. The PIB card holders were also eligible for using facilities under the Central Government Health Scheme (CGHS) even though they were the employees of private firms.

Foreign jaunts were another subtle lure. Before globalization, visits abroad were rare. It was a great attraction for the journos. There was big rush for free jaunts sponsored by foreign players. As per rules, you get a foreign exchange allocation by the RBI for 20 dollars—enough to bring many of fancy goods from abroad. Jaunts with ministers for international events and in the media entourage of the President and PM were more sought after. Those were a statement one's access to the PMO and a status symbol. There were many intrigues and lobbying while drawing up the list. Some editors objected to the government picking and choosing its favourite scribes for jaunts. They often resisted encroachments on their rights. In one case I remember a jilted editor had changed the correspondent's beat.

The ruling extablishment had always used the occasion to befriend and bring round influential regional media owners. Some owners were included in the PM's entourage in the garb of editors. Such owners used the opportunity to do things like fixing business deals abroad. The arrangement in those days was that while the accompanying scribes could travel in the same VIP flight free, they must pay for the local accommodation. There were no other expenses. Yet in some cases, the most favoured ones were obliged with accommodation arrangements by the local Indian mission. Rajiv Gandhi's days as prime minister were jolly good for the jaunt addicts. His aides got the foreign exchange rules relaxed to help the accompanying Press party. The lucky ones had brought two/three fax machines duty-free. Some journalists did it for their office. Some brought the machines home and sold them for a neat Rs. 20,000 margin for two. Fax machines were then new and cost up to Rs. 30,000 a piece in India.

Many such stories were doing the rounds among the capital's growing tribe of journalists. A prominent Delhi-based regional correpondent who later became the editor of his daily, gave a long list of his foreign jaunts with the prime minister, president and ministers as addendum to his biography. A good thing Narendra Modi did as PM was to put an end to the journos' foreign trips. Modi, for one, did not have any great admiration for scribes. He knew he could better tame the media at its corporate office level.

As the Press corps became larger, the intimacy and informality with the establishment began losing lustre. Many of the new young scribes were not so morally malleable. This crowd, some for ethical and others for political reasons, had refused to be part of the establishment. Despite the change in the complexion of the Delhi special correspondnents, a few old ones kept up the tradition of a cosy relationship. But they were few and were on their last days of service.

It was early in May 1974. We were sitting in UNI along with R. Rangarajan, its bureau chief.

"Don't take leave next week," Rangarajan said. "You are a chief sub-editor. Should not be seen as irresponsible." I just could not understand what he meant. Why should I be present in office next week? He would not elaborate. He had repeated the point the next day. And two days later, there was a morning call from him.

"Go to the office. Something big is happening," he said.

At the *Patriot* office, agency teleprinters were ticking 'flash... flash... flash... India texts nuclear device." Four decades, and it still remains a mystery. Was Rangarajan really aware of the Pokhran text in advance? From all indications, he must have been. But he persistently evaded the issue.

In the 70s, Rangarajan was among the few surviving specimens of the old tradition of the symbiotic relationship with the establishment. He wore khadi and moved in and out at Congress session venues. Seva Dal men or security men in Seva Dal uniform did not stop him. Even after the Blue Star. But not so for the rest of us.

The new crop of newsmen broke this collaborative partnership. May be their editors wished the old tradition to continue. And those close to the media houses went on emphasizing the significance of the 'symbiotic'. relationship at the morning staff meetings. Yet the change in the mindset of the journalist crowd was too discernible to the footsoldiers like us. Sudden expansion of the press corps, entry of a rebellious post-Emergency breed and a feeling that the establishment in South Block was no more a permament monolithic entity have had its impact on the new generation working journalists. The protest generation of the tumultuous 1960s had come of age. It was a mix of the saffron, red and mixed hues of different undercurrents. They all had to obey the line set by their respective media houses but they had stong private views. This was the position even in the early 1980s after Indira Gandhi's triumphant return to power.

"What have you done, Raman?" Shailan Chatterjee was on the line. It was hardly 7 am. He sounded very emotional.

Chatterjee was one of the oldest accredited correspondents in Delhi. In his early days he was assigned to cover Mahatma Gandhi. He had a reputation of being clean and dignified. Both of us were together as Press Council members. If such a person feels so hurt there must be something really amiss in my story in *The Indian Express*. In the afternoon, we met at the PIB launch.

"I felt very sad," Chatterjee said. "A prime minister is a constitutional office. As a reporter you are not expected to denigrate that office even if a dacoit happens to sit there. The position itself has some sanctity. You can report if a serious politician criticizes the PM. A reporter should not himself assume the role of the opposition. Your editor can do so in his editorials, but not in your report. "

Chatterjee truly represented the traditional school of media *mimaamsa*. And he ably expounded its cardinals. He did not stop there. A reporter's job, you know, is to report facts. We should not get into agitative journalism as some glossy journals and local rags are doing. After all, a daily newspaper is different.

What had hurt Chatterjee was a page one anchor in *The Indian Express* about the misuse of IAF aircraft for the Congress Party's election campaign. It was an investigaatie sort of byline piece. As per the then existing rules, the PM's close relatives, officials and security staff could accompany him in the IAF aircraft. If party colleagues accompany the PM in IAF aircraft during the election campaign, a bill could be sent to the ruling party. The Congress Party had repeatedly avoided paying the huge arrears. In those days, the mainstream dailies had dismissed such stories as gutter journalism. Clearly, Chatterjee's outbursts represented the recurring clash between the two concepts of media role: that of the traditionl media and the conscientious kind.

Ramnath Goenka's *Indian Express* was the the first major mainstream English daily to experiment with adverserial journalism. The Congress Party and government condemned the critical reports as asmear campaign by a partisan media owner. They had maintained that such critical stories were aimed at hoodwinking the government into hushing up the fraud charges against Goenka. There were allegations of illegal additions to the Express building on Bahadur Shah Zafar Marg. Goenka's problems with the ruling party began much before the Emergency. The Express group had supported the short-lived Swatantra Party of the big business and Maharajas who were in a running battle with the Congress. Later it had sided with the Syndicate group within the Congress against Indira Gandhi.

In spite of this, senior Congress leaders did not show any animosity towards the Express scribes. This may be as a show of nicety or not to alienate the scribes at a personal level. At the AICC office and central hall, they often showed extra regard to us even on a day a highly unpalatable byline story appeared on page one. There were exceptions though. Gujarat Congress MP Vithalbhai Patel, a former Swatantra activist, had suggested to me to leave this 'fraud of a daily'. He had just come out after asking a question in the Rajya Sabha on Ramnath Goenka. That evening he rang me up and offered his help to fix a job in a 'better' newspaper. Incidentally, Vithalbhai was the chief reporter when this writer was a sub editor in a Gujarat daily in Ahmedabad. But otherwise, Congress leaders were cordial, never vindictive.

At the Express, there was reluctance to refer to Goenka—even at the height of the building demolition controversy. Senior colleagues mentioned his name in hushed voices. The idea was to insulate the group chairman's problems with the government from the content of the daily. Barring his official statements, the Express avoided using its columns for personal wars. When questions on Goenka or references to him came up in Parliament, the news bureau was told not to cover it. Instead agency stories were used in full. Simultaneously, instructions were also sent to outstation centres to use 'agency stories in full'. This was a careful move to maintain the newspaper's image of independence and fair play.

The problem for us in the Express was that adversarial reporting was a rather new experience for dailies. We were not used to do such stories. It has to be different from the tabloid style. There the message was more through high display and word play. Tabloids did have a licence to do so. The post-Emergency glossies were somewhat different. But we as a daily newspaper had to evolve a more convincing style and format. The main function of a daily was to provide hard news to the readers. So some had cautioned the editor that readers would desert dailies if it was 'magazinised'. Moreover, the Express had to guard against the charge that it was a campaign sheet. Arun Shourie was already doing such long investigative articles. These did have a good readership. But such style could not be a model for adversarial news reports.

So we had to construct our own style and contour. The soft spoken editor Nihal Singh and then B.G. Verghese had set the first rule: no harsh adjectives or adverbs. The language should not be aggressive. Avoid unnecessary adjectives and adverbs. Instead facts should be presented convincingly with ample evidence. Readers would draw their own conclusions. With such guidelines, the easiest way to present exposure stories was to get a known personality to state the revelations you have dug out. Even that was not always feasible. The other was to use the news presentation format of the reporting of CAG and public accounts committee findings. We did borrow heavily from this style. Such precautions apart, those in the establishment and their acolytes did not take kindly to the Express. We were dubbed as 'anti-Congress' on Akbar Road and *'khilaf likhnewalas'* on Ashoka Road. But face-to-face, they were all very cordial. Fortunately, soon some other dailies had also begun relaxing the strict ban on digging out critical stories.

But tastes and demands of the readers were quietly undergoing change. When the Bofors scandal broke, those who had earlier dismissed it as scurrilous writing were forced to follow up it later. Even the highly respected *The Hindu* had to launch investigations of the scandal. Soon *The Hindustan Times* had to send a person to distant islands to try counter-investigation stories against

V.P. Singh. And digging out adversarial stories, even if vetted, had become part and parcel of Indian media. Big dailies began setting up investigative teams. Some even had an investigative editor. Just have a look at the newspaper files of the pre-Syndicate days. You will find the difference.

The 80s and 90s were marked by a sharp divide within the Capital's press corps, especially among the under-40s. A highly politicized set with their loyalty to political parties and commitment to individual leaders had arrived. This was never so before the Emergency when reporters seemed keen to wear a political tag. Ugly scenes and mindless intrigues became the order of the day. Everyone seemed to know the other's affiliations. He was Arjun Singh's man, a relative of M.L. Fotedar, in the pay roll of A.R. Antulay, Bansi Lal's spy, Murli Manohar Joshi's *chhela* and Chandra Shekhar's camp follower. When Chandra Shekhar held press conferences at his South Avenue house, the camp followers managed the arrangement. They drew up the invitees' list. One could easily fix appointments with the leader through the *chelas*.

L.K. Advani invited the friendly correspondents 'for tea' at J.P. Mathur's Rajendra Prasad Road residence on the eve of every Parliament session. It was supposed to be to familiarize the issues that might come up in the session. Tea, samosas, pakoras, jelabis—all hot and made at home—were freely served. Barring a couple of 'non-aligned' reporters like D.P. Kumar (*The Statesman*) and me (*The Indian Express*), the rest were the converted types. One could count a whole set of pro-BJP crowd in attendance. It was all informal. Advani and Pramod Mahajan, then a rising star, K.R. Malkani, Sunder Singh Bhandari, Jai Dubashi, K.L. Sharma and many others came and left. No agenda. Everyone was free to air their views. Just gossip. Mostly idle talk. But occasionally differences on policy fine-tuning within the BJP came to the fore. Once J.P. Mathur sought our views on the BJP's move for a tie-up with the Shiv Sena. That was the beginning of an arrangement which is now 25 years old. At another meeting, the issue of BJP's support (before the rath yatra) to V.P. Singh had come up. Advani seemed to know the names of each of the two dozen journos. He was friendly and patronizing. During about 90 minutes or so, never ever did Advani showed any ill will to any political leaders, even the Congress rivals. Committed journos present reported so many murky tales about the Gandhi family and its captives in the media. Some referred to them by name. Since 1992 they stopped calling me. The black-listing happened soon after some of us in the Press Council had submitted a minority report against the partisan behaviour of sections of the media during the Ayodhya agitation.

The intense polarization had its echo even at routine press briefings. One day we were with Congress working president Kamalapati Tripathi. The grand old man had to be helped climb the two steps to his office room at 24 Akbar Road. Once during the briefing, Dinanath Mishra (*Navbharat Times*) asked him how he felt as working president. Tripathi was made working president by Indira Gandhi after a few electoral setbacks in the early 80s. Apparently, this was a move to please the Congress old guard. Tripathi stared at Dinanath for a while and shot back:

"I have never attended *shakhas* to know such things," the grand old man quipped with a smile. Everyone laughed.

No one had expected such a retort from a person like Tripathi. Even he at that age was aware of the RSS background of the reporter. Apparently, senior functionaries knew or briefed as to who was friend, foe and neutral. As scribes became more partisan, their profiling had become common The schism was so sharp in those days. At formal press conferences, rival groups came in strength to embarrass the leaders with unpleasant questions. Journos freely dubbed some questions as 'plants' by the friendly ones to emphasize favourable points.

Outside of briefings, there was an organized network to spread scandals and juicy stories about the rival leaders and scribes. From where such gossip emerged, nobody knows. Or that was not even considered important. Some were hard allegations with substance but not fit for an official statement or press briefing. So the best way to spread such scandals was to put it into the grapevine. A committed journo may first pass on the story to a friendly scribe of a popular daily. It might also be 'leaked' to a regional language daily. The Congress side, at least in those days, had directly passed on anti-BJP stories to the friendly representatives of dailies. They did not need the help of an anonymous third party to spread negative stories.

Apart from printable stories, the BJP side had specialized in dissemination of anti-Congress smear campaigns through a network of the word-of-mouth. The Congress side also had its share of such oral vilification. But they were no match for the BJP-RSS network's bush telegraph. They had turned it into a subtle art and developed as a perfect operating model. It begins with a casual conversation during which one of them would just throw some hints. Or make vague insinuations. If you seek more details, they just smile and shy away. This heightens your anxiety. Soon you come across another friend who also hints at the same story. A chuckle, a conspiratorial tone and the similar kind of whisper. When more people talk about the same tale, you tend to believe it. Only the discernible could see a pattern in this protracted hearsay war.

The 1980s had given birth to gossip columns in some periodicals and dailies. Half a dozen reporters had launched such weekly whisper pieces variously called 'Gup-shup', 'Khabaram' and 'Behind-the-News.' Both in English and Hindi. All of them had drawn heavily from the rumour networks of the day. Some of them still continue. They simply lapped up such tales and added more spice. I remember the target once was a retired Andhra Iyankar who had worked either in PIB or a local newspaper. He was regularly seen in the Parliament House canteen and PIB speaking accented Enghish. He was cynial of everybody. But he seemed to hate the RSS.

"A Dhawan man," a friend at PIB launch whispered. "The fellow goes around in a car." The friend conspiratorially looked around to ensure no one was listening. Those days only half a dozen senior special correspondents had cars.

Indira Gandhi's former aide R.K. Dhawan, as per the yellow grapevine, wanted the Iyankar to spy on all those who were critical of the Congress. Soon it spread from ear to ear and the old man invited suspicious looks from everyone—everyone in the press crowd except himself. A couple of weeks later, a piece appeared in a gossip column of an English daily.

"I have something important for you," the call was from Kamal Bhat who was press adviser to Morarji Desai when he was the Prime Minister. In the afternoon we met at INS. Bhat had a list of special correspondents whose telephones were tapped. When there were no mobiles, tapping the land line was the only way to monitor the activities of political adversaries and anti-establishment journalists. On top of the typed list was Virendra Kapur followed by Janardan Thakur and Vijay Sanghvi. P. Raman figured only towards the end. I had never identified myself with any group and did not indulge any political acitivity. Then another list appeared after a few months. That was also from the anti-Congress camp. This time many old names were found missing and new ones added. Apart from the paranoia, this highlighted the emergence of crusader journalism in the capital.

Women correspondents who ask searching queries at briefings instantly became objects of insinuations. Most of them had come to political reporting after a sound grounding at the news desk or were local reporters. They had just broken into what was considered the rough and tough male zone. 'She smokes', 'she drinks', was 'close to some politician'. Such were the kind of hushed comments. One day, a young reporter of an English daily walked with an AICC general secretary asking some questions. And that was enough for the rumour mills to churn out vicious comments. True, that was a transformational stage in political reporting. So many changes had taken place in a short period.

Subhash Kirpekar of *The Times of India* covered Congress and at times BJP. He was moving around on an old scooter. This writer was often his pillion rider. One day he arrived at the AICC office in a brand new car for the regular briefing.

"Antulay's gift," someone commented. Soon the rumour mills began working overtime. Then came more details. Like the 'NE-118' was delivered at Kirpekar's house along with bill and insurance policy in his name. Antulay's gift soon became a subject of gossip at the PIB, central hall and INS corridors. A.R. Antulay, a former chief minister and union minister, was a crucial figure once close to Indira Gandhi. Kirpeker was seen frequently moving with Antulay and other Maharashtra Congress stalwarts. Thus throughout the 1980s, Kirpeker's car was seen as a symbol of politician-media nexus.

Years later, in 1993 I was settling my accounts with Bennet, Coleman & Company. I had resigned as political editor of *The Economic Times* to join *Business Standard*. In the office car loan ledger

I found Kirpekar's NE-118 next to my name and the outstanding dues he had to pay to the office.

This was a big shock to me. Here was a man who was misunderstood by the entire press corps. For a decade he was the object of vilification. But the truth was that what was allegedly Antulay's political bribe was actually paid by Kirpekar himself from his hard-earned salary in instalments. For days we could not meet. We were told he was ill. Then before I could confess my self-guilt to him, he had died at a small nursing home. When his body lay, I just closed my eyes and silently apologized to him for the long-held misunderstanding.

After this shock, to me all other stories of political bribes to the journos became suspect. However, there were also proven cases. Some beneficiaries had admitted payment. And so some paymasters did concede such 'help'.

"In some deserving cases, we had to help our journalist friends," Rajendra Sharma, a close Advani aide and in charge of the BJP office in Parliament house, had once admitted. "They were our cadre who became journalists of small papers. Even without our help they might have worked for us. But that was a small matter." Sharma, an engineering graduate, was Advani's ear and eyes. Unlike Deepak Chopra, Sharma had never courted controversy.

Separate lists of those in Congress and BJP pay rolls were very much in circulation. Among them were big and small names – most were familiar faces whom we met every day. Supposed to have been prepared by IB of the day, these lists showed wide discrepancies and errors. There were also some apparent mixups. There was a suggestion to carry the fading lists as an addendum to this book. Then I thought it was unfair to do so. It would not serve any purpose after three decades and under an entirely changed situation. Some of them are no more. In any case, today's politicians are smart enough to waste time on small, faceless scribes. They can better manage things at the CEO's level without hassles.

But this writer can cite a personal experience without injustice to anyone. It was a few months before the 1996 Lok Sabha polls. One morning there was a call from J.P. Mathur, the one who looked after the media liaison in the BJP. He was an RSS *pracharak* of the traditional mould. It was much before the smart fixers like Pramod Mahajan and Ram Madhav took over the operation. Mathur said they were trying to get some intellectual journalists to help the BJP collect, collate and publish 'speaking points' against the Narasimha Rao government. These were to be printed and circulated among the BJP campaigners to marshal a hard attack on the ruling party. They should be brief, crisp and to the point with facts and figures. Some of these were to be used as catchy slogans and in posters. I was to be part of a journalist team that could also contribute to planning the BJP's campaign strategy. Remember, it was about two decades before the Modi-Amit Shah team had handed the campaign work to big money-driven professionals and event managers.

"We will certainly give you some money as expenses," Mathur reassured. This writer's anti-establishment byline stories and rather friendly interaction with the pro-BJP journalists might have prompted him to make such an offer. I politely avoided getting involved in their work. Clearly, Mathur's suggestion did not fit into our idea of the profession. We did not want to mix political participation with journalism.

13

Pretenders on the Prowl

'Kaaka Krishna, pika Krishna, ko bheda pika kaakaya?
Vasanta kaale sampraapte kaaka kaaka pika pika'

(The crow is black, koel is also black. How do you distinguish the crow from the koel? Spring comes, the crow craws and the koel sings)

The power of Delhi's accredited correspondents in those glorious days was legion. It was the transformative period. And there have been exaggerated stories about the authority enjoyed by the PIB card holders. They could dash into the cabins of the union ministers at will. The senior bureaucrats obliged them when asked for favours. Corporate received them with gifts. They could get licences, quota or import licences just for the asking. That was the kind of aura the accreditation card carried. Much of this was a hangover of the good old days when a small band of two dozen accredited correspondents had enjoyed a symbiotic relationship with the ministers and power centres. This cosy relationship had begun breaking up even before the Emergency. Yet the fad continued to prevail. Even in the 80s, sub-editors in offices used to seek the special's help for favours ranging from railway reservation to posting and transfers of relatives. Circulation managers used to ask for our help to punish the Haryana cops who had blocked the newspaper delivery vans.

It was such exalted stature that led to a mad rush for PIB cards. It began in the 70s and within years reached unmanageable proportions. Big dailies had launched more editions and hence sought more cards to meet the regional requirements. Some media houses had separate economic dailies. It was then decided to give a composite quota for each media organization which could distribute it among the sister publications. There were also fresh demands from the regional dailies, both English and languages, for bigger accredation quota. May be, some of them wanted to use it as an additional lure to their managers in Delhi whose principal job was to look after advertisements. This period also found a sudden rise in circulation of Indian language dailies. Every rise in the literacy rate had forced multiplier effects on circulation of the language dailies. All this had led to the mad rush.

The accreditation committee could not do much when the media houses themselves pushed for a situation which led to the misuse of the accreditation. There were many smart men in safari suits among us who had never done any journalistic work. Those glib talkers convinced owners of local newspapers that they could enhance their advertisement prospects in Delhi for free. All that they wanted was to give them an authority letter for a PIB card. They used it to lobby for business firms and arrange transfers and postings. They went around in big cars even while a senior correspondent of class 'A' dailies moved in second hand Fiats. The smarties had little interest in briefings on chasing stories. But when they made an appearance with great pomp at ceremonial press conferences, they asked stupid questions.

And so the tribes of pretenders swelled. Some were even found organizing press conferences for business firms. Among them were failed property dealers, estranged aides of politicians and printing press owners. Some had used the card for small-time liaison work and hoped to widen their networking in Lutyens' Delhi. At the coffee house, journalists were frequently asked how to get PIB cards. Some were prepared to offer money. Then the accreditation panel decided that the applicant must produce copies of his journal and a charterd accountant's certificate as proof of being a genuine journalist. Yet many had managed to circumvent the rules. You may not believe it. Even as late as this century, a friend engaged in multiple dealership showed us a temporary PIB card in his name.

So much so, we had too many curious characters among us moving along Parliament corridors, party offices and the bhavans around Vijay Chowk. For an outsider, it is impossible to say the touts from the genuine reporters—like a crow from the koel. Some were smart and intelligent. Others so stupid to enquire from us whether liquor would be served at the evenings's corporate briefing. We normally leave such functions to the business bureau.

Look at this tall, grey-haired goggle-wearing gentleman. He claims to be associated with Amnesty International apart from his job with a north eastern daily. And he was always willing to produce a bunch of identity cards as proof.

"I have to go to Colombo next week," he would say, pointing to an Air-India ticket displayed prominently on the front pocket. You can examine if you disbelieve him.

"Unfortunately, this will also clash with my engagement in Taipe. Tell me, which one should I settle for?" That was his way of boasting. There was no dearth of insinuating comments about him, including things like he was doing the worst kind of work for the high and mighty.

Then there was the one in his 50s who would never miss a briefing—at the AICC, offices of the BJP, CPI(M), CPI, Janata and BSP. Some say he was working with North Block or with the Delhi administration. He wrote down every word with high speed in long hand. Both question and replies at briefings. He was very particular about collecting all documents, statements and tour programmes of the party leaders distributed at party offices.

"Where do you work?" one day he was asked. He mentioned the name of an obscure Urdu paper. He was so nice a man, always polite and soft-spoken. Later we were told he was working for the 'two-letter' agency or IB.

We had another man working for a different agency. Some say it was the 'three-letter' agency or RAW. But he suddenl;y disappeared after a Bengali scribe clashed with him during the briefing. The fellow had defended a union minister during the spokesman's reply which was not the job of a reporter. This irritated other journalists. And from the next day he stopped coming.

Some time later, we were privy to a two-page list of shady journos similarly helping different agencies, Indian and foreign. Most were accredited correspondents. There were a couple of senior editors. I had taken a photocopy of it. Half of those in the list were so-called freelancers and power pedlars. There were some known names, those working with mainstream newspapers. We had found it difficult to believe the names because at least a couple of them were known to us. The list was neatly arranged in columns with the name, organization for which the person worked for and the agency they help. Then we were told of more names. Some of them were coming to Parliament only to collect the voluminous question-answers and other official documents. Recently while scanning the old papers and political notings for my weekly column, I recovered the old list. A look showed that about half of those known persons had either died or left Delhi. A couple of them still enjoy the government's patronage.

We also had another character. He joined reporters' ranks through a reverse process. Always in safari suit, this eager-to-please guy was once at the business desk of a big English daily. Apparently, he found lobbying and favour pedalling a more profitable career than getting tied to the desk. For one, he was rarely seen at normal briefings or other sources of news. He, we were told, specialize in cultivating joint secretary level officials. His name appeared in the PIB list but the person was sighted on budget days in Parliament corridors or annual events like release of exim policy.

Come Parliament session, and the complexion of the crowd changed. In those days any MP could issue passes to their aides and separate ones for the library on their behalf. The hangers-on were of three kinds – plain lobbyists for the corporates. There were former MPs like R.K. Amin or those in final years as MPs. Then there were smaller ones. The bold ones even identify their bosses. Short-statured and frail, Desai (forgetting the first name) was a regular even during the off-session period. He never concealed his personal commitment to Dhirubhai. No one else in the organization. He did not find anything wrong about lobbying for this great 'institution.' He once told us about Amin's role. 'If you have any adverse reports about him, tell me'. He continued the work even after Dhirubhai's death.

Desai had once revealed how he along with an aide went round UP during the 1991 Lok Sabha elections to disburse money to both the Congress and rival candidates. His boss wanted both sides to be kept happy. At Allahabad, they had to wait for half a day at the circuit house for V.P. Singh to return. But, he said, Singh had bluntly refused to accept the corporate money.

"No, no, we won't accept funds, they would say," Desai said.

"Then they call an aide to tell them to go with me." That was how they operated. But V.P. Singh was so firm. For some time, Desai had looked after the interests of friendly MPs, mainly from Gujarat. Their names and telephone numbers were given to a garrage operator in South Delhi. The MPs could just ring them up and a DLY/DLZ car would arrive at the flat with the driver. The MPs were often invited for lunch at preferred haunts. Once this writer was present briefly at such a dinner at Taj Man Singh.

Lobbying comes in varied forms. Once a long-time friend came to this writer with an interesting project. It aimed at laying a plastic/acrylic undersea pipeline from the Gujarat coast to the water-scarce Kutch and Saurashtra. The story gave details of the cost-benefit of the scheme. And it was totally maintenance-free. Editor T.N. Ninan at *The Economic Times* wanted to carry it with graphics. But by evening it was found that it was a project once found technically unsound and the man was simply using me to push the case again.

In those days, Parliament's central hall was a venue for individual statements by the MPs and ex-MPs. It was a *laissez faire* kind of atmosphere. Party bosses had not yet come down on such free expressions by the individual leaders. This writer had seen lobbyists carrying neatly typed statements or request letters to ministers favouring their firms. They got these typed on the individual MP's letter head and then got their signatures. Often, the lobbyists themselves released them to the press. Their messengers handed such letters to the concerned minister. I have seen the liaison men carrying the letter heads of some MPs.

All this was happening over quarter of a century ago. Now who cares for a middle level scribe to put across a major project? Or will a lowly aide be deputed to distribute money to politicians? Can you find lowly lobbyists any more? Now deal makings and project pushings are done at the highest level. Nothing below the level of the minister or PMO. When 'ease of doing business' is the *mula mantra*, everything else becomes irrelevant. The humble liaison officer who worked at the level of reporters and undersecretaries, has given way to mighty MNC lobbyists and diplomats. They officially allocate a multi-million dollar budget for lobbying and buying support. This was what Walmart had admitted. Otherwise how could one explain the sudden cancellation of India's deal to buy and indigenize production of 124 multi-role combat fighters from French Rafale by the Prime Minister during a brief Paris visit? The original deal was finalized after decade-long negotiations and field trials. This is the best case of lobbying power of the modern MNCs and domestic corporates.

True, there were some activities by the media pretenders which may not be categorized as illegal. During the session, some of them appeared in Parliament, collected the speeches and parliament answers of their client MPs, made them into news reports and personally handed these to newspapers — all for a consideration. They even circulated the statements of their MPs to regular reporters. Ram Naik had a systematic arrangement for media publicity. And an aide of Vikhe Patel, with or without his knowledge, was offering professional seats in his educational institutions for the sons and daughters of obliging reporters.

Going back to the ignoble media touts, national jamborees of the big two political parties were really great events. Suddenly the tribe gots activated. The Congress had it two-day AICC sessions. The four-day plenary session was a massive event. The BJP's national executive and national council were even bigger, both in the size media 'opp'. Those with a PIB card and reporters from states got free accommodation in 4-star—and 5-star for the biggies and more enterprising ones—hotels as per the local availability. The imposter scribes often managed to wrest better hotels than even regular special correspondents of dailies and agencies. On such occasions, organizers avoided displeasing even the acknowledged fakes. Some even managed to get free air tickets from the organizers. At BJP's Bombay session at the peak of Pramod Mahajan's glory, I have seen media pretenders moving in special labelled cars.

Who says the might of the media has not grown? After every BJP session when the scribes vacate the hotel, the counter clerks asked whether they would like to have duplicate hotel bills and receipts. This was to enable the reporters reimburse the tarrif from their respective offices. Some people took advantage of the double benefit. After the Baroda BJP jambooree, I was witness to Yubaraj Ghimire, then working with *India Today*, refusing the duplicate bill.

He had an argument with the BJP workers on 'corrupting' the journos. On special occasions like Advani's rath yatra, organizers had taken care of the shopping lists of the accompanying correspondents. Some journos were so embarrassed that they went shopping without the official guides.

In those pre-liberalization days, business bodies, even public sector units, organized dinner briefings. Active political correspondents normally avoided them. In any case, that was their busiest hour to wind up the day's reporting. But lowly touts gatecrashed. And the organizers would avoid unpleasant scenes on such occasions. In those days, the lure of minor gifts were so strong among the journos.

One day, the reporters at the AICC office were led to a briefing by a certain Bhup Singh. Bhup Singh? Who is he? We wondered. Then we were told he was the convener of the weaker sections cell of the AICC.

Bhup Singh tailor was a mohalla level Congress worker in Delhi. He was in Tihar Jail with Sanjay Gandhi during the early days of the Janata rule. He had mobilized crowds for Sanjay's rallies in Delhi during and after the Emergency. When the Congress returned to power in 1980, Bhup Singh was brought to the AICC office and made chairman of the weaker section's cell. Suddenly he became a big man. Even the office in charge Kotnala, who had walked out of the old AICC office at Jantar Mantar along with Indira Gandhi, stood up in his seat when Bhup Singh arrived. Such was his awesome clout in AICC.

In his room with a large picture of Sanjay Gandhi (no Indira Gandhi), Bhup Singh told us about his plans to distribute blankets to the shelterless of Delhi. This, his said, was being done on directions from Sanjay, obviously to give it an aura of authority. He then distributed the gift-packed blankets to the journalists present. And the DD camera men rushed to capture the event.

"What nonsense!" shouted Debu Sarkar of *Newstime*. "We won't take it. These are meant for the poor, not reporters." The irrepressible Sarkar was an emotional type. We all left the poor men's blankets on the table and walked out.

The curious part of the story was yet to come. After we left, some hangers on among us and touts carried the blankets to their vehicles. Later we were told that the bureau chief of a big English daily had also accepted the poor men's blankets.

There were also occasions when the conflict of interest played havoc with conscience. It was normal for the jaunt organizers to make nominal gifts to the visiting scribes. All members of a press party at Amul dairy were given a packet of their new products. For years, such gifts had become 'normal'. This was seen more as a courtesy, especially when they were given to all members of the media team. But it became a case of corruption if one person was given fabulous gifts in exchange for out of the way publicity favours for a pariticuar firm. That should be the rule for news persons in such circumstances.

In the early 90s, we were shown a list of those editors and business reporters to whom a prominent corporate house had gifted shares when they had issued IPO. An Income Tax official about to retire had approached some scribes with the details. Finally it came to me. It was startling. There were many important figures who relentlessly preached media ethics and business morality and corporate responsibility. We all know dog won't eat dog's meat. But I tried to push through the information in the form of an article protecting the scribes' identity and that of the corporate.

"Do you find anything substantial in your piece?" asked the executive editor, rather innocently. He had come to my desk with the hard copy. I told him what I had written was a diluted form and there were names with even PAN card numbers. I showed the photocopies of the documents. He smiled as he went through the lists.

"Come on, Raman," he said. "Don't be so naïve." And walked away waving at me.

Perhaps, the executive editor was right. One should not be so naïve. After all, that was the harsh reality of journalism. Many of those executive editors were more 'executives' than editors. Some editors were merely exalted fixers. If one didn't learn such truths even after moving among them for three decades, it is certainly one's own fault. However, during the period this writer had the privilege of working with a dozen editors, executive and managing editors and resident editors. But most of them had earned high respect and integrity, especially the early ones.

Within a year or so, the executive editor who had suppressed the story left the media group to become vice-president of a corporate house. That much for the nexus.

Then we had the other exctreme. Around the same period, Times House had issued an office order asking the journalists and advertisement executives to deposit the Diwali gifts with a designated person, and of course, get a receipt for it. When the journos resented it as a silly naive gesture, it was withdrawn. Many felt this was an overreaction to the gifting IPO shares by the corporates. Normally, fabulous corporate gifts are never delivered at offices. But when the residences are found locked they deliver these at offices.

A.N. Prabhu, who was the resident editor of two Delhi dailies —*The Economic Times* and *The Hindustan Times*—later told me of his bitter experience with handling share rates carried by the daily. He had got some letters to the editor complaining about the higher figures for some corporate shares. After monitoring, the allegations were found true. The practice had continued even after seeking explanations from the stocks editor.

"This does not fall in our range," finally the editor told his RE. It was just before the Harshad Mehta-led stock inflation hit the market. And the RE got the right message. Such things were going on beyond the powers of the editor.

Some of us had made conscientious efforts to keep out of the murky world of power brokers. But the system is such that it drew everyone into its vortex. One day a familiar face in the AICC complex came to me with a request. He thought I could help him appointed as member of Capart. A journalist of the tout category had told him 'Raman dada' was close to Prime Minister P.V. Narasimha Rao. It was absurd. Those were the days when my byline stories critical of the government appeared regularly in *The Economic Times*. But the guy would not believe it. He thrust a copy of his biodata on me.

Months later, a gentleman in brown khadi kurta knocked at the door. He was all smiles. He showed me the notification appointing him as the CAPART member. We were so happy but told him I had not done anything for him. But he just would not believe it. He took out a basket of lichis. Surely there was a conflict of conscience. Could one accept a gratification for something for which one had not done anything? He said the lichis were from his farm in Bihar, and it was only a humble gesture. This was the kind of dilemma some of us had encountered.

We had a slightly different kind of problem with Jayalalitha way back in the 80s. She had come to Delhi after her good showing in Tamil Nadu. She had not yet been sworn in as chief minister. After the press meet with lunch, we all got a surprise gift: an 'Aristocrat' suitcase, a rather proud possesion in those days.

"What is this?" some of us asked the officials. "We won't take such gifts from politicians. That's plain bribing." The entire press core had refused to take it. Such a thing had not happened so far. Giving gifts at political briefings would set a bad precedent. There has to be a difference between a gift by an individual politician and a token gesture by a state-run institution like a handicraft board.

In the mid-80s we discovered another unfair practice. Some ministers frequently invited political reporters for lavish lunch briefings often at five-star hotels. On many occasions, the briefings did not produce any story worth reporting. Then one day the cat was out of the bag. The ministers forced the public sector undertakings under them to pay the bill. A senior accounts assistant of a leading private hotel had passed on the copies of the reminders sent to the PSU for non-payment of the bills. It had mentioned the minister's name. Enquiries revealed that it was an old practice. The then PMO had put an end to the practice after *The Indian Express* had carried a byline story on page one.

For touts and power pedlars, elections were the boom time. Large crowds of ticket seekers from far and near descended on the pavements of Akbar and Ashoka Roads, Congress and BJP headquarters respectively. Those from neighbouring states arrived in big cars and vans along with their entourage. They brought along local lords to demonstrate their popular support. It was a big mela with golgappawallas, samosa sellers and ice cream vendors doing roaring business. And that is the prime time for the touts to make the killing.

Some ticket seekers also brought along local journos under the notion that editors of their mofussul papers had access to the top party bosses in Delhi. Their first task was to find out from the journo-touts whether their name figured in the short list that came up for consideration of the centaral parliamentary boards. Even if an aspirant failed to get the ticket, names appearing in the final list helped them stake claims for future elections.

The tout's work began with an imperious appearance before the crowds. Ticket hunters came to him seeking his good offices to influence the high command. That was the early period when media persons' influence on the decision-making of the political parties was over-rated. The journo-touts took the biodata and asked a few searching questions to make things look genuine. The aspirant was called privately and the first instalment paid. Similar deals were struck with others on Ashoka Road. One of the stock-in-trade for the smart tout was to go to a general secretary while he alighted from the car and move along with him a few feet. This would give the waiting aspirants an impression that the man was pretty close to the leader. Often the smarter touts would get back to the ticket hunter and seek additional documents in support of their claims. These included a petition signed by a few big men from his constituency. This would strengthen their claim. State correspondents of newspapers often camp in Delhi during the period to lobby for their nominees.

The touts usually check with the final list of party nominees. If by sheer chance one of their client's name figured in the list, he would seek his share from the ticket seeker. All this was the position until the mid-90s. Perhaps the new generation ticket seekers must have come of age. I don't know whether the institution of journo-touts still thrives.

14

Pariahs and Press Dharma

"Anything interesting?" the bureau chief asked.

"They have announced an all-India bandh," the reporter said.

"Oh, nothing much. Give two paras. Or you can even drop it."

The reference was to the decision taken by the National Campaign Committee of Trade Unions to launch joint action plans. It followed prolonged negotiations among the RSS and Left unions. It was the first joint action by the two ideologically antagonistic groups. The dumping down of this politically significant story was decided by a person who later became editor of three big English dailies. It was not his decision. That has been the accepted editorial policy of the mainstream English media. Some other contemporaries dumped such stories on the city page as an 18 point lower case single column.

However, two days later the same story had appeared as second lead on page one of the same daily just because the announcement had come from a senior BJP politician. Mind you, it was a time when the Left together had commanded over 40 MPs in the Lok Sabha and the BJP just two. This only illustrates the media's traditional bias towards what they dismissed as *pariah* parties and groups. Mainstream dailies which Kanshi Ram had called '*Brahmin-Bania press*,' always had such fads and fallacies.

"Have you looked at his copy?" the news editor asked the chief reporter. I was sitting in NE's cabin after the afternoon shift.

The cub reporter had filed a three-page foolscap story on the opposition's all-India rally against the price rise. It was in the usual format with the leaders' speech as intro and with photographs of large crowds that had attended it. The chief reporter looked at it and smiled. The fresher apparently did not know that when the *pariah* parties sponsor a big really, the focus had to be on the disruptions it caused to the public, how the school children suffered and the 'unruly' behaviour of the mobs. It is even better if you can estimate the loss of production due to the disruptions. That was the standard unwritten rule everyone should know.

If you join as a chief sub editor or reporter, this is the first thing you have to learn before familiarizing yourself with in a newspaper's working system. Individual dailies have their own unwritten lists of individuals and institutions—some to be ignored, dumbed down or played up. As chief sub, this writer had kept an updated list of such personalities and organizations ready for reference in case of doubt. This training had come in handy when censorship was imposed during the Emergency. Every directive, through the agency clicker or phone, was kept under a clip and tickmarked before the final pages were released for printing.

All successful editors should know the mind of the proprietors. Obvious and subtle preferences are never said, only inferred. But there is a universal, permanent list of the *pariahs*—trade unions, Left parties, BSP and rural issues in that order. A new addition to this internal censorship list was the anti-reform remarks. In the early period after heralding the reform, jarring voices against it was blasphemy. The bar on visiting critical economists like Joseph Stiglitz and Naom Chomsky still continues. All these blacklisted groups get a stepmotherly treatment in the mainstream media.

"What else can you expect from the Bania press?" Kanshi Ram had asked the audience at the Ambedkar fair in Jabalpur in 1980. "The Manuwadi press has the bania's money and brahmin's brain. Both are poison."

He was entirely right. Print media, not to mention of the government-owned TV and radio, had totally ignored his BSP. His 'DS-4' (Dalit Shoshit Samaj Sangharsh Samiti), forerunner of the BSP, was referred to at editorial meetings and news rooms with hate and sarcasm. Beat reporters of the Left parties, BSP and trade unions routinely encourntered the same query from the editors to chief subs: "Anything interesting?"

'Anything interesteing' means anything negative worth highlighting. This includes dissension in the ranks with some groups making disparaging remarks. Reporters are repeatedly encouraged to look for such sidelights. On reports of the all-India bandh, there is no need to tell the chief subs to dump it on an inside page with drastic cuts. An innocent reporter in *The Statesmen* in the pre-1990 days gave a detailed report of the workers' demands in a positive tone. And an acting chief sub in a dak edition let it go. Both received a memo the next day. He had shown the memo to some office-bearers of the DUJ. Santhosh Bahadur Verma, a senior sub-editor who had produced the morning edition of *The Times of India* during its pre-New Media days, put an all-India bank strike on page 1. And this marked his eventual exit from the daily.

An enthusiastic reporter of *The Hindustan Times*, a JNU product, had filed a story about the agonies of the families at the railway colony during the historic all-India strike when L.N. Mishra was the minister. The chief reporter threw the typed sheet in the trash can and gave her a piece of his mind. She quit in protest and joined an NGO. Perhaps the worst case of this decade's media boycott of trade unions relates to the Gurgaon's Maruti plant. Barring *The Hindu*, all English dailies persistently refused to carry the workers' version of the strikes, arrests and torture of the workers. This shows the intensity of the media's collective prejudice to what they dismiss as *pariahs*.

Sections of the well-placed middle class generally treated trade unions as disruptionist. They caused a 'nuisance' through their frequent *dharnas* and strikes. That is how the media has been depicting workers' protests throughout. Reflected here is the true class character of the media owners of English and regional newspapers. Remember they are also industrialists. There is big money in newspaper business. Hence the owners have an intrinsic class bias against the organized working class. We have all sensed it constantly throughout our professional life—in the newsroom and at editorial meetings. We had frequent derisive remarks like 'what do those BMS jokers say?'

Till two decades ago, newspaper establishments were subject to trade union actions. Stiff collective bargains, go-slow, *dharnas*, strikes and lockouts were not uncommon. Most newspaper unions were affiliated to central trade unions. Therefore newspaper managements had always hated the unions. As one who has witnessed strikes, closures and vindictive reprisals, this writer can say with authority that the shop-level bitterness and confrontation constituted an important factor in this perpetual class conflict. During an unusually prolonged strike in *The Statesman*, C.R. Irani had brought musclemen to counter the workers. Arun Shourie had posted 'Gujar bouncers' in the basement of the Express building during the strike. One day insiders in the building stopped bringing tea and snacks on rumours that workers outside were conspiring to poison those inside the building. Such was the deep mistrust and tension during direct actions by the press workers. The gate-level bitterness has certainly influenced the newspaper owners' attitude to the coverage of trade union news in their dailies.

The mainstream media's traditional prejudice towards the communists falls under the same category. Those covering the Left either have to repeat 'nothing interesting' or dig out some negative stories. The media's *pariah* bias towards the 'Reds'—that was the derisive term used in the headlines of Indian English dailies for communists until the 70s—has a variety of reasons. This was the position when this writer began his profession as sub-editor. Obviously, we had borrowed the term from the US and UK dailies for whom communism was anathema.

Such deep untouchability towards communists had a long history. It was part of the cold war, and the Indian media by and large went by the Western propaganda machine and its phraseology. There was a time when they were described as 'anti-social' and instigators of violence. Remember, until the mid-60s those with communist leanings were denied government jobs on adverse police verifications. The old communists, on their part, never trusted the mainstream media. They had to evolve their own propaganda methods to keep in touch with their ranks and reach out to other sections. The CPI and CPI(M) make it a point to issue long statements after the meetings of their apex bodies. This is to deny scope for misquoting and misinterpretations. At times they had a few friendly reporters but the party bosses knew they were of no use as the newspaper hierarchy had tight control of news at every level.

"We have clarified our poisiton in the statement," the then CPI(M) general secretary E.M.S. Nambudiripad once said. "We don't know what will appear in your dailies tomorrow."

"So do we," S. Bannerjee of *The Statesman* quipped. "We file our report. The rest of it is not in our hands." Everyone laughed.

Traditionally, the problem with the communists was how to counter what they felt was the false propaganda by the 'bourgeois' press. Hence they never bothered about pampering the press. Unlike the two big players, they refused to provide free five-star accommodation to reporters during their party congress. They never tried to cultivate the editors or newspaper owners.

The communist old guard never bothered about being media savvy. PTI correspondent K.P. Srivastava had once asked Bhupesh Gupta for the ideological reasons for the CPI supporting Indira Gandhi.

"You first read Lenin's book on state and revolution and then come to me," he said with all seriousness. The old communists always expected media men also to be as proficient in Marxist treatises and have their level of intellectualism.

The CPI began getting some respectability when it became part of Indira Gandhi's alliance. Perhaps from the V.P. Singh days, the mainstream media began putting the Left almost on par with the regional parties. This change in approach had marked a marginal relaxation of the untouchability. As the regional parties began asserting their hold in state after state with considerable say in the politics at the centre, the Left too began getting better media treatment. True, the new generation Left leaders are certainly more media savvy and never missed an opportunity to express their views on electronic media or print.

Such 'untoubability' and inane mistrust also extends to the Left-led coalitions. This became more explicit after the Left's own aversions to the economic liberalization. True, the Janata coalitions were inherently unstable and disruptive. This was the deep imprint left in the national psyche by the first Janata experiment under Morarji Desai. When in 1989 V.P. Singh took over in the aftermath of an anti-corruption movement, the corporate media waited a few days before pouncing on the *khichdi* government. The dominant section of the media had provided full background music to the Ayodhya agitation. This had forced the Press Council to consider the transgression. The anti-reservation agitaion by the upper caste students during the V.P. Singh regime was even led by sections of the media. That much for the National Front government. Media had predicted the collapse of the Deve Gowda regime even before the prime minister took the oath.

Perhaps the worst instance of the mainstream media's utter irresponsibility and bias happened in 1997 during the UF government under Gujral. It was a classic case that speaks volumes of our new obsessions, changed priorities and the very concept of news. Fifty odd eminent persons were present at the Golden Jubilee celebrations of independence organized by the national committee on commemoration. The only surviving president R. Venkatraman in his keynote address had made several constructive suggestions to commemorate the eventful era. But not a word about the former president's address or the historic significanace of the celebrations appeared in sections of the media. Instead they reduced the solemn occasion to one of those routine reporting on the Lalu corruption and infighting in the UF. A English daily of the capital devoted almost an entire report on Atal Bihari Vajpayee's political attacks on Gujral. A multi-edition English daily led the story with the delay in issuing press releases and the nitty-gritty of the briefing. The whole tone and tenor was that of another political tamasha. Another largely circulated daily followed this up with the details of the 'waste' of public funds on the 'gala freedom bash.' It lamented the waste of Rs. 5 crore on observing the quit India movement on August 9 at the August Kranti Maidan in Mumbai and films and presentations on the movement by Girish Karnad and Shyam Benegal.

For media, the Bahujan Samaj Party has been even more 'untouchable' than the 21st century communists. As early as 1980, Kanshi Ram had concluded that the 'Manuwadi' press was only concerned with the 'Brahmin and Bania' value system. Things had not improved even when Mayawati ruled UP both with the BJP support and on her own brute majority. Unlike other regional parties like SP, TDP and BJD, Mayawati did not bother to buy, cultivate or coerce media. Her strength, she believed, lay in her hold over her Dalit constituency. Using that vote power she could rope in other communities. It is another matter that her 'sarvajan' strategy flopped after its initial success. But her party extensively uses mobiles to spread the Bahujan messages. When in power, she used government machinery to defend its performance and her policies. But not beyond that. During the elections, BSP used traditional campaign tools like loud speakers, cycle rallies, distribution of posters, pamphlets and flags. Folk songs and skits are other favourite tools. All this is intended as substitutes for the 'manuwadi' TV and print media.

For the same reason, the BSP minimizes press conferences and other kinds of media shows. It issues official statements without bothering how these are presented in the media. BSP press notes are mostly carried by the local press if at all. Mainstream media uses them only if there is 'anything interesting' in them. For the media's content controllers, the BSP is not 'people like us'. There is certainly a mental block between the two sides. For the post-globalization New Media, there is the commercial factor. Inhouse surveys by the media houses consistently emphasize the fact that the proportion of English newspaper readers among the Bahujan is negligible. Thus BSP stories have minimal market value. True, BSP's own mistrust of the Brahmin-Bania media and the party's highly centralized decision-making system and style of disseminatation of information have also to be blamed for the wide mismatch between the Dalit party and the mainstream media.

The vast rural belt and backward regions have always been in English media's negative list. Its readers are entirely urban except those areas in the suburban peripheries. Perhaps a few copies or early editions going to the rural areas. This may be mostly by post. This vast *pariah* hinterland becomes news only when negative things happen. If five people are drowned in a ferry accident in Mississippi, it is a double column on our foreign page. But if '20 die as country boat capsizes' in Chhattisgarh, it is a headlineless 'if brief'. Very few English dailies have rural reporters. Barring a Sainath, most other rural experts are preoccupied with things like agricultural commodity trade, virtues of fertilizer subsidy cut, GM crop introduction and drip irrigation. The rural belt is seen as markets for the fast moving consumer goods and durables.

All this certainly raises a serious ethical question involving the press *dharma*. It is one thing to deal with the strikers and slogan shouters at the gates of the respective newspaper. But should this prejudice and enmity be extended to the normal news coverage of the entire working class? The Second Press Commission refers to such tendencies on the part of the newspaper owners and editors. Quoting a US press panel report, it asserts that a newspaper is a 'public service and public carrier'. It disfavours the idea of personal or class prejudices influencing the media coverage. Here is a conflict of interests of a reverse kind—clash between the corporates' inherent discord with their ideological rivals and the newspaper *dharma* of honestly informing and educating readers without prejudice to the personal interests. Should readers be denied their legitimate rights to unprejudiced presentation of information by it?

Take, for instance, a group of residents protesting against the power distribution company against, say, inflated bills. Could the company deny power to the protesters on the premise that they protested against it? Enterprises are governed by different rules and regulations, from quality control to consumer courts. They have to observe all such myriad rules. If the media is made a purely private business and news is made a consumer product, should the former be also prepared to abide by the normal business regulations? There is certainly a dichotomy between the philosophy of the New Media and the elaborate journalistic norms and ethics prescribed by the Press Council and recommended by the press commissions.

15

A Muffled Watchdog

This writer became a member of the Press Council when it had still enjoyed its pristine stature. That was in 1985. Ours was the third council after it was reconstituted under the 1978 Press Council Act. The Indira Gandhi government had dissolved the council during the Emergency. The Emergency excesses and onslaught on the freedom of the press were the compelling reasons for the demand for a more nuanced press council. With this in view, the Second Press Commission which had already started work, had to be reconstituted with members like Nikhil Chakravartty and Girilal Jain.

This was the background in which the media, government and the public at large had treated the council with high esteem. In its early phase, it had gained in authority with the presence of members like L.K. Advani, Ram Jethmalani, George Fernandes, Edward Faleiro, Mamen Mathew, H.V. Kamath, R.K. Karanjia, V.N. Gadgil, C.R. Irani, B.G. Verghese, Prem Bhatia, Raghuvir Sahay and M.J. Akbar. Its adjudications on complaints were taken seriously. Newspapers had carried the council's decisions on a regular basis. Some newspapers had found it necessary to make editorial comments on the council's verdicts. Regional dailies had made it a point to publish the council's comments against the local rival newspapers. To an extent, this had served the purpose of naming and shaming the wong-doers.

Cases involving some of the largest media houses were disposed of during our time. Often top Supreme Court lawers had appeared before the inquiry committee to argue cases on behalf of their influential clients. In B.G. Verghese vs *The Hindustan Times* case, the council had passed a harsh judgement against the Birlas, the owners. This was by far the most controversial case that had evoked wide media attention. In *The Hindustan Times* vs *The Times of India* case, L.M. Singhvi was hired to argue the case on the former's behalf. Such was the importance the media had attached to the Press Council even during the 1980s. Then why is the Press Council so ineffective today? How come we are left in the dark about what is happening in the council? Why do the media houses wholly ignore the activities of this quasi-judicial body which was meant to be an effective watchdog?

There have been suggestions in the recent past for scrapping the council if it has not been able to achieve its objective for which it has been constituted. On the other, many have proposed that the council should be given more teeth to make its decisions binding on all parties in disputes. The latter want the council to be armed with punitive powers. Then there are suggestions to include broadcast and social media in its ambit. However, there have been persistent divergent views on all such proposals. Private broadcast media barons have already said they will not accept any regulations by any body, statutory or quasi-judicial. Instead, they have set up their own 'council' for self-regulation.

However, if the experience of the TV media is any indication, the self-regulation itself is far from satisfactory. Both News Broadcasters' Association and Broadcast Editors' Association have been ineffective in disciplining the erring channels. Former Press Council chairman Markandeya Katju challenged the two outfits to state how many licences they had cancelled for the violation of ethics by the fellow channels that had crossed all limits. He had cited several cases of misdemeanours. Only in one case—India TV—a fine of Rs. 1 lakh was imposed for manipulating an interview. But soon after this, its head was taken back into the association. Not only this. The person who was punished for manipulating an interview, was honoured by the government with a 'bhushan' award for 'excellence'. "The NBA is so weak, so feeble in exercise of power that it cannot confront intimidation by its own members," says Abhishek Upadhaya, senior editor of *Dainik Bhaskar* and a media critic. With such experience how can one expect any effective self-regulation in print media?

The harsh truth is that the Press Council, after the post-

Emergency euphoria, has become an unwanted child. Its main stakeholders, i.e. media houses, do not feel comfortable with it. They, at least a dominant section of it, simply want to ignore the council's existence. Why? Perhaps you will not get a formal explanation. But senior editors who are part of the media establishments feel free to pour their hearts out to us, the harmless middle-rung journos. They just hate any constraints being imposed on the media by 'outside' institutions except the judiciary. Many who sit there in the council are journalists working under them as employees. Some are their sacked editors. Who are they to tell us what is wrong and what is right? Running a newspaper, they assert, is a multi-million business. Those close to the media houses say that the newspapers are under pressure from the government, advertisers and various other interest groups. They will, in any case, have to be tackled tactfully. Where is the time for us to listen to the old-style pontifications by a few laymen sitting out there? At Times House, a trusted editor had ones alleged that a few working journalists and former editors were manipulating the Press Council decisions.

This is outlandish. The 28-member Press Council has representatives of the INS, apex body of the media houses, Editors' Guild, small and medium newspapers body and working journalists. In addition, there are MPs, a nominee of the Bar Council, Sahitya Akademi and University Grants Commission. Why should such members allow four working journalists fix decisions of the council? The plain fact is that a dominant section of the media houses just do not want any kind of watchdog—a statutory body like the Press Council or a mechanism for self-regulation.

Clearly, the 36-year-old Press Council is in an identity crisis. Or call it an existential crisis. This is the sentiment behind the clamour for giving more teeth to the council. Every time a new chairman (who must be a Supreme Court or High Court judge) takes charge, the incumbent calls for giving more punitive powers to discipline the media. This writer was privy to the council members going to the new chairman Justice Sarkaria to sensitize him about the complexities of the council's relationship with the stakeholders of the media. A similar incident happened in the case of his predecessor Justice A.N. Sen. Both were quick to grasp the point. But Justice Markandeya Katju, who had the distinction of being the most outspoken chairman, stuck to his view throughout his tenure. He had even written to the prime minister seeking amendments to the Press Council Act to arm it with more punitive powers. This was against the sentiments of the council from its inception. The council before us and after had considered the issue and found the more-teeth demand even more dangerous. First, one cannot rule out the possibilities of a few members ganging up at the behest of the vested interests and resort to witch-hunting the newspapers or journalists.

Second, the government can also use its levers to rally its favourites and misuse the council's punitive powers to harass the unfriendly media. The Information and Broadcasting Ministry had on many occasions written to the council to recommend amendments to Section 14 of the act to vest it with penal powers. Each time the council had rejected the idea. Third, in case the council moved against any newspaper, it could go to the high courts to contest the order. The council would thus get bogged down in a web of litigations in different courts. In case the higher judiciary strikes down its adjudication, it will be seen as a jolt to the council's moral authority and its collective wisdom. It is also likely that the courts may find its intentions *mala fide*. This will place the council in an embarrassing position.

The successive governments have always been too eager to use the Press Council to settle the score with the editors and media. Information minister H.K.L. Bhagat had even encouraged the friendly members of the council to make the necessary recommendations. Take Markandeya Katju's letter to the prime minister. The opportunity was grabbed the UPA's information minister Manish Tewari. In his 'clarifications' to the Rajya Sabha in 2013, Tewari had spoken of amending Section 14 of the act that gives the council powers to 'warn, admonish or censure' a publication, editor or journalist if they were found guilty of violating standards of journalistic ethics or public taste. The amendment could also have empowered the council to recommend to the government suspension of government advertisements to the guilty newspaper and cancellation of the journalist's accreditation. In extreme cases, the amendment proposed suspension of the very registration of the impunged newspaper. Katju as per his recorded statements was more harsh. He wanted the council to have powers to impose fines on the guilty. Such harsh powers could be a convenient tool in the hands of the executive to keep the media under its hegemony.

When the Press Council bill was envisaged, misuse of executive powers against the media was a dominant theme. The council's rules and procedures were shaped with this danger in view. The council adjudicates on two kinds of complaints—against the media for violating the ethics and against the executive or private groups for attacking the press for their vested interests. After receiving a complaint, the council secretariat issues notices to the defendants and collect evidences from both sides. The inquiry committee of the council at its hearing examines both sides. They argue their cases, often bringing in additional evidence. The whole process is to provide full opportunities to both sides. Then the inquiry committee forwards its findings to the council which in its full meeting scrutinizes and endorses the recommendations. The hearing is done in public and all statements and evidences are public documents. The idea is to have fair play and prevent any misuse of powers to settle the score with the media, government or members of the public.

There are similar elaborate safeguards in the procedures for the formation of the Press Council. The Chairman has to be a retired judge of the Supreme Court or high court. All stakeholders in media like the Indian Newspapers Society, Editors' Guild, small and medium newspapers and working journalists are selected in a balanced proportion. Names are given by their respective recognized associations. The government can only issue the orders. The rules also strictly prohibit the same newspaper group having more than one member, in the council. Supposing the Editors' Guild and working journalists associations recommend names from the same media house, one of the nominees gets eliminated by draw of lots. All this is to avoid any particular group monopolizing the council. So the apprehension of manipulating the council's decisions is wholly fallacious.

Despite such safeguards, there may have been instances of partisan interests playing out within the council. But then this is not due to the council's structural defects. Such things happen when the polity remains sharply divided in a highly charged political atmosphere. It could happen to any panel. True, nominating bodies like INS and Editors' Guild have often been not serious enough to send the best talents. Some of their nominees were so busy they only made an occasional appearance. Some MPs were very serious and active. But many took it as just another committee. We had a sharply divided council in the aftermath of the Ayodhya violence during the Mulayam Singh government. The council had received complaints about the highhanded manner in which the Mulayam government had acted against the press. It had then formed an investigating committee to find out the truth. Some members of the committee were bent on admonishing the UP government for its actions against sections of the Hindi media. It was then decided that the partisan behaviour of the sections of the media and the sensationalism and hatred they had indulged in should also be probed. Sections of the Hindi media had done it as part of their partisan build-up in favour of the Ayodhya movement. Every day duing the kar seva movement, these dailies came up with stories with sensational headlines.

The committee had visited Agra, Faizabad, Ranchi and Lucknow to collect evidence. In all places, partisan crowds had appeared before the committee to present their version. It had all the trappings of a tutored narration against the Mulayam government's repressive measures and justifying the rabid communal campaign indulged in by sections of the regional media. As a result, we three members, K. Vikram Rao, famous Hindi poet and journalist Raghuvir Sahay and I, were forced to present an alternative report. We had highlighted both the Mulayalam government's actions and the rabid competitive communalism indulged in by sections of the Hindi media violating journalistic ethics. This was the worst case of the misuse of the council by sections of its members for partisan political interests.

Looking back, such aberrations could have been avoided had the nominating bodies like INS, Editors' Guild and Small and Medium Newspapers Association had nominated men of stature to the council. A similar episode took place when Justice Markandeya Katju was chairman. An imquiry committee had found fault with the actions of chief minister Nitish Kumar when he was part of the NDA. The issue had to be reopened when some other members had taken exception to it. Finally the decisions had to be reviwed. In a politically divided polity, there is always scope for aberration in the working of such institutions. The remedy is not to muffle the Press Council or boycott it altogether but to improve its quality by making it more effective and giving it a higher stature. The media barons boycotting the council have another reasonable option. They can initiate a debate to make the watchdog body more effective by seeking structural changes in its composition.

In our time, we had made a landmark decision. We decided to open the hearings of the council's inquiry committees to the public. Before this, proceedings were confined to the concerned parties. The media was not allowed to report its proceedings but only the final adjudication. The issue was debated both within the council and outside. There were apprehensions that the members would not be free enough to express their views if all that they said was carried by media. Some felt that the council's verdict would lose sanctity if it was known that the adjudication was made by a divided house. Despite this, the public hearing did have a salutary effect. There was a sudden spurt in the number of complaints received at the council's secretariat obviously because of the wider public interest this had evoked. Newspaper reporters also had begun attending the proceedings and some reports about the daily hearings appeared in the press. However, for reasons best known to the media houses, this healthy practice was discontinued. This was another case of deliberate devaluation of the press council by the media houses.

As briefly mentioned earlier, a complaint filed by *The Hindustan Times* against its rival *The Times of India* had created a big storm in the media world. It was over an advertisement campaign conducted by the latter on its pages. It was widely seen as distasteful. The advertisement showed a man climbing bare stairs drawn on a circulation chart and tripping suddenly on the ground below. The accompanying caption said: '**H**umpty-**T**umpty had a great fall' with 'H' and 'T' (**H**industan **T**imes in bold letters. It had also showed HT's circulation figures falling at the time. Clearly, it was part of a bitter circulation war between the two media giants. When the issue came up before the inquiry committee in which this writer was also a member, both the complainant and defendant had appeared in strength. Leading lawyer L.M. Singhvi had appeared for HT. On the TOI side about a dozen officials, including the editor Dilip Padgaonkar, had come. The latter's argument was that there was nothing distasteful in that 'artistically' presented advertisement. The whole story had represented the emerging trend of 'comparative advertisement', the TOI side asserted.

The next day the TOI had carried a rather long report of the council proceedings, throwing doubts about the very fairness of the adjudication. Soon the newspaper had also carried articles on the virtues of 'comparative advertising' to what it said create a better awareness among the consumers. On its part, the council after hearing the arguments of both sides and studying the documents presented, came to the unanimous conclusion that *The Times of India*'s advertisement was in bad taste and expressed concern over such tendencies. While other dailies carried the verdict, the impugned daily later came up with a highly defiant version of it. And that was the beginning of a long saga of determined boycott of the media watchdog. It often reached such a ludicrous level that even the high court orders on the Press Council were treated as blasphemy. In April, 2016, the council had issued a bailable arrest warrant to the Secretary Information and Broadcasting Ministry after his refusal to appear before the council in a case. But the latter went to the Delhi High Court which promptly stayed the council's order. This was a rather rare intervention by the high court. It involved the union government. Why was the story dumbed down? Herein lay the bitter side of a determined boycott. As this book goes to the press there were some feeble signs. Some dailies have made a brief reference to the Press Council seeking report on the Kashmir violence. We do not know whether it is a change of heart or happened by default.

Did the council lose its relevance after having lost its track and getting lethargic? Has it become non-productive and turned a white elephant? Some have asked this question. This writer, to his surprise, found that the council since our time had been even more active and discerning in its deliberations. They were admirably diligent in disposing of the complaints. It did enormous work and was also active in non-routine functions. For instance, the council had drawn up appropriate guidelines on a number of critical issues affecting the profession. These included issues like exit polls, portrayal of women in media, right to reply, changes in the Official Secrets Act and a report of the problems of small and medium newspapers. Even a casual look will convince one of the enormous inputs they mustered to arrive at the right conclusions. It is worth mentioning the sensible norms the council has recently drawn up for those doing the business and commercial reporting. Perhaps, this may not be to the liking of certain media houses that are known for mixing news with business. But if truthfully followed, it will enhance the media's integrity.

The Press Council's separate guidelines for the financial reporters, editors and owners in accepting gifts and facilities like loans, preferential shares and such other favours have been totally ignored. While presenting company reports, the council recommended, the writer should make it clear that it was based on the firm's official version. Another significant suggestion was that no newspaper owner, editor or reporter should use their position to promote their other business interests. The council's recommendations on mixing advertisements with news was similar. How many media houses had allowed their newspapers to carry these important guidelines? Perhaps such proposals are not to the liking of certain media houses. Media observers like B.G. Verghese and Ajit Bhattacharya had attributed the 'New Media's' business interests to their dislike for the Press Council. This mismatch is an extension of the three-decade long confrontation between the dominant media houses and government on similar contentious issues.

In the happier days, after every coumcil meeting, the secretariat used to send out a press release on the major adjudications and special reports, if any, to the media. News agencies promptly released the verdicts. Delhi dailies had regularly carried them. Then came the boycott. Since then the council chairman and secretariat had made special requests to the editors to at least carry those adjudications involving the respective newspaper. Barring *The Hindu* and a few others, most others had ignored even this request.

Rather than giving sharper teeth to the watchdog, what is immediately needed is an amendment to the Press Council Act, 1978, to make it obligatory on the part of the newspapers to carry the council's adjudications concering the respective newspaper. This will make the readers aware of the omission and commission on the part of their newspapers.

But let there be no illusion. No such thing is going to happen. Ministers may talk of giving more powers to the council. Those like Markandeya Katju may lament 'yellow journalism, cheap sensationism and highlighting frivolous issues'. They all overlook a crucial point. Media houses in India, both electronic and print, have grown enormously powerful since the Second Press Commission report came out during the Janata rule. In the past 38 years, the media houses have acquired unchallengable financial and political clout.

Unlike in the pre-liberalization days, many media houses have established deeper intrinsic links with the corporate entities in different ways. A recent report had said that BCCL, publishers of *The Times of India* has a stake in 350 companies by way of its ad-for-equity scheme. This includes some biggies and real estate firms. This meant media houses getting an easy financial stake in a large number of private firms and thus raising issues of conflict of interests. A report of the Press Council sub-committee on paid news had recommended effective measures to stop the practice. But Paranjoy Guha Thakurta, a member of the PCI panel, says that the council had suppressed the report, obviously under pressures from the newspaper owners. Later it was released which had angered the interested parties.

Second, unlike earlier, the whole character and philosophy of media has undergone tectonic changes. Many of the lofty ideals enshrined in the Press Commission report and the Council's 'pontifications' have been swept away by New Media's commercial philosophy. The media houses are setting their own rules of the game without consultation or wider debate. They brazenly reject the old dictum that journalism is 'a public service and a profession'. Much against the Press Commission's dictum, the editor is no more the 'ear and eye' of a newspaper. They are merely executives hired to run the paper. Newspaper publishing has become a multi-million industry. If a publication is treated as solely a commercial business, the newspaper becomes a consumer product and 'news' marketable 'content'. The form and marketing of the 'content' will be decided not by ethical press dharma prescribed by the Press Council but market surveys and consumer tastes and behaviour.

The story of the Press Council vs. New Media will not be complete without the reference to a cosy arrangement between the establishment and big media houses. In olden times the successive governments had used collective class actions like 'diffusion of ownership' and newsprint quota to hoodwink the media. Mass action is passé post-liberalization. Media taming could be more focused and unobtrusive through direct targeting. If a media house brings out too many 'negative' stories with a view to enhancing its visibility, the Enforcement Directorate could send an innocuous notice. Or a few queries by a CBI official. Suddenly you will find even the brave ones singing the songs of praise. Look at the fall of the great interrogator Arnab Goswami. When he was angrily shouting at Sushma and Vasundhara on the Lalit Modi case, it was explained that the media house gave enough freedom to its different publications if that was necessary to gain TRP edge. Then suddenly Arnab went silent. The roaring lion on the screen has turned into a tame mouse. This has been last year's most telling case of effective media management. Possibly, the 21st century cannot produce a Ramnath Goenka.

16

Why is it Dysfunctional?

Every time there were prolonged disruptions of parliamentary proceedings, they would come up with the usual statistics: How many hours of business lost during the session and how much of the tax payers' money was wasted. Parliamentary researchers had put the 'loss' of money due to the opposition boycotts in the first few weeks of the 2015 winter session at Rs. 12 crores. It was calculated on the basis of six hours per day for the Lok Sabha and five hours for the Rajya Sabha. The cost of every hour lost has been put at Rs. 25 lakhs.

There are more impressive statistics. The winter session of 2015, which was mentioned as a classic case, was allotted 54 hours. But it met just three hours in two weeks. It passed just eight bills. Some of the bills were passed in less than five minutes. As for the Rajya Sabha, half the scheduled time was lost with just 1 per cent of the question hour being 'productive'. If this is an accountant's narrow view, we do not in any way lack the manager's wage cut orders. Hence it was suggested—ably supported by a few editorials—that if a section of the MPs obstruct proceedings and stay away from the House, their pay and allowances should be cut. If such punishment is not enough, there was the call for a strict no-work-no-pay rule to punish the erring MPs. Then there are other bright ideas: impose collective fines on the MPs to recover the 'lost money'; change the House rules for automatic suspension of membership and include a declaration in the candidate's form—kind of a 'bond'—pledging to accept all such rules, if elected. Finally, the Speaker, like a good HR manager, should hire and fire the MPs.

Incumbent speaker Sumitra Mahajan, was quick to take the cue. During the 2015 winter session, at one stroke she suspended

25 of the 40 Congress members of the Lok Sabha as a punitive measure. Sonia Gandhi was not exaggerating when she described it as the 'blackest day' in the history of the Indian Parliament. As expected, neither the pay cut threat nor firing of the MPs could frighten them into submission. On the other hand, it only further emboldened the opposition to turn more aggressive. The result was even more disruptions.

The Indian parliamentary system works more on healthy conventions than hire-and-fire rules. When direct telecast of proceedings was introduced, we were assured that naming and shaming in public would disuade the MPs from rushing into the 'well'. But that just did not happen. Some management gurus argued that abolition of the whip system will 'free' the MPs from the strangle-hold of party bosses. Along with this, they suggested revoking of the 'obsolete' anti-defection law. The last two suggestions find no supporters either in opposition or treasury benches. Both sides realize that such quick remedies will prove to be more pernicious than the disease itself. It will only open the floodgates for *'aaya ram-gaya rams'* and unbridled use of money power. Mass suspensions and punitive measures by a control freak speaker can only put parliament's very legitimacy to question. Let's be frank. The problem is political, and if parliament becomes dysfunctional, it only reflects the collapse of dialogue in a sharply divided polity. Every time the proceedings got paralyzed it has been due to arbitrary actions and high-handed style of the ruling camp.

We in the media should also take our own share of the blame for the dysfunctioning of this important democratic institution. The decline began much before the emergence of the post-liberalization New Media. The latter's deliberate downgrading of this vital democratic institution for news coverage only worsened the process. It was a time when news was sought to be made largely entertainment. Newspapers were being redefined and revamped on the basis of perceived reader interest. Everything was decided on what the inhouse readership surveys said. And who cares for the drab debates in Parliament? Readers were concerned about the 'end product', not unnecessary details. Parliament coverage became the worst victim of the reader survey-based news planning.

During those the transition days correspondents were repeatedly told by the new media planners to look for colour and drama.

Those days, MPs of all shades had the same complaint—media's failure to reflect the work done on the floor of the House. We the footsoldiers could only listen to the complaints. At newspaper offices, news editors and coordinators blamed the new tribe of 'invisible decision-makers' for the change. They dictated how the daily should be, not the editors or news editors. Media's refusal to give due importance to parliamentary coverage was the main factor that had led to the dysfunction of this institution.

Look at the newspaper files of the pre-24-hour TV era. You will find how diligently the dailies had covered the House proceedings. The fourth estate had kept a regular watch on both Houses. A dozen reporters were present in the press gallery even during the debate on private members' bills. And now? With the great communication revolution and facilities for quick transmission, all that you get from certain big dailies is a couple of 'hangama' stories, if any, and bare facts like 'three bills adopted in ten minutes'. A golden rule in yesteryears was that during the debates—from President's address and to adjournment motions—names of every speaker should be mentioned with party affiliations.

Newspapers devoted one page for Parliament during the session. About one-sixth of the space was reserved for answers given in the two Houses during the question hour. Most dailies had separate boxes for the answers. Answers containing crucial information are packed in tightly edited briefs after culling out the unwanted details. We carried about 15 to 20 answers every day. During my news desk days, I remember how we had to ensure no item was missed on the Parliament page. Reporters with a nose for news could dig out separate stories from the huge answer bunch. Then there were starred questions where members could ask supplementaries. These always yielded separate stories if the issue was explosive. During the inter-session period, it was a routine for us to take out the answer piles and dig out unpublished information and turn them into page-one story-breakers.

At the Express, once we did such a story on public holidays for the year. Most of a particular community's holidays that year fell on Sundays or other holidays. As a result, other communities got more holidays from the 'restricted' category. It raised such a hue and cry that the ministry had to revise the criteria for apportioning holidays. Zero hour yielded surprise stories. Smart MPs had often alerted friendly scribes about the awkward issues they would raise. Hyper active MPs had taken full advantage of special mentions to corner the government on the least expected issues. In case we fail to file a story, the desk would take the agency take. The idea was not to miss any story.

And now? Those dailies with the New Media mindset have done away with the very concept of a Parliament page. Instead of comprehensive coverage, today's readers have to rest content with whatever the reporter or editors want you to know. It was this media attitude that had caused frustration among the parliamentarians. Watch the plight of the second rank MPs. They speak in parliament and ask questions about their constituencies but not a word comes out either in newspapers or on electronic media. People in their constituencies hardly know of their hard work. To overcome the problem, some MPs resort to the practice of collecting their speeches and questions in Parliament and printing them in booklets to distribute in their constituencies. MPs have to prove they are active in parliament. It was not so before the New Media had devalued the parliamentary coverage. Under the good old format and news selection priorities, even AIR and Doordarshan mentioned the names of all those who had participated in debates. Most often one sentence was given to each speaker. People in their constituencies thus knew what their MPs were doing.

Even such veterans like Chitta Basu and A.G. Kulkarni used to give the transcripts of their special mentions for publication. Agencies and dailies duly carried such stories. Does any newspaper today carry individual MPs' addresses unless they are controversial enough or the respective media house has a special interest in them?

In situations like the prolonged boycott of Parliament on the issue of the telephone scam under Sukh Ram, even the offer of a debate in the House had no meaning for the ordinary MPs. After all the acrimonious debate, what will get highlighted in the media—electronic or print—was the speech by a couple of big shots from either side. The round-up story that appears in the morning will have to be led by the PM's or the minister's reply. Official opposition views, in most cases, appears as adds on. Very few made it a separate story. On most occasions, not a word of the individual members who have done painstaking homework to highlight crucial points, gets mention. The outcome of the debate, in any case, does not depend on the points raised in the House or quality of debate but its brute numbers.

The stress of the post-TV daily newspapers is not on providing facts and full information to the readers but sensationalism and controversy. Parliament has been the worst victim of the New Media's reader ('consumer') interest-centred news evaluation. This distorted system by the fourth estate has been the major reason for the erosion of Parliament.

Pariament is one of the four pillars of democracy. Media is traditionally treated as the fourth pillar. With this in view, journalists and media establishments are provided with several facilities by the state. These include press gallery passes to its journalists, postal and telegraph concessions and land for the media houses at cheaper rates. All this was to enable the fourth estate present a full and fair account of the happenings at other pillars. This apart, readers do have a right to know the full proceedings of the House. No crucial information should be held back from the readers due to personal bias or deliberate devaluation of an institution. This is especially so in view of the social media's quick and scrappy communication skills. Apologists of the New Media argue that average readers are interested in what they call 'end results' (see: 'Snake Was A Rope'), not a comprehensive account. Selective reporting of the proceedings and misplaced emphasis on drama and 'colour' have certainly contributed to the erosion of Parliament.

However, it is absurd to put the entire blame on the media. A dysfunctional Parliament is a reflection of the sharp divisions in the polity. The system is such that the bosses of all parties impose the official views on its members without giving an opportunity for airing individual opinions either within the party or in parliamentary panels. There was a time when even middle-level MPs like Moolchand Daga (Congress) and Maniram Bagri spoke freely on issues but obeyed the party whip while voting. And today? MPs are forced to adopt rigid partisan position even in Public Accounts Committees. As a result, some PAC reports got stuck.

The refusal of the ruling parties—whoever in power—for dialogue and consensus while pushing their agenda is the main factor that leads to Parliamentary logjam. In a situation where the ruling party enjoys only a nominal majority, the opposition can rightly question the government's right to arbitrarily push decisions that would have consequences on future generations. There is another crucial factor. It is the very legitimacy of the ruling parties to pushing basic policy changes under fragile coalitional conditions. Such policy shifts should ideally be effected only through honest dialogue and wider consultations. In the US, they call it bipartisan agreement. Many countries have such institutional systems. Stealth and ruse could not be a substitute for honest consensus.

Take the issue of passing the Aadhaar bill. The government side knew the opposition would block it in the Rajya Sabha. So the NDA managers tricked them by pushing the bill through the 'finance bill route'. Such one-upmanship and crude stealth tend to further heighten the mutual mistrust. The Manmohan Singh government too had unsuccessfully tried such stealth on the Indo-US nuclear deal. On mega scams—whether it was Sukh Ram, A. Raja and company or Lalit Modi and his friends like Vasundhara Raje and Sushma Swaraj—both the BJP and Congress governments had brazenly refused to concede demands for debate. Speakers routinely help the treasury benches by disallowing debates on contentious issues that entail voting. Normally such decisions could have been arrived at all-party meetings with the speaker. In some parliaments as in UK, a few days are earmarked for the opposition to decide the topics to be taken up for debate. As against this, the trend in India is to accord diminishing space for the opposition. All this happened even when there was scope for a *modus videndi.*

Arrogance of power overtook the ruling politicians whoever in power. I remember as early as July 1966, both houses of Pariament had to be adjourned due to pandemonium as the government refused to debate a strike in UP. However, the issue was resolved following conciliatory moves by Speaker Hukam Singh. Manmohan Singh's trusted ministers had often told us off-the-record how determined he was to stake the very survival of his government on the issue of the nuclear deal. With such a live-it-or-take-it approach, how do you expect the cooperation from the opposition? Even on the eve of the crucial voting on the nuclear deal, Manmohan Singh was rigid. At a late night meeting with Arun Jaitely, he compromised on the nuclear liability clause with the understanding that this single hurdle could be 'managed' at a later stage. And the Parliamentary logjam had ended on that compromise. Look at the performance of the monsoon session (2016) which adopted all but one scheduled bill, the controversial GST legislation. All this illustrates two aspects of the parliamentary confrontations. First, compromises are possible if both sides are genuinely keen on meaningful dialogue. Second, the onus of ensuring a logjam-free session is more on the ruling party than opposition.

In Indian conditions, the opposition, whoever it is, has a valid argument. We have a badly divided multi-party system with wide, sweeping powers for the executive. This is an anachronism of the Indian system. In countries like the US, all major decisions by the executive, especially international agreements, will have to be statutorily ratified by the legislature (Congress or Senate). A Bush decision to sell out all major sea ports in the US to a Saudi firm had to be cancelled when the Senate objected to it. Even a person like Bush did not stand on false prestige. We breast-beat too much about the opposition blocking economic reform measures like scrapping of labour protection laws. But in the US there are many blocked bills at a given time. Indian lawmakers have no powers to scrap any such government decision. They can, if they choose, only pull down the PM but not reverse his executive decisions. This is another anomaly.

Right from the Rao days, opposition was nursing this hurt feeling. L.K. Advani, Prakash Karat and JD(U) leader Sharad Yadav were advocates of statutory ratification powers for Parliament in the case of all international agreements. Rightly or wrongly, misuse of executive powers by ruling parties under fragile coalitions has been the contributory factor that has led to blockade of parliament.

Last but not least, there is a deep-rooted misconception about the role and function of Parliament. For over two decades we were led to believe that Parliament's sole function was to enact reform bills and endorse or oppose the executive's decisions. Hence MPs are increasingly being called 'law makers' as if that is their only function. Parliament and legislatures are also the voice of the people. It is designed as a forum where important matters of public interests and constituents' concern are raised and debated. Legislatures in many functioning democracies have special days in a week fixed for topical interests. Germany's Bundestag does it on a priority basis. In the US they have a mechanism to almost equally time for government and opposition parties to raise their respective points. And in India? A recent study said that members of the Lok Sabha wanted to raise 127 and 253 issues during the zero hour in the winter and monsoon sessions (2016) respectively. This reveals the irrepressible demands for raising the constituents' concerns on the floor of the House. But the middle-level MPs get shabby treatment. Question hour, call-attention and adjournment motions and 'special mentions' are sufficiently indicative of this crucial role. Refusal to allow debates on misdemeanours by the executive and overemphasis on reform bills contribute to the logjam.

Last, there is a dire need for appropriate changes in Parliamentary procedures to suit the badly divided multi-party situation. More than constructing a massive new building or mindless suggestions like scrapping or shifting the question hour, what is needed is building higher standards and sound conventions. These could be evolved only after strenuous consultations. In the early 1990s, the system of standing committees was introduced. It had worked fairly well despite the present move to devalue it. There can be a consensus on compulsorily referring all bills to standing panels. In the past three years, just 29 per cent of bills were referred to standing panels. This is in contrast to 60 per cent in the 14th and 71 per cent in the 15th Lok Sabha. Another reform is to stop the practice of instant passing—or same-day adoption—of bills. It denies the opportunity to scrutiny the legislation.

Glossary

Block: Wooden block on which embossed lead plates are fixed for printing.

Body matter: Type set in the running body as against in headlines.

Bottom: News story, usually in three or more columns in size, at the bottom portion of a daily.

Bromide: Photographic paper coated with an emulsion of silver bromide on which printouts are taken.

Case: A tray in which the compositor keeps individual metal types of a particular size and style.

Compositor: One who sets up lead types for printing.

Copy Holder: One who reads out from set matter to the proof reader colleague.

Crown size: Size of the paper or print area smaller than demy.

Demy: Size of printing page 17.5" by 22.5".

Dummy: Designer's layout of a page.

Em : The square of a body of any size of type used as a unit of measurement.

Flong: Special soft cardboard used for making stereotyping or imprinting locked up page.

Forme: Type matter, blocks, etc assembled in a case and ready for printing.

Frame: Steel frame into which matter is arranged for printing.

Galley: A tray for holding composed type.

Galley Proof: A printer's proof taken from the type in the galley for correction.

Hold Over (H/O): Copy or composed matter kept apart for possible use later.

Intro/Lead: Beginning of a news story usually highlighting the main theme.

Italics: Letters set slanting to the right

Joiners: Compositors who join the body matter and headlines which are usually cast by different machines.

L/c: Lower case or small letters. The lower section of the cubicled wooden case where small letter types are kept.

Linotype: Typesettng machine operated by a keyboard that casts an entire line on one solid slug of metal.

Ludlo: A hand-operated machine to set headline types and caste them in lead.

Lock-up: To finish page making by locking up the frames around.

Make-up man: One who makes the page as per the layout during the hot metal days.

Matter: Types set up/copy to be set in type

Monotype: Type setting machine that casts letter-by-letter in lead as per the punched tape.

Morse Code: A telegraph code used internationally for transmitting texts

Narrow: Another word for galley proof.

Page Proof: Proof of the final page ready for printing.

Privy Purse: A regular payment to former princes in lieu of the integration of their 'kingdom' with the Indian Union.

Proof: Trial impression made from composed type for correction.

Proof machine: An inked roller operated by hand to take proof.

Plates: To make a stereotype in hot metal from types or another plate for printing.

PRRM: A cooperative coffee house popular among middle class intellectuals set up at the initiative of Gulzarilal Nanda under his Price Rise Resistance Movement.

Punch: Make holes in a tape by an electric typewriter which when fed into a machine will produce letters.

Reader: One corrects the proof.

Spot News: Huge boards on which latest news was displayed and put up in front of newspaper offices.

Stick: A palm-sized steel case in which lead types are arranged by fingures.

Stone: A metal-topped table on which composed matter is arranged for printing

Take: Pages in teleprinter roll-outs.

Through (TP): Establishing connection with the other side.

Trunk Booking: Long distance telephone call where the operator had to connect lines across sectors.

U/c: Upper case or capital letters.

Index

Aadhaar bill 198
accredation quota 164
Adanis 84
Adi Shankara 89, 90
Advani, L.K. 54, 140, 142, 157, 161, 182, 199
  media fans 144
  on the Jinnah remarks 147
  phenomenon in BJP 146
AICC 160, 165
AIR 148, 196
Aiyar, G. Subrahmanya 34
Aiyar, Mani Shankar 20
Akbar, M.J. 42, 55, 182
Ali, Aruna Asaf 105
Ambani, Dhirubhai 141
Amin, R.K. 166
Anand Bazaar group 110
Anand, S.K. 132
Andrews, C.F. 37
anti-BJP stories 158
anti-colonial campaigners 36
anti-Congressism 108
anti-Emergency campaign 21, 102
anti-Sikh riots of 1984 21
Antulay, A.R. 111, 157, 160-61
ASEAN in Laos 78
Australian Press Council 120
Avadi session 17
Ayodhya agitation 158
Bagri, Maniram 197
Bahuguna, H.N. 140
Baluchistan 79
bania's money and brahmin's brain 175
Bannerjee, S. 178
Bansi Lal 157
Bar Council 184
Basu, Chitta 196
Beg, Arif 145
Behl, Raghav 87
Benegal, Shyam 179
Bengali dailies 23, 151
Bennet, Coleman & Company Ltd. (BCCL) 57, 160, 191
Bhagat, H.K.L. 185
Bhagwat, Mohan 146
Bhagwati, P.N. 76
Bhandari, Sunder Singh 146, 157
Bhartiya, Shobhna 56
Bhat, Kamal 159
Bhatia, Prem 182
Bhattacharya, Ajit 190
BIMSTEC 78
BJD 179
BJP 14, 65, 71, 144, 159-61, 165, 168, 172, 198
  campaigners 162
  jambooree 168
  media liaison in the 161
  move for a tie-up with the Shiv

Sena 157
national council 143
party president 147
politician 174
workers 169
block making 131
Blue Star 153
Bofors scandal 44, 80, 111, 156
Bose, Subhas Chandra 37
Braddleman, Lawrence 127-29
Brahmanism 135
Brahmin-Bania media 180
breaking scandals 111
Brexit referendum 72
BRICS 78
British dailies 117
British-owned English dailies 31
BSP 165, 175
minimizes 180
Bulletin format 90
business lobbyists 86

CAG, reporting of 156
Calcutta 144
Canada 89, 129
cartoonist 114
casteism 20
CBI and enforcement agencies 74, 87, 192
Central News Agency (CNA) 132
Century News Digest 129
Ceylon 126
Chakravarti, Prithvis 142, 145
Chakravartty, Nikhil 101-02, 182
Chandra Shekhar 46, 54, 141, 157
channel Jihadi 75
Charlton, Evan 34
Chatterjee, Ramananda 37
Chatterjee, Shailan 154-55
Chatterjee, Somnath 146
Chaudhury, Sanchin 49
Chhattisgarh 180
China 126
1962 war with 76
Chomsky, Naom 175
Chopra, Deepak 161
CIA agents 104
CIA project 109
Coffee House intellectuals 102
Cohen, David 102
colonial administrative provinces in India 31
colonial rulers 32
commercialization of news 70
communists, pro-China 128
compositors 112, 131
Congress 14, 28, 37, 65, 71, 100, 102, 105, 153, 158, 160-61, 168, 172
leaders 129, 132, 155
leadership 123, 126
Nehru-dominated 107
Party 126, 142, 155
election campaign 154
rivals 158
session 19
split in 1989 20
style PMO control 147
Congress(O) 108
copy editors, modern 131
corporate pressures 13
corridors of power 14
counter-investigation stories 156
CPI 102, 105, 165, 177
CPI(M) 105, 165, 177
crass commercialization of newspapers 63, 92
crime, accidents and suicides 119
crime and politics 21
Cross-Bar' French technology 19
Cuba 126
cut-throat price war 93

Daga, Moolchand 197
Dalit party 180

Dalit Shoshit Samaj Sangharsh Samiti 175
Dalmia, Ramakrishna 47
Das, C.R. 33-4
Dasgupta, Swapan 144
Dasmunshi, Priyaranjan 20
Dayal, John 45
Debhar, U.N. 17
Delhi dailies 122
Delhi Press 133-39
Delhi Press Club 47
Desai, Morarji 140, 159, 167, 178
desi media 37
Deve Gowda regime 179
Dharmarajan, S. 141
Dhawan, R.K. 159
Dhirubhai's death 166
dictatorship and communist regimes 72
Diego Garcia 126
Dilli Durbar 24
Doordarshan 196
Dua, H.K. 43, 45
Dubashi, Jai 157
Dubey, Suman 20, 43-44
Dutt, Dev 45, 141

editorial 137
  management 61, 136
  meetings 144
  pieces 138
  policies 122
  policy 174
  Strong 123
editors 13, 14, 149, 152, 190
  assistant 114
  'associate' 114
  conservative 21, 120
  consulting 114
  'joint' 114
  'senior' 114
election-eve scam taint 80
elections, 12th and 16th general 73
emergency 76, 106, 110, 155, 157
  after the end of the 123
  national 78
  regime 44
English dailies 23, 35, 36, 104, 117, 123, 166
English media 100, 103
  'market' 97
ethics and practices 92

Faizabad 187
Faleiro, Edward 182
FERA cases 43
Fernandes, George 182
Fernandes, Naresh 87
First Press Commission 53, 64
footsoldiers 13, 154
foreign news 95
Fotedar, M.L. 157
Fowler, H.W. 118
freelancers and power pedlars 165
French Rafale 168

G-20 Summit in China 78
Gadgil, V.N. 182
Gandhi, Devdas 33, 42
Gandhi family 158
Gandhi, Feroze 44
Gandhi, Indira 19, 29, 44, 53, 61, 73, 80, 107-08, 126, 141, 148, 155, 158-60, 169, 182
  triumphant return to power 154
Gandhi, Mahatma 37-38, 154
Gandhi, Rahul 58
Gandhi, Rajiv 20, 43, 73, 143, 152
Gandhi, Rajmohan 101, 108
Gandhi, Sanjay 24, 169
GenX owners 48
GenX periodicals 111
George, T.J.S. 125, 128, 130
Ghimire, Yubaraj 168

Ghosh, Girish Chandra 33
Giriraj 123
Gjuarati dailies 24
Goenka daily 47
Goenka, Ramnath 43-45, 54, 62, 85, 144, 155, 192
Gokhale 34
Goswami, Arnab 61-62, 192
guilty newspaper 185
Gujarat Summit of foreign investors 74
Gujral 179
Gupta, Shekhar 55, 69

Haji Mastan 104
Hegde, K.S. 145
Hindi daily 32
Hindi hinterland 50
Hindi journalism 22
Hindi journalists 21-22
Hindi media 187
Hindi poet 22
Hindi writers 22
Hindi writers and journalists 50
Hindi-speaking middle class homes 135
Horniman, A.G. 33
hot metal typesetting 112
human rights violations in Kashmir 79

IAS and army 113
India mainstream media 75
India Press Agency 102
Indian and Eastern Newspapers Society (IENS) 23
Indian language dailies 21, 92, 164
Indian media 63, 76, 78-79, 103, 157
Indian National Congress 34
  in 1955 16
Indian newspapers 31, 35, 117
Indian Newspapers Society 159, 186
Indian-owned newspapers 36
India's post-world war generation 100
information imperialism 74
information monopoly and content distortions 82
information order 82
intellectual journalism 99
intelligence agencies 77
intrigues and lobbying 152
investigative journalist 71
Irani, C.R. 45, 177, 182
Iraq war 42

Jacob, General 145
Jacob, Paul 129
Jain, Ashok 43, 48
Jain brothers 56-57
Jain, Girilal 47, 48, 54, 80, 113, 182
Jain hawala scandal 147
Jain, Punit 51
Jain, Samir 48, 56-57, 61, 144
Jain, Shanti Prasad 47
Jain, Vineet 57, 68
Jaitely, Arun 199
Jana Sangh 108
Janata coalitions 178
Janata Party 29, 165
Jayalalitha 172
Jethmalani, Ram 182
Jinnah's remarks 146
JNU types 22
Josh, Baba Sohan Singh 32
Joshi, Murli Manohar 142, 145, 157
Joshi, Prabhash 22
Joshi, Shyam Manohar 51
journalism 60, 82
  adverserial 155
  agitative 154
  courses 113
  footsoldiers of 144
  formula 72

gutter 155
harsh reality of 170
meaning of 110
responsible 36
tradition of critical 85
journalist crowd, mindset of the 153
journalistic ethics 94, 185
journalistic norms and ethics 181
journalistic values 72
journalistic work 164
journalists, accredited 152, 185
journalists and advertisement executives 171
journalists, new generation working 154
journalists of Telugu dailies 17
journalists, talented 110
journalists, younger 151
journo-touts still thrives 173
journos, 'corrupting' the 169
journos, middle-rung 184
JP movement 21

Kakkar, B.M. 125, 127, 130
Kamath, H.V. 182
Kansal, Rahul 58
Kanshi Ram 174
Kapur, Virendra 160
Karaka, D.F. 101, 108
Karanjia, R.K. 104, 109, 182
Karat, Prakash 199
Kargil operation 77, 80
Karnad, Girish 179
Kashmir violence 189
Katju, Justice Markandeya 183, 185, 188, 191
Kesari, Sitaram 141
khilaf likhnewalas 156
Kirby, John 79
Kirpekar, Subhash 160-61
Krishnamurthi, S. 120, 149
Kulkarni, A.G. 196
Kumar, Ajay 49
Kumar, D.P. 23, 142, 157
Kumar, Krishan 133

Lala Hardayal 32
Lalu corruption 179
language dailies 35
Left and Right 101
Left parties 175
Left unions 174
Left writer 107
Left-of-Centre weekly 104
Leftwing economic analysts 100
lino operator 112
lobbying power of the media 51, 168
lobbyists 167
Logistic Support Agreement (LSA) 81
Lohyaist mould 22
Lok Sabha elections, 1991 166

Madhav, Ram 162
Madhya Pradesh 141, 145
magazinization 96-97
Mahajan, Pramod 162, 168
Mahajan, Sumitra 193
Maharajas 123, 155
mainstream English media 174
mainstream media 82-83, 155, 177, 179-80
Majithia, Sardar Dyal Singh 33
make-up man 137
Malhotra, Inder 49
Malkani, K.R. 146, 157
Malviya, Madan Mohan 33-34, 42
Mankekar, D.R. 50-51, 93
'manuwadi' TV and print media 180
Marathi dailies 23
market intervention 97
Masani, Minoo 107

Mass action 192
Mathai, T.P. 106
Mathew, Mamen 182
Mathur, Girish 100, 107
Mathur, J.P. 146, 157, 161
Mathur, Rajendra 22, 49
Mayawati 179
media 68, 74, 150-51, 158, 184, 186-87, 194
  traditional school of 154
  barons 65
  centre 20-21
  circles 56
  commentators 96
  conservative news presentation 100
  contemporary mainstream 148
  crowds 19
  dharma 77, 79
  domination 64
  erring 61
  ethics 170
  'good' 84
  gossip 13
  honeymoon 75
  houses 24, 67, 69-70, 98, 111, 153, 163
  houses in India 191
  imperialism 65
  integrity 190
  management 192
  'monopoly control' of 53
  organizations 20
  owners 83, 97, 152
  patriotism 78
  portals 65
  publicity 60
  systematic arrangement for 168
  strategy 111
  savvy politicians 140
Mehta, Balraj 13, 100
Mehta, Feroz 34
Mehta, Harshad 171
Mehta, Vinod 50, 110
Menon, V.K. Krishna 104-05, 125, 127-29, 132
Menon's articles 126
Mishra, Dinanath 49, 144
Mishra, L.N. 176
Mitra, Chandan 144
MNC lobbyists and diplomats 167
Modi, Lalit 192
Modi, Narendra 50, 73, 81, 153
Modi, Piloo 101, 108
Modi-Amit Shah team 162
Moraes, Frank 47, 50
Moral Rearmament Association (MRA) 109
Morse code system 19
Mulgaonkar, S. 44, 50, 118
Mundasseri, Joseph 17

Naik, Ram 168
Nambudiripad, E.M.S. 177
Naoroji, Dadabhai 34
Narasimha Rao, P.V. 25, 102, 162, 171
Narasimhan, V.K. 44-45, 50, 62
Narayanan, Edathatta 55, 105, 117
Narayan, Jayaprakash 21
Narendra Modi-Amit Shah dispensation 145
Nath, Vishwa 133-37, 139
National Front government 179
Nautiyal, Nand Kishore 106
Nayar, Kuldip 45, 48, 50, 124
NDA 188
NDA government 122
NDTV Hindi, shutdown of 83
Nehru, Arun 20
Nehru baiters 123
Nehru family 44
Nehru, Jawaharlal 17, 37-38, 76, 105
Nehruvian 141

Nehruvian concept of planning 135
Nehruvian economic and foreign policies 52, 107
Nehruvian model 52
Nehruvian mould 123
Nehruvian socialists 53
New Media 41-42, 180-81, 194, 197
    commercial philosophy 191
    mindset 196
    post-reform 92
NewGen owners 48
news bureau 155
news desk 41
news editor 114
news market 84
news network management 41
news transmission hurdles 29
newspaper business 97
newspaper claiming 39
newspapers 13, 18-19
    in India 31
Ninan, Sevanti 87
Ninan, T.N. 49, 55, 144, 167
Nitish Kumar 188
non-Left journals 103

Obama, Barak 57
online news portals 83
Organization of Islamic Cooperation (OIC) 79
outsourcing system 139

Padgaonkar, Dilip 42-43, 46-47, 189
page maker 139
page making 131
    under the lino system 112
Pakistan 80
    a terrorist state 78
    border clashes with 77
Pal, Bipin Chandra 33
Pandita, Kedarnath 43
Panikkar, K.M. 33, 42
Pant, K.C. 150
Parliament corridor 142, 166
Parliamentary logjam 198
Parliamentary reporting, old-style 96
partisan dailies 83
Patel, Aakar 75
Patel, Jayesh 84
Patel, Vikhe 168
Patel, Vithalbhai 155
Patil, Vasantdada 30
Philipose, Pamela 88
photo offset machine 139
photo offset printing 117
photo setting 117
photographs and graphics 131
Pillai, Shankar 55
plate making machine 112
PMO 152, 167, 172
Pokhran text 153
political briefings 172
political coverage, 'balanced' 144
post-Emergency glossies 156
post-Emergency Janata sweep 29
Prasad, Krishna 50
Prasar Bharati 90
Premchand 37
press briefings 158
press cards 20
Press Council of India 14, 43, 45, 67, 69, 90, 120, 154, 158, 181-84, 186,
Press Council vs. New Media 192
Press Council's separate guidelines 190
Press Information Bureau (PIB) 13, 66, 151, 154, 159, 166
    accreditation committees 14
    card holders 149
    officials 24
press rooms 16, 20
Press Telegram Authority Card 27
press telegrams 19, 26, 29

press workers 117
print media 83, 86-88, 92-93
Privy Purses 52
  abolition of 53
pro-Left newspapers and diplomatic missions 103
professional pressures 14
proof marking 114
proof readers 113
  colleague 114
PRRM coffee house 134
PTI 19, 114-15, 148-49
pulse scam 84
Purie, Arun 69

Question hour 200

Radhakrishnan, 39
Radia tape story 50
Rahejas 50
Rai, Lala Lajpat 33, 37
Raj 33, 37
Raja, A. 198
Rajagopalachari 52, 101
Rajamani, N. 149-50
Raje, Vasundhara 192, 198
Ram, Jagjivan 17
Ramachandran, C.P. 54, 100
Ramaswami 123
Rangarajan, R. 80, 153
Rao, K. Vikram 145, 187
RAW 165
rebellious journals 101, 124
recorders 18
Reddy, Rammanohar 88
reform bills 200
regional dailies 25
Reliance 141
reporter, chief 114
reporting, adversarial 156
Rig Vedic people 135
rival media giants 93
Roy, Arun 97
RSS 158, 174
  controlled Jana Sangh 76
  hardliner 146
  line of Indian history 135
  oriented recruits 22
  pracharak 161
Russians 126

Saari, Anil 127-28
saffron channels 75
Sahay, Raghuvir 22, 50, 182, 187
Sahitya Akademi 184
Samachar Bharti news agency 22, 144
Sen, A.N. 184
Sanghvi, Vijay 141, 160
Santhanam, K. 107
Sarkar, Avik 14, 144
Sarkar, Debu 169
Sarkar, Jadunath 37
Satpati, Nandini 53
Second Press Commission 35, 41, 48, 54
Sen, Samar 100
Sengupta, Arindam 96
Shah of Iran 104
Sharma, K.L. 157
Sharma, Rajendra 143, 146, 161
Shenoi, T.V.R. 144
Shourie, Arun 46-47, 156
Shyam Lal 47, 113, 119
Singh, Arjun 141, 157
Singh, Arun 20
Singh, Hukam 198
Singh, Khushwant 42
Singh, Manmohan 81, 198-99
Singh, Mulayam 187
Singh, Nihal 46-47, 62, 156
Singh, Ram 109
Singh, Ramsubhag 149-150
Singh, S. Nihal 45, 50

Singh, V.P. 73, 146, 157, 166-67, 178
government 83
Singhvi, L.M. 183, 189
Sinha, Murlimanohar 33
Sinha, Sachidananda 33
Sinha, Yashwant 145
Sister Nivedita 37
social media 63, 73, 83-84, 87, 91
Soviet papers 127
Soviet Union 104, 106, 126, 132
SP 179
special correspondents 60
spot news 119
Srivastava, K.P. 141, 178
Star News 90-91
Stiglitz, Joseph 143, 175
Sukh Ram 196, 198
Sullivan, Margaret 71
Sunday magazines 111
Swachch Bharat campaign 74
Swaraj, Sushma 192, 198
Swatantra Party 52, 76, 107, 123, 135, 155
Syndicate leaders' clashes 126

Tagore, Rabindranath 37, 44
TDP 179
tele-communication 19
telegram counters 25
telegrams, era of 26
telegraph address 29
telegraph office 26, 30
teleprinter (TP) operators 27
teleprinters 19, 26
Telugu dailies 24
Tewari, Manish 185
Thakur, Janardan 28, 160
Thakurta, Paranjoy Guha 191
Thapar, Karan 84
Thapar, Romesh 101, 106
Thimmaya episode 103
Think Tanks, private 127
'three-letter' agency 165
TOI Ombudsman 76
TP operator 28
trade unions 175
transcribe 18
Tripathi, Kamalapati 158
trivialization 96, 97, 98
Trump, Donald stunning victory 72
Trump's brash campaign 73
TV and online news 87
TV and social media 96, 120
TV media house 91
TV news 91
and social media, Indian conditions 97
news channels 89, 90
Tyagi, Mahavir 76, 123

Uber and Ola 139
UK 89, 126, 128
UK documents 128
UNI 115
University Grants Commission 184
Unnikrishnan, P. 114
UP government 187
UPA 185
government 80-81
Upadhaya, Abhishek 183
US 79, 89, 128, 200
US and China 126
US forces 81
US media 104
US nuclear deal 198
US policies 106
US, presidential campaign in 86
US-China collusion against India 127

Vadra, Robert 80
Vajpayee, Atal Bihari 50, 73, 81, 140, 179
rule 147

Vajpayee, Upendra 13, 45
Valiullah, Raof 29
Varadarajan, Sidharth 87
Venkatraman, R. 179
Verghese, B.G. 45-46, 50, 62, 90-91, 156, 182, 190
Vidyarthi, Ganesh Shankar 33
Vidyasagar, Ishwar Chandra 33
Vijayan, O.V. 105
Voice of America 126

Walmart 167
weekly whisper pieces 159
Western propaganda machine 177
women crime reporters 21
women journalists 21
working journalists 186
writers and columnists 60

Yadav, Sharad 199

Zafar, Bahadur Shah 32